FENG SHUI

A HOMEOWNER'S GUIDE TO ABUNDANCE

Jane Langof

Published in 2024 by Feng Shui Concepts
Contact: www.fengshuiconcepts.com.au

Title: *Feng Shui – A Homeowner's Guide to Abundance*
Author: Jane Langof
PRINT ISBN: 9780975627648
EPUB ISBN: 9780975627617
Subjects: Feng Shui | Interior Design | Design & Construction

Book Production Services: www.smartwomenpublish.com
Registered with the National Library Australia

Contents

How to Say 'Feng Shui'

Feng Shui is a complex art. Navigating the pronunciations of 'Feng Shui' can be as nuanced as the practice itself. There are a few different ways to say it, all correct, which vary depending on where you are in Asia. Spelled phonetically, they are foong shway, foong soy, foong shoy and fung shway. It's definitely not 'feng shooey'—sorry to my friends who insist on this version!

I use the pronunciation 'foong shway' or 'foong shoy', depending on whom I'm speaking to.

Foreword

In the heart of Sydney's vibrant Chinatown, amidst its bustling markets and lively streets, lies a philosophy that has influenced the course of my life and that of my community—Feng Shui. As a community leader deeply connected to Chinese history and traditions, I've seen the transformative power of this ancient practice firsthand.

My journey from taking over the family business in Haymarket to leading cultural tours in Chinatown taught me the importance of creating spaces that attract success and nurture the soul. Feng Shui is more than superstitions and knowing where to place a plant or mirror—it's about engaging with our environment on a meaningful level. Although the principles of Feng Shui originate from Chinese traditions, they offer universal value, reaching across cultural and geographical boundaries.

Meeting Jane Langof through her work on the Chinese Garden of Friendship reinforced my belief in the value of Feng Shui in connecting diverse communities. Her book, *Feng Shui: A Homeowner's Guide to*

Abundance, demystifies this ancient practice, making it accessible and relevant to everyone, regardless of their background or familiarity with Feng Shui.

For those of us in the Chinese community, and indeed anyone interested in enriching their living environment, Jane's book offers a fresh perspective. Jane's approach stands out because of her exceptional ability to harmonise Feng Shui principles with a commitment to practical design aesthetics. This book breaks down the barriers of complexity that often surround Feng Shui, offering a clear, practical guide to creating spaces of abundance and harmony. Jane has a way of making Feng Shui approachable, peeling back the layers of mystique to reveal its practicality. Her book is a guide to understanding the energy of our spaces and how to make them work for us.

As the 'King of Chinatown,' a title the media named me for my contributions to the community, I have seen how community and culture can bridge the gap between the past and the present. Jane's book extends this bridge even further, offering a path to abundance and wellbeing, and a journey toward transforming our living spaces into areas of profound impact and personal growth.

Let Jane's expertise lead you through the practical applications of Feng Shui. Whether you're seeking to enhance your living environment or invite more positivity into your life, this book promises to be an invaluable resource on your journey to abundance.

I am proud to write the foreword for *Feng Shui: A Homeowner's Guide to Abundance*, a book that reflects the profound teachings of Feng Shui and its principles for a better life.

King Fong, OAM
President, Chinese Australian Historical Society Inc., 2013–2018

Preface

I haven't always been a Feng Shui master. My first career happened somewhat by chance. In my last year of high school, a friend in my economics class suggested we apply for cadetships at accounting firms. Motivated by the idea of starting my career early, and the glamour of city life, I threw my hat in the ring for several cadetships and secured a job at an accounting firm in Sydney. Although I had been an A-grade student at school, working full time while studying finance and accounting turned out to be a huge struggle. There were times when I stared at my computer, thinking, *kill me now*! I felt like a square peg in a round hole. I did not have an affinity with my accounting career until years later, when I became CPA qualified and moved up the corporate ladder.

There were two things I enjoyed about my corporate work—helping people and collaborating with a team—but I realised that accounting and finance were a long way from what I truly cared about.

During my time in the corporate world, my husband and I renovated our first home, a townhouse in the pretty suburb of Hunters Hill in Sydney. I fell in love with the creative process of interior decorating and design, and would pore over home-design magazines and spend weekends browsing homeware stores. I even started applying my creativity at work, injecting fun into my workday by rearranging my office and obsessively colour-coding files on my bookshelf. The idea of studying interior design crossed my mind at the time, but with my demanding job as a financial controller, this wasn't an option.

In 2006 my husband and I had our first child, and I left my corporate career to focus on our family. One day a friend told me about her encounter with a psychic, the renowned spirit medium Kerrie Erwin. Knowing that I had experienced a lot of change in my life, my friend suggested I also get a psychic reading. My friend was amazed at how Kerrie had been able to connect to the spirit world and relay astonishing details about her late mother. This ignited my curiosity—my father had passed away when I was a teenager, so I was curious to see if Kerrie could communicate with him on the 'other side'. I also wanted to know whether she had any insights about my future, because I was at a crossroads.

Meeting Kerrie Erwin changed the trajectory of my life. As soon as I entered her incense-filled room, she connected with my father in the spirit world. She described his appearance, his life's challenges, a war injury from a bullet in his leg, his proudest moments, and the circumstances of his passing. The level of detail Kerrie relayed about my father was so specific and accurate that I knew she could not have guessed. She had my attention. And what she said next blew me away.

Kerrie told me that my corporate career was over. She said that returning to my former role in accounting would be soul-destroying. My spirit guides told Kerrie that I should study interior design.

I loved the idea. I began researching the best courses and found a wonderful design college in Sydney. It was a joy to unleash my creativity and study a topic I was passionate about, but after the first half of the course, the college announced there would be an extended break before I could complete my qualification. This unexpected pause in my formal education led me to explore other avenues.

Frustrated by the delay, I decided to visit Kerrie for another psychic reading. This time she told me to study Feng Shui and combine it with my interior design practice. I thought this was a brilliant idea. Feng Shui had fascinated me for years, and as soon as I commenced my studies and opened the classic texts, I was hooked. I felt an instant connection, like I was made to do this work.

Kerrie also told me that one of my spirit guides was an ancient Chinese master called Fu Chen. She said I could call upon his guidance to inspire my work. I found this very intriguing and exciting, like a calling from destiny.

I continued my studies in both Feng Shui and interior design and started to apply the principles to my own home. I noticed huge shifts in energy for my family and me. I had just had a new baby, yet I found that I started to have more energy. My husband got an unexpected promotion, and my new business was taking off.

When I looked back at the changes that had occurred, I realised how powerful Feng Shui was. I wanted to take my practice to the next level, so I went overseas to learn from the grand masters. I travelled to Singapore and Hong Kong to study Feng Shui, the I Ching and Chinese astrology. In my practice I have been influenced by many different masters and grand masters, including grand master Raymond Lo, grand master Stephen Skinner, and Feng Shui architect Howard Choy, the principal of the European College of Feng Shui.

Throughout the years, as I deepened my expertise in Feng Shui, I discovered its principles extend far beyond home design. As my business expanded, I began to offer consultancy services in various settings, including residential homes, commercial businesses and community spaces. Many of my clients come to me because they recognise the importance of Feng Shui to their customers. I've worked with commercial clients like investment bankers to create a welcoming environment for their Asian clientele. I've collaborated with the government agency Placemaking NSW to enhance community spaces like the Chinese Garden of Friendship in Sydney. And I've also had the pleasure of working for resorts, casinos, hotels and clubs.

In 2014, I became an accredited Feng Shui master through the International Feng Shui Association in Singapore. Now I am grateful to share my knowledge and experience in a holistic way to help people create positive change in their lives. I'm proud to have worked on award-winning projects in Australia and internationally, and that my business, Feng Shui Concepts, has been the recipient of multiple awards.

Each Feng Shui master has their own unique way of communicating their insights. I have met Feng Shui masters who have a direct communication style that can be perceived as blunt, some being so straightforward they'll tell you that if you're living in a house on a cliff, you might as well start digging your grave. Such direct communication isn't everyone's cup of tea. While this approach may be effective in delivering a message, it can be worrying for many people, and I speak as someone who has been on the receiving end of that style of communication.

The irony is that the Chinese approach and my cultural Filipino heritage share a common trait in this regard. Filipinos are also known for their blunt, no-nonsense communication style. If you put on a few kilograms and show up to a family gathering, you can bet that one of your aunties will likely tell you, 'Hey, you're getting fatter!' before shoving you towards a table full of deliciously rich foods and urging you to 'Eat more, eat more!'

I have always had an innate curiosity about the practice of Feng Shui, thanks to my strong connection to my Asian roots. However, I am the product of two vastly different cultures. My paternal family is European, originating in Slovenia, and I grew up in the multicultural melting pot of south-western Sydney. With my east-meets-west cultural background, I feel perfectly aligned with the disciplines of Feng Shui and design.

As a Feng Shui master, I always aim to strike a balance between delivering my insights with clarity while being sensitive to my clients' feelings and preferences.

Introduction

There's much chaos in the world right now. Many people are feeling out of control. The Covid-19 lockdowns we experienced in the early 2020s taught us a big lesson that we won't forget in a hurry: the importance of home.

You might have realised that the design of your home is not working for you, and you're ready to make changes. During times when you were confined to your home during the lockdowns, it might have become clear that certain aspects of your floor plan could be improved. Perhaps you found that your living space didn't function well. Perhaps you sensed that the energy in your home was affecting you and your family in a negative way. Now is the time to do something about it, whether it's to make simple Feng Shui adjustments to your existing home or build a new one with the best energy flow possible.

If you're intrigued by the ancient Chinese art of Feng Shui, you're likely drawn to the prospect of creating a home that not only looks beautiful but also brings wealth, health and wellbeing. Perhaps you're on a journey to become your best self, whether you are seeking patience in challenging moments, harmony in your family dynamics, or a deeper connection with your partner. Ultimately, the goal is to cultivate a space that helps you feel happier and more fulfilled in your life.

Perhaps you've done some research on Feng Shui and found the topic confusing. And it's no wonder! There are so many myths, misconceptions and conflicting views on Feng Shui in the public domain. This book will help you understand the principles of Feng Shui that are relevant for a home in modern times. I will take you on a journey of discovery, uncovering as much depth of knowledge of Feng Shui as possible, however it's important to note that Feng Shui is an Eastern practice meeting the needs of a Western audience. While it may not always align with modern scientific methodologies, its transformative effects are evident. I will give you examples that will demonstrate how positive changes can be made, and explain what you need to know about this ancient art.

Feng Shui is an art and metaphysical science that originated in China thousands of years ago. It is a coalescence of ancient principles, design insights, practical knowledge, formula, and symbolism. Feng Shui has many layers of complexity and takes many years to master. It is an ancient tradition that shares many underlying principles with acupuncture and Chinese medicine, practices that have gained substantial evidence and recognition over the years.

Feng Shui is a powerful tool that enhances the energy in your surroundings; however, I want to make it clear that it's not the answer to all of life's problems. Feng Shui is not a cure for cancer or a solution to domestic violence, but it can positively influence many aspects of your daily life, contributing to a more harmonious and balanced environment. The purpose of this book is to show you how to elevate your energy levels and create an environment that will support you to reach your fullest potential. I offer practical tips and useful guidance to help you transform your home into a sanctuary of abundance, promoting prosperity, happiness and wellbeing for you and your loved ones.

The book is divided into two parts, both designed to help you understand and implement Feng Shui principles in your home.

In Part I, you'll gain a solid foundation in the origin and basic principles of Feng Shui. I'll provide clear explanations without any fluff or confusion. You'll learn about the value of working with a Feng Shui master and how to get the right assistance. I'll also explain why the cookie-cutter approach to Feng Shui is incorrect, emphasising the need for a more personalised approach that considers the unique aspects of your home and lifestyle. Furthermore, I'll show you how Feng Shui can add value to your property.

In Part II, you'll learn how to apply Feng Shui principles to every room in your home. I'll guide you through a step-by-step process to improve the energy in each space. You'll discover common issues that can disrupt the energy flow, and I'll provide solutions and remedies to mitigate those problems.

Finally, you'll learn the importance of aligning the energy in your home with changes in your mindset and daily habits. This holistic approach to Feng Shui is about harmonising your external surroundings with the energy within you, fostering improvements in all aspects of your life.

Whether you are new to the concepts of Feng Shui or have dabbled in it before, this book will provide you with the knowledge and tools to create a more abundant home. So, welcome to my world, and let's get started.

PART I

A Journey Into Feng Shui Secrets

'Everything is energy and that's all there is to it. Match the frequency of the reality you want, and you cannot help but get that reality. It can be done no other way. It is not philosophy, it is physics.'

This quote is frequently credited to Albert Einstein; however, its authenticity remains a subject of debate. Nevertheless, it's a powerful statement, and I'll embrace it, because Feng Shui operates on the premise that energy is everywhere, constantly affecting our thoughts, emotions and daily lives.

Some people dismiss Feng Shui as a pseudoscience, but regardless of whether you believe in its principles, the influence of Feng Shui on your daily life is undeniable. While it may be difficult to measure the effects of Feng Shui using traditional scientific methods, it's hard to ignore the countless stories from people who've seen a tangible shift in their lives after implementing its principles into their surroundings.

Choosing to embrace Feng Shui, or not, is entirely personal. But remember, it's a practice that has stood the test of time for thousands of years and has found its way into the hearts and homes of many cultures worldwide.

In Part I of this book, you will learn about the fundamentals of Feng Shui. In Chapter 1, we'll look at how Feng Shui can lift your home's energy from abysmal to auspicious, then in Chapter 2, I'll unpack some Feng Shui secrets. Chapter 3 will explain the importance of mapping the energy in your home, and in Chapter 4, I'll show you why it's essential to balance Feng Shui with practical design. And finally, in Chapter 6, I'll reveal my unique approach to Feng Shui.

Are you ready to transform your home into an abundance magnet?

Let's begin.

CHAPTER 1

Transforming your Home into an Abundance Magnet

An abundant home is more than just a physical structure; it is a space that nurtures your health, wealth and happiness. It provides opportunities for you to thrive and flourish in all areas of your life.

Feng Shui can help you achieve this abundance by harmonising the energy flow within your space. By making subtle changes, you can unlock the potential of your home to improve relationships, increase productivity, and foster feelings of empowerment. I will guide you through the principles of Feng Shui and show you how to apply them to your own living environment to create a place that supports your goals and aspirations.

From abysmal to auspicious

A home is intended to be a sanctuary, a haven of abundance that nourishes the mind, body and spirit. Often, when I first meet clients, I find them feeling drained—low on energy, burdened with stress and feeling disconnected from their loved ones. Such depletion can manifest in various ways, including outbursts of anger, a decline in motivation, or a diminishing sense of joy in everyday life.

When applying Feng Shui principles in designing spaces, I've observed that the energy in people's homes tends to fall into one of four categories: *abysmal, average, adequate* and *auspicious.*

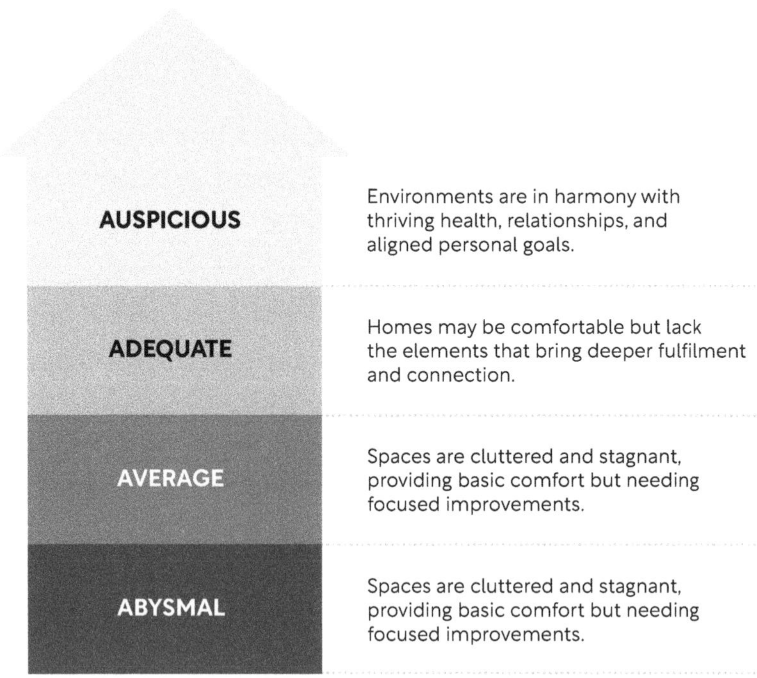

1: Four types of energy in a home

Unfortunately, too many people find that the energy in their homes is stuck at the lowest level: *abysmal*. This level often manifests as a state of utter depletion, characterised by signs of depression, persistent health issues and overwhelming clutter. The atmosphere in these homes feels dysfunctional and even toxic, sometimes appearing beyond repair. However, despite these daunting conditions, there is always room for improvement and transformation through Feng Shui.

When people are stuck at this level, they may feel trapped. It's as if the system is working against them, creating a vicious cycle that's tough to break. At this level, people may not even realise how much the energy in their surroundings adversely affects their well-being.

There's a myth that many people believe: Feng Shui is a foreign concept that doesn't apply to them. However, the truth is that Feng Shui is about the flow of energy in one's surroundings, making it relevant to everyone, regardless of their belief in it. Once people understand this, they can begin to move up to the next level.

The second level, *average*, is where life feels just bearable. Homes at this level are often cluttered or disorganised, leading to a feeling of overwhelm. It's not an ideal state, but it's also not the worst. People here often think about taking control, yet something usually holds them back. To move beyond this level, it's essential to shift the energy flow within the home, which can be as simple as undertaking a spring clean or decluttering.

Moving up to the third level, *adequate*, people find a comfortable energy balance in their homes, yet there's still room for improvement. They might feel somewhat unfulfilled and recognise that their relationships could be deeper and more connected. There's an underlying sense that life holds more than they're currently experiencing. At this level, small but meaningful adjustments can make a significant difference. By rearranging spaces to encourage open communication, introducing calming elements, or creating areas for family interaction, you can transform an adequate environment into one that supports and enriches your life. While this level may feel okay, remember that the right energy flow can elevate your home from simply adequate to a space of abundance and deeper fulfilment.

At the highest level, *auspicious*, a home radiates peace, vitality and prosperity. This is where good health flourishes, relationships resonate with harmony, and the environment aligns with your goals and aspirations. Living in an auspicious space means thriving in an atmosphere that supports and elevates every aspect of your life.

The ripple effect

Creating an abundant home can lead to a remarkable ripple effect, enabling you to positively influence not just your own life but also those around you. By optimising the energy flow within your living spaces, you create an environment that fosters well-being and opens the door to new possibilities.

Some might consider the pursuit of creating an abundant home as superficial, given the serious issues the world faces right now. However, don't let guilt overshadow your desire to find joy in your surroundings. While it's natural to focus on other priorities like work and family, nurturing your living environment elevates your own vibration and energy. When you look after your energy, your energy looks after you.

What's next?

In Chapter 2, you will learn about the history of Feng Shui and its fundamental principles. I'll give you an overview of this remarkable practice and share with you some aspects that have intrigued and excited me.

CHAPTER 2

Feng Shui Decoded

Feng Shui, which literally translates to 'wind and water', is a complex art based on formula, culture and arrangement. Ancient Chinese masters found that different energy patterns affected the human body and mind. They observed that when people were aligned with positive energy, they experienced periods of good fortune. When they were aligned with negative energy, they experienced misfortune and obstacles. From these observations came a defined set of rules, systems and guidelines that form the basis of traditional Feng Shui theories.

True Feng Shui is not based on superstition or religion. It is an Eastern philosophy that originates from the foundation of Chinese metaphysics, a branch of philosophy that explores the nature of reality and the universe. Feng Shui is deeply inspired by the principles of Taoism, an ancient Chinese philosophy that emphasises living in harmony with the Tao, or 'the Way'. Taoism teaches that everything in the universe is interconnected and constantly changing, influenced by the balance of yin and yang—opposite yet complementary forces. Chinese metaphysics, which encompasses acupuncture, Chinese herbal medicine and traditional Chinese medicine (TCM), is guided by these principles.

Feng Shui focuses on the energy flow within your environment, and how it affects your wellbeing. Similarly, acupuncture and TCM use the principles of energy flow and balance to promote health and wellness. Acupuncture, for example, involves the insertion of thin needles into specific points of the body to stimulate the flow of energy. TCM uses herbs and other natural remedies to balance the body's energy and promote healing. As research advances, more scientific evidence is emerging to support the efficacy of these modalities.

These practices share a common philosophy that the human body and the environment are interconnected, and that maintaining balance and harmony between them is essential for optimal health and wellbeing.

Due to its esoteric nature, Feng Shui encompasses various schools of thought. Its ancient texts were written poetically, requiring interpretation, with practices traditionally passed on from master to student. The interpretive process involves correlative thinking, which differs from the analytical thinking many in the Western world are accustomed to. This has led to confusion and difficulty in understanding Feng Shui, resulting in conflicting information in books and on the internet. Feng Shui can be a highly effective tool for improving the energy and harmony of your surroundings, provided you approach it with an open mind and guidance from a trusted practitioner.

Feng Shui lite vs Feng Shui extreme

There's a surface-level view of Feng Shui, which I refer to as Feng Shui 'lite'. Adherents of Feng Shui lite think that by simply placing a lucky object here or there, such as golden ornaments and money toads, they will receive great wealth. Or if they have an element of bad Feng Shui, their life is doomed. There's also a common, overly simplified approach to Feng Shui that incorrectly applies the same energy map to every home, ignoring the unique features and specific orientation of each residence.

At the other end of the spectrum is an extreme, rule-driven approach to Feng Shui, where every rule must be followed to the letter, to the detriment of practicality or design. I've seen instances where people, misled by extreme interpretations of Feng Shui, end up making choices that reverse the very benefits they seek. Through my experience, it's become clear that without proper understanding, Feng Shui's potential can be unintentionally misdirected.

For instance, I had a client share a story about her friend who received Feng Shui advice from a family member. The advice, though well-intentioned, left her too scared to use her newly built kitchen, fearing it would stir up negative energy. Instead, she resorted to setting up a makeshift cooking area in a corner of her dining room, complete with buckets and a microwave. This situation is a far cry from the true essence of Feng Shui. Rather than creating fear, Feng Shui is meant to cultivate an atmosphere of peace and positivity.

I have encountered many who perceive Feng Shui as a collection of superstitious practices, without understanding the structured system behind it—one that can be aligned with beautiful, functional design. In my practice, when I explain my Feng Shui approach to clients, there's often a sense of relief. They are reassured to learn that I'm not about to transform their property into something resembling a Chinese restaurant, unless of course, that's what they're trying to achieve.

Learning Feng Shui properly isn't something that happens overnight. It's a profound discipline, anchored in centuries of tradition and extensive knowledge.

While some might assume it's as simple as picking up a book and following a few guidelines, truly understanding the nuances of Feng Shui is far more challenging. The art of Feng Shui involves much more than just applying basic principles; it demands an in-depth understanding of complex theories and practices. Even among seasoned Feng Shui masters, there are often debates and differing viewpoints, further illustrating the depth and complexity of this ancient art. This richness is what makes Feng Shui a lifelong journey of learning and application, continuously evolving as one delves deeper into its wisdom.

Feng Shui's journey west

During the 1970s, a religious leader and scholar, Professor Lin Yun, introduced to the United States a unique form of Feng Shui, known as Black Sect Tantric Buddhist School of Feng Shui, or more commonly, Black Hat Sect Feng Shui. This approach is a standardised system that became popular because it was so easy to understand and implement. According to this system, every home has the same energy map determined by the location of its main entrance. However, it doesn't necessarily factor in the unique features of an individual home, such as design, orientation or the effects of time.

The Feng Shui industry owes a debt of gratitude to Professor Lin Yun for introducing Feng Shui to the West, but with the rising awareness and availability of information about traditional Feng Shui, we are now ready for more.

The popularity of Feng Shui in the West coincided with the emergence of the New Age movement, which emphasised personal transformation, healing and spirituality. As a result, modern Feng Shui consultants often integrate New Age practices into their approach. For instance, decluttering, which emerged as an antidote to materialism, has become a significant trend. And while space-clearing and sage-burning techniques are not part of traditional Feng Shui practices, they are highly effective in rejuvenating the energy in a space. I incorporate them into my own practice with valuable results.

Qi: the invisible breath of life

Feng Shui is the study of the flow of *qi*, or life-force energy, which impacts your spiritual, mental and physical wellbeing. Qi is present in all things—both seen and unseen—that exist around you. All living and non-living objects, including yourself, vibrate at a unique rate of energy that connects everything in the universe.

By examining the flow of qi in your home and surroundings, you can enhance positive energy and minimise negative energy. Your surroundings reflect your energetic vibration, and vice versa, your energetic vibration can impact the home and surroundings you attract.

Qi can be classified into two groups, positive and negative. Positive qi is beneficial for your health and wellbeing, and examples of this include fresh flowers, beautiful artwork, a serene garden, your favourite music, or a cool breeze on a sunny day. Negative qi can be harmful and manifest as clutter, bad odours, stagnant water, or even things in your home that you simply don't like, such as decor that doesn't resonate with you, or gifts you've never wanted. It's essential to recognise and address these energy-drainers to cultivate a more harmonious living space.

These tangible forms of qi, like the decor and belongings you surround yourself with, are just one dimension of Feng Shui. Beyond what you can see and touch, there are intangible, unseen forces at work, shaping the energetic essence of a space. Personal experiences and emotions, too, play a role. Strong emotions like anger and grief, for instance, have an undeniable impact on the human body and can potentially imprint the energy of a space. It's these unseen energies that can determine whether the environment in a home naturally supports areas of your life like finances, health and relationships.

A Feng Shui practitioner assesses the flow of qi, or energy, within your home and surroundings, offering guidance to harmonise these energies towards a more balanced environment. This may involve suggestions regarding furniture placement, colour choices, adding or removing objects, or other nuanced adjustments to enhance the energy flow. The aim is to create a home that resonates with balance and positivity, fostering enhanced wellbeing, success, and prosperity.

Yin and yang: balancing the dual forces

Yin and yang are two powerful forces that influence the flow of qi. These forces represent the dualities of nature and how things function in relation to each other. The yin and yang symbol, which depicts two complementary halves, is often used to symbolise balance and harmony.

Yin
Soft materials
Curved forms
Neutral tones
Shaded areas
Quiet spaces
Intimate nooks
Matte textures
Natural materials

Yang
Hard surfaces
Straight lines
Vibrant colours
Natural light
Active zones
Expansive areas
Reflective finishes
Manufactured materials

2: Yin and yang balancing the dual forces
The yin and yang symbol represents a state of balance, harmonising calming energies (yin) with dynamic forces (yang). Each half contains a dot of the opposite element, emphasising the interdependence and presence of both energies in every space.

Yin and yang have distinct characteristics associated with different aspects of the natural world. Yin is often associated with darkness, dampness, coldness, slowness, night-time, passivity and contraction, while yang is typically described as light, hot, warm, fast, bright, active and expansive.

Yin houses can be cold and dark, lack vitality, and leave residents feeling drained and unmotivated. Conversely, yang houses are livelier and more energetic, and are often characterised by busy people engaged in active pursuits. For instance, busy apartment blocks on main roads tend to have higher levels of yang energy compared with quiet homes in remote locations. Continuously living in a predominantly yang environment can lead to sleeplessness and heightened stress. It's not about favouring one over the other, but finding the right balance.

Understanding the interplay between these two forces is a key aspect of Feng Shui practice. By creating balance and harmony between yin and yang energies in your space, you can create an environment that is more conducive to the flow of positive energy.

The wisdom of Chinese metaphysics

According to the fundamental concepts of Chinese metaphysics, the universe is made up of five elements: fire, earth, metal, water and wood. These elements are regarded as the fundamental building blocks of nature and interact with one another in various ways. The interactions between these elements are believed to be responsible for the cyclical patterns observed in nature and human life. Understanding the roles and relationships of these elements is key to comprehending Chinese metaphysics, and its application in various fields such as Feng Shui and traditional Chinese medicine.

Each of the five elements is associated with certain colours, shapes and materials that Feng Shui practitioners incorporate within a space to create balance, and each has a specific quality of energy, or qi. The five elements are also linked with specific directions, seasons, physical organs, emotions, and even phases of life. By understanding these multifaceted connections, Feng Shui practitioners can more accurately address and rectify energy imbalances. These imbalances can be identified in the energy map of your home, which I will explain in the following chapter.

Let's delve deeper into each of these five elements, exploring their unique attributes and how they can be introduced into a space for optimal balance and harmony. Within the realm of Feng Shui, every physical object around us resonates with the energy of one of these five elements:

Five elements

1. WOOD

Symbolising growth and vitality, the element of wood is represented by the colour green and takes on a rectangular form. By introducing plants or incorporating timber furniture into a space, you can invite an ambiance of growth and vitality.

2. METAL

Associated with sharpness and precision, metal is represented by the colour white and circular shapes. Incorporating metallic accents into a space may enhance focus and clarity.

3. EARTH

Associated with stability and grounding, the element of earth aligns with the warm tones of yellow and the square shape. Including earthy materials such as clay or stone into a space can create a sense of stability and grounding.

4. WATER

Symbolising fluidity and adaptability, water is characterised by the colours blue and black, and wavy, organic shapes. Water elements can promote a sense of fluidity and vibrancy.

5. FIRE

Associated with passion and transformation, the element of fire is represented by the colour red and triangular shapes. By adding features like fireplaces or using candlelight, you can ignite a space with warmth and dynamic energy.

The cyclical nature of the five elements is based on the concept of *wu xing*, which means 'five phases' or 'five elements' in Chinese. This concept describes the dynamic interactions between the five elements of fire, earth, metal, water and wood. The relationship between the five elements is illustrated in this model.

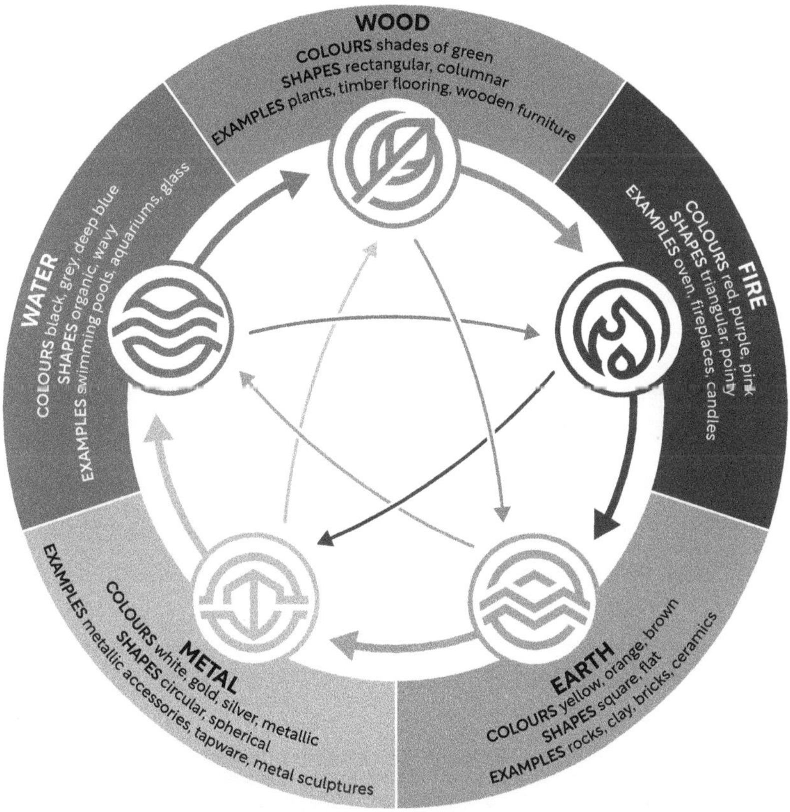

3: Five elements

This diagram shows the Five Elements of Feng Shui—Wood, Fire, Earth, Metal, and Water—and how they interact. Through a cycle of support and balance, each element either helps to nurture or keep the others in check. This ensures a balanced and positive energy flow in your space, which is reflected in the choice of colours, shapes and materials around you.

To illustrate how the five elements are interconnected, let's look at the productive cycle. For instance, in this cycle, water provides nourishment, encouraging the growth of plants, which embody the wood element. Wood, in turn, fuels fire, allowing it to burn and generate heat. As fire burns, it produces ash, which enriches the earth. From the earth, we extract metal, and metal, when it condenses moisture, contributes to the formation of water. Thus, the cycle continues, with each element supporting and creating the next.

This cycle highlights the interdependence of the five elements, as each one contributes to the growth and development of the others. For example, without water, there would be no nourishment for plants to grow and become wood, and without wood, there would be no fuel for fire. Alongside the productive cycle, there's also a destructive cycle and control cycle. In these, each element can balance or suppress another. For instance, water extinguishes fire, fire burns wood, wood depletes water, and so forth. These counter-balancing actions maintain harmony among the elements.

The energies in your home are connected to these five elements. If there is negative energy that needs to be addressed, a Feng Shui practitioner will recommend elements to neutralise its effect. On the other hand, if the energy is positive, certain elements can be used to enhance its impact and promote an even more positive energy flow. For instance, if a Feng Shui practitioner finds the energy of conflict in a room associated with the wood element, they will suggest neutralising it with the fire element. This can help to restore balance and harmony in the space.

In Feng Shui, it's not strictly necessary to have all five elements present in every room. The key to creating balance is using the appropriate elements most suitable for the particular space and its intended purpose. For example, a living room may benefit from a combination of fire, earth and wood elements to create a cosy, nurturing and welcoming space. On the other hand, a home office may benefit from a combination of metal and water elements to create a more focused and productive environment.

It's important to note that the specific combination and balance of elements in a space can vary based on the individual needs and preferences of the occupants, as well as the specific Feng Shui principles being applied. A Feng Shui practitioner can help determine the most appropriate elements for a particular area based on various factors, such as the layout, orientation and purpose of the space, as well as the energy and flow of qi within it. We'll take a closer look at how to blend the five elements into your design in Chapter 4.

One of many influencing factors

Before we delve deeper into Feng Shui, let's consider its role in your life, and what other factors complement it.

Feng Shui emphasises the importance of the energy in your surroundings and its influence on your moods, psychology and luck. While luck allows good things to happen by chance, it is not the sole enabler of positive events. Fortunate outcomes result from a combination of factors, including a positive mindset, motivation and self-mastery.

The following Chinese proverb offers insights into the various factors contributing to your life.

> *First is a man's destiny,*
> *Second is his luck,*
> *Third is his Feng Shui,*
> *Fourth is his virtue,*
> *Fifth is his knowledge.*

Each factor plays an important role. Let's take a moment to explore each one.

1. Destiny

According to Chinese tradition, the energy at the time of your birth shapes the course of your life. While you do not have control over this conceptual energy, you can learn to work with it and harness its power. Gaining insight into your birth chart through Four Pillars of Destiny (Chinese astrology) can reveal your inherent strengths and guide you in making choices that align with your true path. This understanding empowers you to navigate life's journey with greater awareness and purpose.

2. Luck

Luck may appear to be an uncontrollable force, but your mindset, actions and perseverance influence it significantly. When you maintain a clear vision of your goals and take consistent actions to achieve them, you attract positive outcomes and opportunities.

In other words, by actively pursuing your aspirations, you set the stage for good luck to find you.

3. Feng Shui

This ancient practice is all about the energy in your surroundings and its impact on you. By understanding and applying the principles of Feng Shui, you can cultivate an environment that boosts your wellbeing and success. As you read this book, I invite you to approach Feng Shui with a sense of curiosity and light-hearted exploration. The journey to harmonising your space should be as enjoyable and uplifting as the results it brings.

4. Virtue

This refers to your interactions with others. By treating people with kindness, compassion and integrity, you build strong relationships that positively impact the world around you. Consider how being of service to others can enrich your own life. Engaging in acts of kindness and service not only benefits those around you but also cultivates a deeper sense of happiness and fulfillment within yourself. This cycle of virtue and wellbeing reinforces the idea that our own happiness is interconnected with how we treat and serve others.

5. Knowledge

Education is an essential aspect of personal growth and development. By seeking out knowledge—and continuously learning—you can expand your horizons and open yourself up to new opportunities. Mindset mentor Rob Dial puts it well when he says you're either 'green and growing or brown and dying'. This analogy highlights the importance of constant learning and growth. Like a plant that needs to grow to stay vibrant, our minds thrive when we keep learning and exploring.

Feng Shui is a key element in creating a life of abundance, but it's part of a bigger picture. When it's combined with a positive attitude, determination and a commitment to personal growth, the impact is much stronger. This holistic approach offers a comprehensive way to live a life that is rich and rewarding, in harmony with the natural flow of the universe.

What's next

Now that we've looked at some basic concepts, it's time to move past the simplistic views to understand the more advanced techniques that tap into the deeper aspects of Feng Shui. At the centre of these is the energy map, a powerful tool we'll explore in Chapter 3.

CHAPTER 3

Map the Energy in Your Home

Abundance starts with a Feng Shui energy map, a tool that highlights the energy dynamics within your home. These energies, subtly influencing your psyche, are pivotal in driving success, wealth and opportunities. However, when these energies are out of balance, they can fill your space with tension and unease.

When I first learned that every home has a unique map of energy, I was fascinated and eager to learn more about my own. Think of it like a personalised horoscope for your home. This Feng Shui tool provides invaluable insights into the potential of your home and how well it supports your physical and emotional wellbeing, relationships and finances.

Creating an energy map is an essential step towards achieving Feng Shui abundance. While it is a technical process that often requires guidance from a professional, the benefits it brings are significant. An energy map can help you make informed decisions about the planning and design of your home, inspire your decorating choices, and provide insights into the best property investments. It can help you determine the best location for your main functional areas like your entrance, bedroom and kitchen. This tool will allow you to discover the best ways to arrange your spaces to maximise positive energy.

The benefits of an energy map don't stop there. If you don't have the flexibility to make big changes, an energy map can guide the subtler aspects of your home's design, such as colour schemes, furniture choices and material selection. It offers inspiration for everything from room layouts to curtain colours, enabling you to make the most of your living space, regardless of its size or constraints.

If you have family members with specific issues, like a history of illness, you can use the energy map to make informed decisions about which rooms are best suited for them. Or let's say you have a child in their final years of high school. An energy map can help you find the best place for their desk to support academic success.

My client Tracey felt overwhelmed when she and her family were about to move into a new home. With three children, she knew that one of their biggest challenges would be deciding who got which bedroom. The kids were already squabbling over who would get the larger room or the one with the better view.

I suggested using the energy map to help with the decision. By analysing the unique energy flows in each room of the new house, we were able to determine which spaces would be best suited for each child based on their individual needs.

Tracey was thrilled with the outcome. Not only did the energy map help her make a well-informed decision, but it also provided a way to settle the disputes between her children. With the energy map as our guide, we were able to create a peaceful and harmonious living space for the whole family. The squabbles subsided, and the kids settled happily into their new rooms. Tracey is grateful for the Feng Shui input in helping her make the best decisions for her family, and she's even noticed an improvement in their overall wellbeing since moving in.

Robert, a property developer, called me as he began planning the construction of duplexes. He wanted to create a space that was beautiful and energetically harmonious. We began the design process by considering the flow of energy within each home. During the design phase, Robert and I discussed the potential benefits of swapping the living space and bedroom on the first floor. By conducting an energy map analysis, I found that this change could activate the wealth sector of the building, thereby improving the energetic flow and unlocking the potential for greater prosperity. While this change required a shift in the original design plans, Robert was keen to incorporate Feng Shui principles into his property development. He ultimately made the decision to switch the location of the rooms. This was a move that not only created a more harmonious living environment, but also set his development apart from others in the area.

Upon completion of the building, Robert made it a point to inform potential buyers that Feng Shui principles were incorporated into the design. As a result, he was thrilled to find that his property generated a significant amount of interest from potential buyers, further highlighting the value and appeal of incorporating Feng Shui principles into a property development.

Uncovering hidden treasures within your walls

Your home, like every home, has a unique profile of energy. The energy map of your home is based on a series of calculations and formulas. These are based on your floor plan, the direction your home faces, the surrounding landscape, the date your home was built and your own birth data.

The energy map is overlaid on your floor plan and divided into segments like a pie chart. Each segment shows the directional sector of north, south, east and west, and the intermediate directions of northeast, northwest, southeast and southwest. Calculations are made, and various formulas are applied to determine the configuration of energy in each room of your home. A Feng Shui master can pinpoint energy zones with great potential, like the wealth sector, that you'll want to tap into. Or there may be toxic energy zones with influence you'll want to avoid.

Each occupant also has a specific profile of energy, based on their birth information, that corresponds to a section in the home's energy map. This indicates how each person's profile relates to the home and whether it supports their health, wealth and relationships.

An energy map is insightful. When clients talk about past experiences, they often align with the potential I see in the energy map.

My clients, Jen and Steve, were desperately trying to start a family. They contacted me as a last resort. They hoped that changing the energy in their home would bring them more luck in terms of fertility. I calculated the energy map of their home and found a large water feature in a toxic-energy zone. Its location in Feng Shui terms contributed to abdominal illness. I advised them to drain and turn off the water feature. Steve loved the water feature, so he wasn't happy with my advice, but he went along with it anyway. Within weeks I received the joyous news that the couple were expecting twins.

An intriguing observation: during Jen's pregnancy, Steve wanted to use the water feature. Not long after he started using it, Jen experienced early contractions. They promptly switched off the water feature, and soon after the symptoms subsided. Jen continued to have a smooth remainder of the pregnancy.

Working with clients through their challenges is hard, but it's also incredibly rewarding to see them find happiness and peace. I remember one client who had left an abusive relationship and was looking for a fresh start. As I walked through her old home, I noticed the energy map indicated misfortune in the bedroom and conflict at the entrance. These factors accurately reflected the difficulties she had faced in her relationship.

To help her start anew, I analysed the Feng Shui of her new home, and we were both thrilled to discover that it had wonderful romance energy. With the right environment and energy, she attracted a new partner and found happiness in a healthy relationship. When I last checked in with her, she was still enjoying the positive energy in her home and was happy in her new relationship.

You might be worried about what your energy map will reveal. Suppose it indicates challenges like separation or financial difficulty. It's important to understand that these are potential indicators, not certainties. Consider them as signposts or lessons you need to learn at a particular time. Let them serve as a prompt to work on underlying issues. A specific challenge projected by your energy map can be addressed with the right attention and action.

On the other hand, there might be a particular room in your home with excellent energy. And if you can enhance that positive energy, it can lead to greater abundance. When you focus on improving yourself and creating good Feng Shui in your environment, you'll be setting yourself up for success in a powerful way.

Unlocking light and energy: home orientation

Orientation is a key factor in Feng Shui, driving many of its calculations and formulas. It refers to the direction your home faces in relation to its main source of energy, which is the active side of the property. For most single-dwelling houses, the active side faces the street. On the other hand, waterfront properties are often measured facing the view because water is a powerful source of energy.

The term orientation refers to the cardinal directions of north, south, east and west, and the intermediate directions of northeast, northwest, southeast and southwest. Orientation also determines how your home interacts with weather patterns, affecting how it receives natural light and responds to seasonal changes.

A well-oriented home in Feng Shui captures natural light and warm breezes, deflects glare and provides shelter from harsh winds and rain. These are the foundational aspects of creating a harmonious environment. However, in the practice of Feng Shui, many people get so absorbed in intricate formulas that they overlook or ignore these critical basics. While advanced Feng Shui formulas are valuable, it's essential to remember the foundational principles that connect our living spaces to the natural world.

In a Feng Shui consultation, the orientation of your home is measured to the degree. A Feng Shui compass, known as a *luopan* is used to read the precise orientation of a building. This is a large, specialised compass with an overlay of Feng Shui information, allowing the practitioner to gather the necessary data for many Feng Shui calculations.

A Feng Shui master takes measurements by standing outside the building on natural ground. For instance, I will stand at the front of a property and verify my compass measurements from different positions. Sometimes the compass will malfunction due to magnetic interference, which can be caused by heavy electrical cabling under concrete reinforcements, power poles, or magnetic influences below ground. Occasionally I need help from a geomancer to balance the earth energies.

Magnetic interferences can also come from the presence of spirits. When this happens, the luopan needle might spin, in which case I collaborate with a spirit medium; essentially, a real-life 'ghost-buster'. There's more on this exciting topic in Chapter 8.

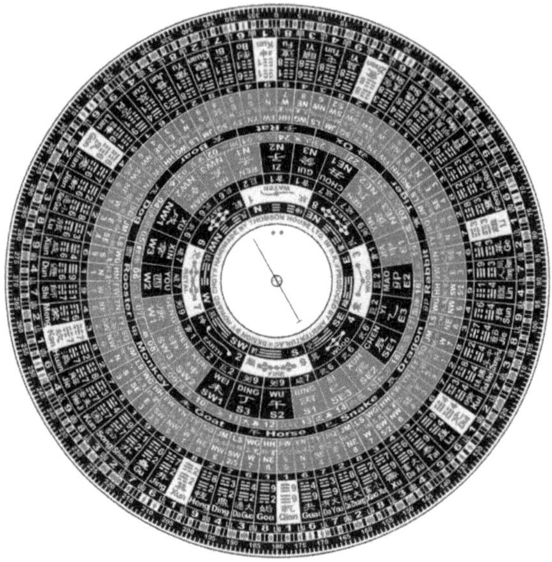

4: The Luopan

The Luopan, a traditional Chinese compass, is an essential tool in Feng Shui practice. It features detailed markings used to assess the directional energy of a space, guiding practitioners in harmonising environments with the natural world. This intricate instrument combines geomancy, astronomy and geography to align living spaces with auspicious energy flows, key to enhancing wellbeing and prosperity. Pictured above is a Luopan designed by Master Howard Choy.

I use online mapping tools such as Google Earth to assist with determining the orientation of a building. When I visit a site in person, I cross-check my luopan measurements with Google Earth. However, there are limitations to solely relying on Google Earth. The application is based on *true* north, whereas a compass, including the luopan, works from *magnetic* north. True north is constant, linked to the Earth's axis. On the other hand, magnetic north is influenced by the Earth's ever-changing magnetic field, originating from its core. If you rely on true north without factoring in magnetic declination, your energy map could end up being inaccurate. A well-informed Feng Shui master always adjusts for the difference between true north and magnetic north, a process known as declination. Declination varies from time to time, and from location to location.

Capturing natural light is a fundamental aspect of good Feng Shui. In the southern hemisphere, homes with a northerly aspect are highly prized due to the sun's path, and the opposite is true for homes in the northern hemisphere. Having lived on the east coast of Australia, I've experienced homes facing all cardinal directions: north, south, east, and west. My current home, with its rear living spaces facing north and the main entrance to the south, has been my favourite. This alignment brings warmth, brightness, and a sense of comfort. Living here, I've found myself feeling happier and more productive, a testament to the positive impact of well-aligned Feng Shui.

Historical figures have long recognised the influence of environmental factors on health. Dr Esther Sternberg is an internationally renowned expert on the mind-body stress connection, and the role environment plays on healing from illness. In her book, *Healing Spaces*, she describes how Florence Nightingale found that natural light and ventilation greatly improved patient recovery rates. This observation led to a revelation that sunlight doesn't just provide warmth; it actively combats bacteria, therefore promoting health and wellness. Nightingale revolutionised hospital design, with large windows to allow greater access to natural light and ventilation. These principles were an inspiration for modernist architects of the 1920s and 1930s, who designed homes and hospitals to maximise sun exposure.

Not every home can have the ideal orientation, but thoughtful design can still maximise natural elements effectively. It's important to understand how your home is oriented: observe where the sun rises and sets, and identify areas within your home that could capture more natural light. The expertise of a skilled architect is invaluable in this process. By combining their architectural knowledge with the insights of a Feng Shui master, you create a formidable team. Together, they can guide you in optimizing your home's design to its fullest potential.

The impact of timing in Feng Shui

In astrology, your energy profile is captured by your date of birth. While the underlying energy of a home is fixed when it is built, the active or manifesting energy within it changes over time. According to Feng Shui principles, energy shifts annually, monthly, daily and even hourly. Significant changes in energy occur in 20-year cycles, and the cycle in which your home was built affects the calculation of your energy map. These cycles of time are based on the Chinese solar calendar—the *Hsia* calendar, also known as the 10,000-year calendar, which is an ancient measure of sun cycles.

The solar calendar, which begins around 4 February, was historically used to help farmers identify the best time to plant and harvest their crops. Feng Shui masters use this calendar to map and predict changes in energy. The lunar calendar, which determines the date of Chinese New Year, is integral to various Feng Shui practices and calculations.

When aligning the solar calendar with our Gregorian calendar, the shifts in 20-year Feng Shui cycles typically start around 4 February. These cycles are important for understanding and predicting energy changes in Feng Shui. For practical purposes, especially when analysing heritage buildings, we can trace these cycles back as far as needed. More recent cycles began in 1964, 1984, 2004 and 2024.

As one cycle transitions to the next, the quality of energy within a home undergoes significant transformation. There are also annual fluctuations in energy, which can be effectively managed. The key is to establish an optimal energy map right from the start. Over time, the energy in a building can change substantially, sometimes shifting from a state of prosperous energy to the opposite. Therefore, at every major change in the energy cycle, like the onset of a new 20-year period, seeking a Feng Shui consultation is highly beneficial. The transition in 2024, for instance, marked the start of such a new period. These transitions are pivotal in Feng Shui, emphasising the need to adapt to and harness new energies.

Recognising the role of energy cycles in Feng Shui, we see the importance of knowing your home's construction date for a Feng Shui consultation. This information is key to creating an accurate energy map.

Sometimes all a Feng Shui master will need to know is the decade your home was built. If the building date falls squarely within a 20-year cycle, it's straightforward; but if it's closer to the cusp of a 20-year cycle, more information will be required.

Ways to find out when your home was built

To find out when your home was built, you can start with your purchase contract. Your local council or water authorities might help too, as they often know when a house first got connected to water. Other places to look are the land titles office or in historical records in the library. Sometimes, you can even find this information online. Don't forget to ask your neighbours, especially the long-term residents, as they might know something about your home's history.

A home's energy map may change if it has been extensively renovated or rebuilt, depending on certain criteria. For example, was the renovation cosmetic or structural in nature? Was the roof removed, and if so, for how long? Share this renovation history with your Feng Shui master.

If you are still unsure when your home was constructed or renovated, a Feng Shui master may be able to test different energy maps to see which one aligns with your experiences in your home. A Feng Shui master can also use alternative techniques if you cannot find any information about the building date.

An essential step for abundance

An energy map is a way of finding the treasure in your home. It guides you to find the best energy for wealth, health and relationships, and helps in identifying and neutralising challenging energy zones. This approach is one of the deeper secrets of traditional Feng Shui, which sets it apart from the more superficial, one-size-fits-all approaches.

Working with an energy map will enable you to elevate your home's energy beyond the fundamental levels of Feng Shui. While you can make significant improvements to your home without an energy map (Part II of my book will help you), delving into the intricacies of traditional Feng Shui offers richer rewards.

Feng Shui is a highly nuanced art that takes many years to master. Unfortunately, a lot of people have been misled into thinking they can study Feng Shui in a few days and become their own Feng Shui master, or a practitioner for others. Learning Feng Shui properly is a long, complicated (and expensive) process. It's not as straightforward as studying a course in college. Feng Shui is an esoteric art with many different theories and schools of thought. Knowing the right masters to follow and courses to study is a challenge. It is infinitely more cost-effective to find a Feng Shui master you trust to help you with the selection and design of your home rather than trying to muddle through it yourself.

What's next

Now that you have a deeper understanding of an energy map and its role as a valuable tool in revealing your home's energy potential, the next chapter will explore the importance of harmonising Feng Shui principles with design. We'll delve into aligning Feng Shui's ancient wisdom with contemporary design to enhance the aesthetics and the energetic balance of your living spaces.

CHAPTER 4

Architectural Harmony: Feng Shui Design

I see a profound alignment between Feng Shui and design principles. When I approach the design of a new home, I draw inspiration from the Feng Shui energy map. Fundamental design principles such as balance, contrast, rhythm, proportion, interest, movement and harmony resonate with the fundamental principles of yin and yang.

However, it's essential to strike a balance: while the energy map provides valuable insights, it should not rigidly dictate a home's design. With a broader perspective, my goal is to weave Feng Shui with design elements harmoniously.

In my line of work, I often collaborate with architects. They reach out when clients want to incorporate Feng Shui principles into their home designs. When an architect comes across a design element that raises concerns, it's my responsibility to examine that feature and offer a

Feng Shui solution that aligns with it. With my background in design, my ambition is not only for my clients to live in their dream home but also to ensure these homes radiate the best Feng Shui energy, while remaining functional, practical and beautiful.

When I step into a room, my attention is drawn to its structural nuances: I assess the placement of windows and doors, the proportion of the space, and the delicate balance between openness and enclosure. Elements like light, focus, contrast and harmony capture my attention and each resonates with foundational Feng Shui principles.

There are questions that both Feng Shui masters and designers think about. How should the furniture be positioned? In which direction should seating arrangements face? Where is the natural light coming from, and how is artificial lighting integrated into the ambiance? Is there interest in the way the furniture and objects are arranged? Does the room reflect the homeowner's personal taste and contain the things they love?

A Feng Shui master should consider your specific needs and the way the home is used. There must be an element of flexibility to achieve a beautiful design that works for everyone living in the home.

Designing with Feng Shui in mind

For the best outcomes, Feng Shui principles should align with high-quality architectural and interior design. The goal is to create functional, beautiful homes or spaces that radiate with an abundance of positive energy. It's vital to balance both Feng Shui guidelines and personal design aesthetics, always keeping functionality and practical concerns at the forefront. In my practice, I bring together these elements, ensuring every design achieves optimal harmony and energy flow.

To illustrate how design and Feng Shui have complementary goals, let's look at one element of a home: the entrance.

Transitions are powerful, both in design and in life. The entrance of your home is more than just a point of access; it's the gateway to your personal sanctuary. From a design perspective, practical considerations matter. Can your entrance be accessed with ease? Does it cater to the needs of the occupants, including those who might need wheelchair access? Ideally, the design of your entrance creates a sense of arrival and gives you a hint of what lies ahead.

From a Feng Shui perspective, the front entrance holds a deeper symbolism. It is the most important area for your wealth. To maximise wealth energy, specific design elements can be thoughtfully integrated. A spacious foyer, for instance, symbolises the capacity to welcome and retain prosperity. Incorporating water features, when positioned according to Feng Shui principles, can attract and stimulate the flow of wealth. The choice between a serene or dynamic water feature should align with the desired energy balance, provide visual delight, and actively channel positive energy.

Entering a home should be an experience, a sentiment that designers often emphasise. A transitional space at the front door, no matter how modest, offers a buffer between the external and internal worlds. This concept resonates both with Feng Shui principles and contemporary architectural tastes.

However, not all homes have the luxury of a foyer. In such cases, it's important to steer clear of Feng Shui pitfalls like having the front door aligned with internal stairs or the back door. But these challenges offer opportunities. With subtle additions, such as a circular light fitting, beautiful artwork, or strategically positioned decor, the energy flow can be redirected.

Feng Shui and design share a yin-yang relationship, with many concepts intertwined. Following Feng Shui formulas or rules too strictly can sometimes lead to impractical outcomes. It's important to remember that if Feng Shui advice makes a space feel odd or uncomfortable, it defeats its purpose. Feng Shui is fundamentally about balance—it's the art of blending design, function and energy in a harmonious and effective way.

I once had a client troubled by a piece of Feng Shui advice she received from a well-meaning friend. She had placed a Chinese statue in her living room, thinking it would improve her relationships, but instead of the expected harmony, she felt that its ornate design was out of place in her modern home. Each time a guest visited, they would ask about the statue, making her question her choice. Seeing her discomfort, I offered a simple solution: remove it. After she had removed the object, her relief was palpable. She said her home felt like hers again, reinforcing that while Feng Shui offers direction, it should never overshadow personal comfort and style. Sometimes the best Feng Shui solution is what feels right for the individual.

Another client once shared her bewildering experience with a Feng Shui recommendation. She had been advised to place sixty-four salt-water cures—glasses filled with rock salt, water and lucky coins—throughout her home. This remedy, believed to dispel negative energies, was overwhelming in such an extreme way. Rather than feeling the peace Feng Shui aims to bring, her home became a cluttered maze of water glasses. Instead of harmony, she felt discomfort and irritation.

True Feng Shui is about enhancing your living space in a way that is harmonious with your lifestyle, without causing disruption. It's not merely about sticking to certain rules; it's more about ensuring these guidelines naturally integrate and resonate with your way of life.

On the flip side, if you're wondering whether prioritising design might overshadow Feng Shui, rest assured. Smart design choices can complement and amplify positive energy in your space. A proficient Feng Shui master will know how to combine these for the best outcome.

Where to begin

If you're planning to work with a Feng Shui master, start by creating a vision board with images of styles or materials you're drawn to for your interior and exterior. Maybe you're drawn to the Hamptons style with its coastal charm, or perhaps you're captivated by the

Danish concept of *hygge*, which exudes comfort and cosiness. It could also be the timeless appeal of natural elements like wood or stone that strikes your fancy. When you're ready for a Feng Shui consultation your vision board can be used as a guide to integrate your design choices with specific Feng Shui recommendations.

A vision board can be created on your computer or phone, or as a physical version like a scrapbook or pinboard. To create one on your computer, use sources like Pinterest or Instagram, where you can find diverse styles ranging from country to urban, minimalist to eclectic. To find material for a physical board, consider flipping through magazines, browsing the architecture and design sections at your local library for ideas, visiting your nearby bookshop, or printing images from online sources. Even if it's a specific piece of furniture or a light fitting you like, add these elements to your vision board for inspiration.

Shaping energy: the art of form and landscape

The overarching objective in Feng Shui design is to create an arrangement that contains and protects qi—the life force energy—and allows it to meander through your home. One of the original and foundational systems in Feng Shui is the form-school system, which is based on observation of the natural environment and the ways in which the physical shape and layout of a space can impact the flow of energy. It relates to the tangible aspects in your surroundings—the things you can see both in your interior and exterior environment. Form and landscape are central to the oldest forms of Feng Shui. The spatial and physical design of a home has always been considered as part of the fundamental principles in Feng Shui. Only recently have formula-based systems of Feng Shui seemed to overshadow form-school principles.

In my practice, form-school principles are a primary consideration in Feng Shui design. Internally, form relates to the layout of the home, the shape of the rooms, the position of the doors, the location of the windows, the furniture arrangements, and the visual aspects of a space.

Externally, form principles to consider include the slope and shape of the land, the angle at which a house is built, and whether the back of the property is open or enclosed. When determining the ideal layouts, a Feng Shui master not only considers sun and weather patterns, but also seeks a harmonious balance of yin and yang. The external features of a property play a vital role in harnessing and protecting the home's energy. At the rear of the home, trees, plants, or other barriers should be present to offer a sense of protection. The face of the home, whether directed towards a street or a scenic view, should remain open and inviting, allowing energy to flow in. Alongside the home, you'll want trees, plants, or neighbouring buildings to work together and give a sense of an embrace.

In Feng Shui theory, the form of the landscape is described through symbolic animal metaphors. These symbolic animals correlate with the four sides of your home. They serve as protective energy guards and depict the ideal landscape from a Feng Shui perspective. Each symbolic animal represents specific physical attributes that practitioners aim for.

Feng Shui animal metaphors

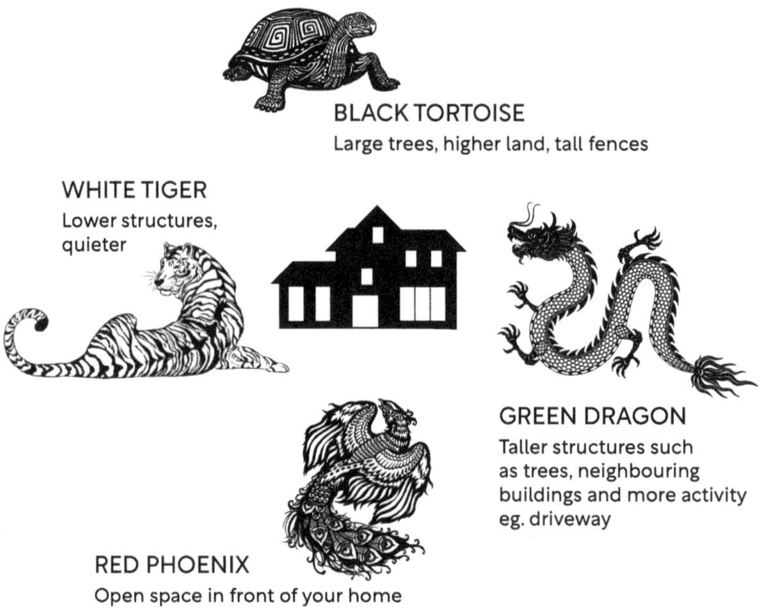

5: Feng Shui animal metaphors

TIGER AND DRAGON—THE LEFT AND RIGHT SIDES OF YOUR HOME

As you stand on the street and look at the front view of your home, the left side symbolises the tiger, representing yin or passive energy. This side should ideally be more subdued or lower than the right side, reflecting the tiger's earthly and grounded nature. On the other hand, the right side represents the dragon, symbolising yang or active energy. It's beneficial for this side to be more elevated or prominent, possibly incorporating architectural elements such as higher floors, elevated decks, or tall trees. Achieving harmony between these energies is a key objective of Feng Shui. But it's not always about achieving a perfect 50-50 balance. For the typical homeowner, balance refers to having more active than passive energy. This arrangement is intended to inspire the occupants to move, work, and engage.

Now, as you stand on your street and look at your home, ideally, in Feng Shui terms, the right-hand side of your property will have taller structures or more pronounced landforms than the left. To achieve this, consider the natural slope of your land and the neighbouring home or landscape on the right-hand side. If it doesn't naturally favour this setup, you might enhance the balance by planting taller trees or placing other tall elements on the right-hand side of your home.

PHOENIX—THE FRONT OF YOUR HOME

The phoenix symbolises the front of your home and serves as a beacon for attracting wealth and opportunities. The ideal representation of the phoenix is an attractive and open space in front of your property, such as a beautiful garden or lawn bordered by a fence or a row of low hedges to contain the energy flow.

The front of your property is a key aspect of Feng Shui as it is the area that typically receives the most energy flow. Therefore, it's important to create an open and welcoming environment that is well-maintained and visually appealing.

This can be achieved with thoughtful landscaping and by keeping the area clean and uncluttered.

TORTOISE—THE BACK OF YOUR HOME

The tortoise represents support, which means creating solid protection behind the home. This could involve planting trees or hedges, or constructing a wall for tangible strength and protection. This may also be represented by land sloping up at the back of the home, regarded as the Feng Shui ideal.

In my experience, some people take Feng Shui animal metaphors quite literally and try to address imbalances by placing statues of these creatures around their homes. Placing a statue of a tortoise in your backyard will not contain the energy flow or provide protection and support. Instead of relying on symbolic statues, which unfortunately lack magical powers, it's far more effective to make practical changes to your environment. Building a fence, a wall, or planting trees at the back of your home offers tangible support and protection, proving much more effective than a tortoise statue keeping watch.

If you do not have the ideal arrangement according to these form principles, you might wonder what this implies for you. If there is a lack of enclosure at the back of your home, it could indicate a lack of support from people who have an important role in your life, such as your boss, or your parents and other family members. If the tiger or dragon is out of balance, this indicates an imbalance of yin and yang. If the left-hand side is higher than the right-hand side, it can indicate that the matriarch or female of the household is the dominant influence in your home.

Historically, this system arose from an era where roles tied to masculinity and femininity were highly prescriptive. The ideal balance back then leaned towards yang, representing the male, being dominant, while yin, symbolic of the female, was more submissive. That is inherent in this model. Of course, times have changed, but it doesn't mean we don't still use the principles of yin and yang.

An excess of yin energy in a home can be just as disruptive as a dominance of yang. Active, decisive yang energies are balanced by the nurturing, softer yin energies, whatever you might think of the masculine and feminine. We tend to be happier when these aspects in a home are balanced, and not when one is over-shadowed by the other.

While the principles of yin and yang are foundational, the environment in which your home sits plays an integral role in Feng Shui. Types of landforms and properties are many and varied. Your home might be positioned on land that slopes from the street towards your house or vice versa. You may have water or a park facing the front or the back of your home. Your home may be on a busy street, in a cul-de-sac, at the end of a T-junction, or on a corner block (I expand on these in Chapter 8).

Building on this, when I assess a property, the energy map and its physical surroundings are interconnected. Let's say I calculate your energy map and find great energy for harmony and relationships at the back of your property. Firstly, I would check to see whether the energy is adequately contained. If not, I will specify a solid fence or boundary wall to hold in auspicious energy. Secondly, I would determine the best elements to use at the back of your home. If the ideal element is fire, I may recommend designing a fire pit with curved seating to encourage friendly get-togethers. If you have young children and you're concerned with child safety, a fire pit may not be suitable, but you could consider a tropical garden with a peaceful Buddha and red flowering plants instead (red being a fire colour). Many possible solutions can be tailored to your specific needs, ensuring we strike a balance that's both stylish and just right for you.

In my practice, I've noticed a pattern with clients living in homes with land steeply sloping down towards the back of the property. Sometimes I find these clients lacking in family support or feeling disconnected from parents. I have observed clients living in homes with an imbalance between the right and left-hand side of the property, where the wife or mother tends to be more dominant. This is not necessarily negative. Sometimes there can be too much yin energy in a property where people spend most of their time chilling out and not working or being productive.

It's possible to argue that many people are doing fine in houses in all types of landscapes. However, a Feng Shui consultation can reveal untapped potential. It is a multi-layered process, where the property's form is merely one of the many aspects we delve into.

Take a moment to reflect: what do you see as the strengths and shortcomings of your home's surroundings? Are there parts of your landscape that seem incomplete, windblown or dark? For example, if your home has land sloping down towards the back, this might indicate a leakage of finances. An imbalance between the right and left sides of the property can reflect in the dynamics within the household. However, instead of feeling overwhelmed, focus on the positive changes you can make. Planting trees or hedges, for example, could help correct these imbalances. If certain changes aren't possible, think about what your landform's features mean in Feng Shui terms. Reflect on their significance in your life and consider any proactive steps you might take to either harness or lessen their influence.

Blending the five elements into your design

In Chapter 2, I introduced the five elements of fire, earth, metal, water and wood. These are the building blocks of nature. Now let's go a bit deeper into these five elements and the roles they play. A Feng Shui master will use the five elements to influence the energetic quality of your home. When it comes to designing homes, the important aspects of the five elements are shape, colour and material.

Shapes and the five elements

SQUARE AND RECTANGULAR DESIGNS represent the elements of earth and wood.

TRIANGULAR DESIGNS SYMBOLISE the energy of fire. Triangular forms are more suited to spiritual or artistic spaces than residential homes. It is difficult to counteract the challenging energies that arise from sharp triangular shapes. While triangular designs are rare in homes, it's advisable to avoid such shapes where possible.

ROUND AND ORGANIC SHAPES represent the metal and water elements, often symbolising wealth in Feng Shui. Curved designs minimise sharp corners and create smooth flow of energy, giving a design a harmonious and fluid feel. This principle of ease and flow is also evident in art-deco-inspired homes.

It is widely considered that the ideal Feng Shui home design is a regular shape, like a squarish rectangle, with no missing parts. Missing corners or missing sectors indicate aspects of your life that may be compromised.

For example, if the southwest corner is missing from your home, it can indicate that the matriarch or mother in the household feels drained or compromised in some way. If the northwest corner is missing, this could compromise the patriarch. While a squarish rectangular house may be the Feng Shui ideal, it isn't always practical or reflective of many homes' unique designs. Consider this: your home might be designed to step in to capture natural light or to accentuate a specific feature in your landscaping. Many apartments are built with light wells or interior courtyards, which bring natural light into homes where it might otherwise be inaccessible. So while some may perceive a missing section as a Feng Shui shortcoming, such a design can enhance your home's energy in a far better way than if the building was a regular shape.

Feng Shui offers ideal design principles, providing guidance on creating harmonious spaces. For instance, a home built with a solid foundation—or at least appearing to have one—is often viewed more favourably than one on stilts or a structure with a cantilevered design. A solid foundation is favourable because of the home's grounding connection to the earth and the stability of nature. There's a natural ease in aligning with the flow of nature rather than defying it with structures that seem unsupported. However, if you think about homes in flood-prone areas, there is nothing ideal in Feng Shui terms about a house that gets flooded, so building a home on stilts becomes practical. In such scenarios, we can introduce complementary design elements to address Feng Shui challenges. For example, in a Queenslander style home, cladding and plants could be used to give the open space around the stilts a more solid appearance.

While unique designs have their charm, in the world of Feng Shui, homes with regular shapes hold more appeal. These conventional forms are typically preferred over more avant-garde or irregularly shaped properties, which can sometimes be viewed as controversial and less appealing from a Feng Shui perspective.

But imagine a world where all our homes were standard squares or rectangles uniformly seated on the ground? Feng Shui ideals prioritise convenience and efficiency, making such homes cheaper to build and more comfortable to live in. The simplicity of a rectangle also lends itself well to practical interior design, from furniture arrangement to hanging artwork. However, architectural diversity is the spice of life, and if you'd like a bit of panache, a seasoned Feng Shui master can guide you in blending tradition with individuality.

Combining Feng Shui with thoughtful design is about creating a home that's both visually appealing and rich in positive energy. It's important to remember that each home is unique, and while traditional shapes are often favoured in Feng Shui, not every space will fit these moulds. Instead of worrying over parts of your home that don't align perfectly with Feng Shui rules, let's focus on the enhancements you can make. Every home has its potential for harmony and balance, and I'll be exploring this in more detail in Part II.

What's next

Now that you see how Feng Shui and great design can complement each other, let me share the approach I use with my clients to infuse their homes with abundance. Join me as we delve deeper into the heart of Feng Shui through the unique model that I have developed as a Feng Shui master.

CHAPTER 5

The Feng Shui Path to Abundance

A friend once made a comment about my job as a Feng Shui master that amused me. She said I simply waltz through homes saying, 'Do this, do that, move this, and throw that'. I'll admit that there's a grain of truth to that perception, especially at the superficial level, but the reality is that Feng Shui is a complex and nuanced art, demanding both skill and deep understanding. There's so much more to Feng Shui than lucky ornaments and rearranging furniture. Behind the scenes, there's a lot of analytical work, more than most people might think.

As we dive deeper into this book, I'm excited to share my unique approach to Feng Shui. This is a method I have developed after years of working closely with clients. This model does not show how all Feng Shui practitioners work; it represents my own unique practice as a Feng Shui master and designer.

I love sharing my model with people who may not fully understand Feng Shui. It helps show the richness of this ancient practice and allows people to appreciate its power. My model is not designed to confuse you with complicated jargon. Instead, it breaks down my Feng Shui process into more accessible ideas. By exploring and using this model, you'll gain a better understanding of how Feng Shui can be used to create your ideal home. I'll outline the key aspects of my method to give you a deeper understanding of the process it takes to create an abundant home, but first I want to begin by drawing your attention to its centre. This is where our journey together will lead.

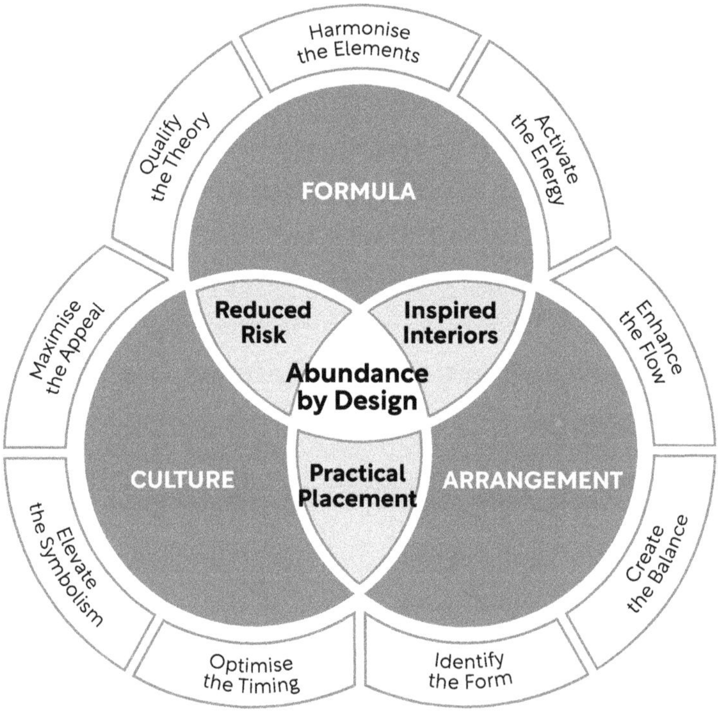

6: Feng Shui method by Jane Langof

Creating abundance by design

Striking a balance between practical design considerations and Feng Shui principles allows you to attain what I term 'abundance by design'. Abundance by design is at the heart of my work as a Feng Shui master. This concept is about inviting more of what enriches your life, far beyond material possessions. It focuses on cultivating thriving relationships, fostering optimal health, encouraging personal success, and inspiring a sense of purpose, all of which contribute to a harmonious and contented home life. My approach is dedicated to creating homes that embody this kind of abundance for you.

Abundance visualisation exercise

Pause for a moment and visualise your favourite space, whether it's in your home or another place that holds special meaning for you.

What feelings does this space evoke in you?

Reflect on the design, colours, textures and objects in this space. How do they contribute to these feelings?

Does this space reflect who you currently are, or perhaps who you aspire to be?

Now, imagine enhancing these feelings. Picture this space transformed into an area that radiates positive energy, channelled into every aspect of your home.

This is the essence of what I strive for in 'abundance by design'. It's about creating spaces that not only look beautiful but also resonate deeply with your personal aspirations and wellbeing.

My Feng Shui model can be visualised as a flower with three petals, each representing a pathway to achieving abundance by design:

- inspired interiors
- practical placement
- reduced risk

As we explore each petal, think about how these elements could manifest in your own space and contribute to an environment that supports and enriches you.

Inspired interiors

At the heart of Feng Shui is the creation of spaces that do more than just look good; they uplift and energise you. This petal is about creating a home that complements and boosts your personal energy, fostering an environment where you can grow and prosper. It's about designing a space that's visually appealing and, more importantly, in tune with your unique character and life goals. In this approach, we consider every aspect of your home's layout and design, from choosing the right colours to arranging your living spaces. Every decision is made to align your home with your aspirations. This isn't just about aesthetics; it's about creating a home that inspires and encourages you to reach your fullest potential.

Practical placement

The second petal is about creating a home that is both welcoming and functional. It starts with understanding your daily routines and interactions. Recognising that each household is unique, we tailor a design plan to meet your specific needs, interests and hobbies. For example, in a home with young children, we focus on fostering a nurturing environment to strengthen family bonds. As life evolves—perhaps when children grow up or the house dynamics change—we adjust the focus, maybe to enhance connections with your partner or friends.

Practical Feng Shui applications can enrich the relationships within your home, helping you rediscover moments of intimacy that might have been overshadowed by the bustling energy of family life. As your lifestyle evolves, a Feng Shui master will suggest necessary adjustments to keep positive energy flowing.

Practical placement also addresses potential sources of negative energy, like the noise of a busy road or sharp corners in your floor plan. These factors may disrupt the energy flow in your home, but with challenges come Feng Shui solutions. For instance, plants can act as buffers, helping to diffuse negative energy like traffic noise, and furniture can be repositioned to restore harmony. Practical placement is pivotal in achieving this balance, ensuring your space resonates with your needs and Feng Shui principles.

Reduced risk

The third petal, crucial in creating a Feng Shui-friendly home, focuses on comfort and peace of mind, ensuring that every aspect of your space is optimised for abundance. A common regret

I encounter with clients is not integrating Feng Shui principles earlier, which often leads to costly errors. Examples include staircases directly aligned with the front entrance, or bedroom layouts that result in unfavourably positioned beds, such as those aligned with a door.

Incorporating Feng Shui not only offers personal benefits in terms of living quality but also enhances your home's appeal to Feng Shui-aware buyers. Even if selling isn't on your immediate agenda, applying Feng Shui principles is a smart long-term investment. I've observed that homes with challenging Feng Shui issues often struggle to meet their market potential.

The importance of reduced risk magnifies during construction or renovation. Preventing expensive missteps from the start is crucial. This is why collaborating with architects and designers familiar with Feng Shui principles from the beginning of a project is invaluable.

Understanding these elements offers a clearer insight into how a well-planned home can nurture positivity and abundance. This is where the harmonisation of the old and new, tradition and innovation, comes in. It's a harmonious blend of traditional Feng Shui with beautiful design, culminating in a balanced, prosperous and stylish living space.

Exercise using the three petals

If you're planning features for your dream home, this simple exercise can help. Take a piece of paper and divide it into three columns, one for each petal. In each column jot down as many ideas as you can.

Inspired interiors	Practical placement	Reduced risk
Focus on spaces that energise and inspire you. Do you prefer large rooms bathed in natural light, or are you drawn to cosy, intimate corners? Do plain white walls inspire you or bore you? Let your imagination guide you. Think about colours, textures, and design elements that resonate with you. Capture every inspiring detail.	Here, think about practical aspects that will make your home more functional and efficient. It might be innovative storage solutions, multifunctional spaces, or energy-saving features. Tune into your personal needs and lifestyle and write down any ideas that come to mind.	Consider how to avoid common Feng Shui mistakes. For instance, ensure the front door doesn't directly face the back door or staircase, and avoid beams over key areas like your bed or desk. Jot down notes on these and other Feng Shui aspects you want to get right to minimise negative energy.

After completing this exercise you'll have a comprehensive list of features to guide your dream-home design. Don't worry about editing or fine-tuning your list just yet. The goal is simply to brainstorm and capture a wide array of ideas.

Three pillars of Feng Shui application

My approach to creating an abundant home rests on three core pillars: Formula, Culture and Arrangement.

Formula

This pillar revolves around identifying the Feng Shui techniques needed to align with you and your unique home. It's not a generic blueprint that fits everyone. It's about understanding your space, your energies, and selecting authentic Feng Shui strategies tailored to the needs of all who live within your home.

Culture

This pillar holds a dual meaning. First, it's about nurturing a culture of balance and harmony within your home. Second, it emphasises the understanding and value of the rich cultural heritage behind Feng Shui. By understanding and appreciating Feng Shui's cultural significance, you're creating a space that you and your family love. And if selling becomes a consideration in the future, the same understanding will resonate with Feng Shui-conscious buyers.

Arrangement

The third pillar deals with the physical design and tangible aspects of your home. It's not just about where you place a sofa or a bed, but understanding how these placements interact with the ambient energy, natural light, and even with other furniture pieces. It's a balancing act, combining adherence to Feng Shui principles with flexibility to accommodate your unique needs and lifestyle.

With these three pillars in mind, let's delve deeper into my process.

Formula: personalised for your unique home

The first pillar of my Feng Shui model, Formula, is structured around three core components:

- qualifying the theory
- harmonising the elements
- activating the energy

Each component guides us through a specific process to shape the ideal Feng Shui formula for your space.

Qualifying the theory

Our journey begins by evolving from a broad understanding of Feng Shui to a tailored approach specific to your home. Depending on your aims—whether to boost health, nurture relationships, or attract prosperity—I pick techniques that resonate with your goals. A popular choice is the flying-star method (or *xuan kong fei xing*). It evaluates your building's energy, drawing from details like construction date and building orientation. Through it, I analyse the shifting energies or 'stars' in your home. If this method isn't feasible, other techniques, like the eight-mansions method (*bazhai*), are at our disposal.

A key aspect of your home's energy profile is your *personal sector*. Each individual has a unique personal sector within their home, a space energetically aligned with their wellbeing. The location of this space is determined by your date of birth, the orientation of your home, and your floor plan. Together, they are indicators of how you may be energetically affected by a particular area within your home.

If, for instance, your personal sector is in your kitchen, you might feel burnt out or exhausted; if it's in the bathroom, you could feel drained of energy. I use this information to guide the placement of objects, identify potential imbalances, and recommend ways to enhance positive energy flow.

Auspicious measurements

In the realm of Feng Shui, there are specific measurements associated with happiness, wealth, and good fortune. Originating from ancient China, the *luban* ruler has been used for centuries to determine auspicious dimensions for constructing homes, furniture and religious artifacts. This tool honours Lu Ban, a legendary builder during the Zhou dynasty (1046–256 BC) who is celebrated as the patron deity of builders and constructors throughout China.

I use auspicious Feng Shui dimensions to guide the design of key architectural features in homes and commercial spaces. These include entrance doors, bespoke furniture pieces—including desks and beds—and items symbolising wealth, such as water features and sculptures.

My clients light up when I ask them to rank their preferences for happiness, prosperity and career—it's as if I'm a genie granting wishes. Designing a three-dimensional object allows us to tap into one or more of these lucky measurements. For example, in my collaborations with internationally acclaimed sculptor Todd Stuart, we create sculptures for clients where each dimension holds a special meaning. They can select a length that resonates with the energy of wealth, a width that symbolises happiness, and a depth that represents career or fame. These sculptures are carefully crafted to reflect the principles of Feng Shui, offering more than just visual appeal. They are designed to harmonise with and enhance the surrounding space, acting as a focal point that draws in positive energy.

When using auspicious measurements to guide home design, it's crucial to ensure that the dimensions are practical. An auspicious front-door measurement loses its benefit if you bump your head on it every time you walk in. A desk designed with favourable dimensions must still be functional and fit comfortably within your office space.

I use the words 'auspicious' and 'favourable' to describe the feeling I want you to achieve in your home. According to the Merriam-Webster dictionary, 'auspicious' means fortunate or prosperous. I use the term 'favourable' to mean the same thing.

Auspicious directions

In my Feng Shui toolkit, I have many techniques to help invite the energy of success into your home. One such technique involves calculating your auspicious directions based on your birthdate. These directions can optimise the flow of positive energy, particularly in areas where you spend a lot of time, like your bedroom or workspace. In Feng Shui, auspicious directions can guide how you position yourself while sleeping or working—for instance, which direction your bed faces or the orientation of your chair at your work desk. This concept taps into personalised energy alignments that can enhance success and wellbeing in your home. I delve deeper into this topic in Chapter 8.

Harmonising the elements

After I qualify the theory, I produce your energy map and harmonise the elements. As you learned in the previous chapter, the energy map is like a horoscope that highlights issues and potential in your home.

Harmonising the elements is about balancing the five elements in your home. The process involves analysing each part of the energy map to find positive energy to enhance and unfavourable energies to reduce.

Take the fire element as an example: it brings warmth, fosters transformation and nourishes spaces. Fire elements include fireplaces, kitchen cooktops, ovens and outdoor fire features like barbecues and fire pits. I apply specific Feng Shui formulas to guide their positioning for optimal energy flow. Fire features can create a warm, welcoming feeling while enhancing the ambiance of your home. Thoughtful alignment based on your energy map will ensure that these elements contribute in a positive way to the energy flow in your home.

Every home has harmful energies to varying degrees. If a toxic energy zone is in an active part of your home, such as the front entrance, its potential impact on you is magnified. Key areas to consider are the front entrance, bedroom, kitchen and living room. When a challenging energy zone falls within a wet area, like a bathroom or laundry, the harmful energy tends to get drained away–an ideal positioning. Meanwhile, if the toxic energy zone is in a spare room you rarely use, its influence is naturally diminished.

The next step in harmonising the elements involves a careful calibration process. This means applying a Feng Shui remedy or enhancement to fine-tune specific energy zones in your home. Remedies in Feng Shui are typically associated with the five elements: fire, earth, metal, water and wood. While traditional cures like Chinese coins and metal chimes are widely used, my approach leans towards incorporating elegant decor that represents the required element. For example, a beautiful plant can enhance the wood element, or a circular metal sculpture can represent the metal element. This approach not only achieves the desired Feng Shui balance but also contributes to the overall aesthetic appeal of your home.

Next, let's explore some examples of the types of energies I commonly encounter, and the remedies I typically use to address them. It's important to remember that these are examples based on my experience, and I always recommend consulting with a Feng Shui master to ensure any remedies are perfectly suited to your unique space. Every home is different, and remedies should be tailored to align with your specific energy needs and configurations.

Conflict and clashing

In some homes, there's a presence of quarrelsome energy that can range from minor disagreements to more serious conflicts. In Feng Shui, this type of energy is often related to the wood element. To counteract it, I recommend introducing elements of fire, as fire can help balance and neutralise the wood energy. One way to do this is by using the colour red, representative of the fire element, as an accent in home accessories. However, it's important to use red sparingly—for instance, in small decorative pieces rather than large areas like a feature wall or kitchen cabinetry, as excessive red can be overwhelming and counterproductive. I delve deeper into the energetics of the colour red and its use in Feng Shui in Chapter 9.

Robbery and reputational ruin

Gossip, slander and theft manifest in various ways, from verbal attacks to physical theft of property or ideas. To deal with this negative energy, I often suggest using the element of still water to counteract its influence in your home. Unlike moving water, such as a fountain or aquarium, which actively circulates energy, still water is calm and tranquil, representing clear reflection and serenity.

One traditional Feng Shui remedy involves placing a few stalks of lucky bamboo in a vase of still water. Other beautiful plants that thrive in water, such as peace lilies (*Spathiphyllum wallisii*) and pothos (*Epipremnum aureum*), are also effective. The key is to ensure that the water is sitting undisturbed in a bowl or jug, rather than constantly moving like a water feature. The water must also be regularly replaced to avoid it becoming stagnant.

Sickness and health struggles

Sickness and health struggles are the most challenging energies. Sleeping in a room with this energy profile is believed to amplify illness, from mild to chronic, making it difficult to achieve optimal health. To counteract this energy, I often recommend using the element of metal. A traditional remedy for this energy is the *wu lou* gourd, which looks like a small brass oriental vase. While this can be an effective remedy, I understand it may not suit everyone's taste. That's why I often suggest metallic accessories, like a lamp or a curved sculpture, which can be functional and aesthetically pleasing. These pieces not only serve as remedies for negative energy, but also add a touch of elegance to a room. The key is to choose metallic pieces that resonate with you and fit seamlessly with the overall design of your home.

Misfortune and mishaps

This type of negative energy can feel disastrous, often manifesting as missed opportunities, accidents or unexpected obstacles. If you find yourself feeling stuck or unable to make progress in meaningful ways, it could be due to this energy affecting a key functional area of your home.

To counteract this, I often recommend incorporating the element of metal. Metal, in Feng Shui, is known for its ability to cut through negative energy and bring clarity. However, it's important to note that a small metal ornament might not be sufficient. While metallic decor can be beneficial, the use of metallic sounds is even more effective as they permeate the energy field of a room. This can be achieved with metal singing bowls, a chiming clock or even piano music.

Bad romance

Like Lady Gaga's song, this dysfunctional energy indicates relationships gone wrong. If your bedroom contains this energy profile, it can indicate infatuations leading to poor relationship choices, infidelity and affairs.

The remedy I use is the element of fire. This can be achieved with the colour red. I generally discourage using the colour red in bedrooms, but if I do need to use it, I will do so in small amounts only.

For example, I might suggest an accent cushion that can be moved aside while sleeping, or placing a red book on your bedside, like *8 Rules of Love* by Jay Shetty.

This challenging energy can be exacerbated by negative Feng Shui features such as exposed ceiling beams or having a toilet facing the bed. If this is the case, the physical Feng Shui issue needs to be dealt with first. This could be as simple as moving the bed or closing the bathroom door while sleeping.

Activating the energy

Now we arrive at the best part of my Feng Shui consultations—identifying and activating the best energy zones within your home.

Wealth sector

The wealth sector is that elusive place every Feng Shui enthusiast wants to know about. The wealth sector varies in each home, depending on its energy map. The good news is that there's more than one. The main wealth sector of your home relates to your current wealth, and the secondary wealth sector relates to future wealth. There is also a sector for distant wealth. You can tap into all of these energies, depending on your home's design.

The trick with harnessing the energy of the wealth sector is to ensure that it's in an active area of your home. Sometimes it's not possible to access a wealth sector if it's in an inactive zone like a storage area or bathroom. The best situation is to have your main entrance in the wealth sector. This means you naturally activate wealth energy whenever you enter your home. You can also enhance positive wealth energy with a water feature, like an aquarium or swimming pool. These elements are especially effective when they are visible from your interior spaces.

Power and authority

The energy associated with power and authority is valuable if you want to advance your career and improve your professional standing. This energy is beneficial if you hold a position of leadership, or if you're looking to establish yourself as an expert in your field.

The best location for this energy is in your home office or study. By creating a space that supports your career goals and aspirations, you can harness the power of this energy to help you achieve success and recognition.

When this energy is in a home office, I often advise clients to incorporate the element of metal into their decor. This can be achieved using round, metallic or white objects. This may include trophies, metallic-framed artwork or metal sculptures. These accents can create a sense of strength and solidity, helping to reinforce your authority and influence.

Healthy relationships

This energy relates to harmonious relationships, love and romance. I often prescribe the element of fire to enhance this positive energy. This may be achieved with candles or by decorating with red accessories. Different shades of red can be used, including pink, purple and maroon. If this energy is found in a bedroom, I tend to avoid the use of red because it is too intense. Instead, I opt for muted shades of pink.

Culture: Feng Shui's significance

Feng Shui, deeply anchored in Chinese culture, is now widespread and practised worldwide. It holds great significance, especially for those with an Asian heritage. The second pillar of my Feng Shui model, Culture, is structured around three core components:

- Maximising the appeal
- Elevating the symbolism
- Optimising the timing

Maximising the appeal

This is about showcasing positive Feng Shui elements in your property and highlighting them to magnify your home's appeal and desirability. Conversely, it's important to identify and minimise any negative features, ensuring they do not detract from the overall harmony and attractiveness of your home.

Elevating the symbolism

The power of symbolism in Feng Shui can be accentuated through intentional designs and motifs that channel positive energy. For example, homes designed with curves indicate a smooth flow of energy and resonate well with Feng Shui principles.

Optimising the timing

Timing in Feng Shui is paramount. Whether it's selecting auspicious dates for important activities such as moving into a new home or planning an auction, the right timing can invite good fortune and positive energy into your space.

Auspicious date selection

Auspicious date selection is used to guide the timing of essential activities. These include daily activities like travelling, choosing lucky days for weddings, opening businesses, buying or selling a home, and even the planned caesarean birth of a child. A Feng Shui master will choose the best days and hours for conducting an activity that energetically supports your success. Feng Shui masters employ professional date-selection methods like *xuan kong da gua*, flying stars, dong gong, 12-day officer method, twenty-eight lunar constellations, and interaction of elements of the days based on Chinese astrology. I often help clients select dates for selling their home, moving into a new home, signing contracts, and starting home-building projects.

Superstition in Feng Shui culture

While true Feng Shui is not based on superstition, it has, over time, become intertwined with some superstitions associated with Chinese culture.

Separating Feng Shui principles from the associated superstitions can sometimes be challenging. Regardless of your belief in these superstitions, it's important to recognise their significance to the Feng Shui community. Such beliefs can influence your home's resale value. Given that your home is likely to be your most significant investment, awareness of this aspect can prevent potential regrets.

Numerology has become intertwined with Feng Shui, with eight being considered a lucky number. The number eight can be subtly incorporated into your home's design or decoration by using patterns of interlocking circles. An example is a garden with two circular patches of lawn set together to resemble the number eight. Conversely, certain shapes and designs have negative associations due to an uneven energy flow. These unfavourable forms include sharply angled designs, triangular shapes and long, thin formations that resemble knives. Being informed will mean you can avoid these elements or minimise their negative impact.

I live in Sydney's lower North Shore, an area that attracts Feng Shui-conscious homeowners. I've observed savvy developers capitalising on this by purchasing properties with the number eight—then developing and selling them at a premium to Chinese investors and Feng Shui-conscious buyers. On the other hand, properties with the number four or those situated at the end of a T-junction, typically sell at reduced prices due to their perceived inauspicious associations. Living in a number four house doesn't necessarily translate to bad luck, but it is helpful to be aware of the number's unlucky connotation.

Arrangement: from chaos to harmony

Arrangement plays a pivotal role in ensuring that your home's energy resonates harmoniously with all its residents. It represents the transformation from chaos to a design that's both practical and inspired by your energy map. In my Feng Shui method, I follow three steps to determine the optimal arrangement:

- identify the form
- create the balance
- enhance the flow

Identify the form

I touched on this foundational element in the previous chapter. To identify the form, I observe the view from inside your home, looking outward. I consider the natural and built elements in the surrounding landscape. Then, observing from the outside looking in, I evaluate how these external factors may influence the energy inside.

Create the balance

Once I've identified the form, I advise you on how to create a balanced environment. This stage involves reducing negative influences and boosting positive energy. Typical actions might involve screening an unattractive view with plants or sheer curtains, or strategically positioning windows to capture beautiful views.

Enhance the flow

This stage focuses on refining the energy circulation within your home. We work to eliminate blockages that might obstruct energy flow, and slow down energy that is moving too quickly. The goal is to let the energy meander freely throughout your home.

What's next

With its deep history spanning thousands of years, Feng Shui is filled with subtle nuances that often vary from one practitioner to the next. That's why it's so important to find a Feng Shui master whose philosophy aligns with your own vision and values.

Mastering Feng Shui doesn't happen overnight—it's a journey. Now, equipped with a new understanding of its principles, you can start exploring the possibilities within your own home. Think about changes that could enhance the Feng Shui of your space, aiming to create a home that's even more welcoming and balanced than it was before.

As we venture into Part II, we dive into the fun part of my book. This is where I will provide insights, room by room. This practical guidance is ready for you to start applying to your home immediately. So, let's embark on this transformative journey together.

PART II

A Room-By-Room Guide to Transforming Your Space

In Part I you learnt that achieving balance between yin and yang is a fundamental goal in Feng Shui. It's about guiding the flow of energy through your home, and containing it in just the right amount to cultivate an environment of support and protection. Instead of allowing energy to flow too quickly in straight lines through your home, we aspire for it to meander gracefully, much like a calm river flowing through a landscape.

This is where design plays a pivotal role. Thoughtfully designing your home to contain and manage energy flow is crucial. Too much energy escaping quickly could signify a leakage of wealth. Imagine your wallet brimming with cash. You wouldn't want it full of holes, letting your hard-earned money slip away. Similarly, your home should be a sanctuary that conserves not only material wealth, but also nurtures intangible qualities like harmonious relationships and good health. Our aim is to harness this positive energy, ensuring it flows smoothly throughout your home.

Building on the foundational concepts in Chapter 4, we explored form and its significance in fostering support and protection in your home's design. These principles can also be adapted to suit each room's unique layout. Alongside these foundational principles, there are a range of specific Feng Shui rules and guidelines designed to elevate your home's energy. In the upcoming chapters, I will delve into these empowering insights, showing you how to apply them to your own space. This journey will build on the model introduced in Chapter 5, combining inspired interiors with practical placement and a focus on reducing risk, all aimed at manifesting abundance in every corner of your home.

Chapter 6 will focus on the active areas: the entrance, living areas and kitchen. Then in Chapter 7, we'll look at the quieter spaces: the bedrooms, office, bathrooms and laundry. Chapter 8 will cover taboos and pitfalls, and Chapter 9 will offer a series of finishing touches, to wrap up our journey through your living spaces.

CHAPTER 6

Enhancing Active Living Spaces

Every decorating and design choice you make has the power to transform the energy flow in your home, influencing your daily life and emotional well-being. These decisions can lead to environments that either foster relaxation or create tension, boost productivity or spark disarray. Certain spaces within your home will have a more significant impact on your energy than others.

In this chapter we will walk through key areas of your home: the entrance, living spaces and kitchen. We start with the entrance, emphasising its importance in Feng Shui for attracting success and positive energy. Practical steps, like a clear path and a well-designed garden, help invite these elements into your home. Living rooms, serving as spaces for both formal gatherings and everyday family life, play a key role in how layout influences relationship dynamics and the overall ambience of your home. Our aim is to find a balance that suits your lifestyle, fostering either vibrant socialising or peaceful relaxation. Then, we move to the kitchen, which is central to your home's health and vitality. A well-arranged kitchen supports your wellbeing and impacts your financial prosperity. We consider elements like the placement of the cooking appliances and colour choices to enhance this space. By applying Feng Shui principles to these areas, we aim to create a harmonious, balanced home that supports a prosperous and joyful life.

Your front entrance: the welcoming gateway

The entrance is the most important part of your home in terms of wealth, career, and your family's success. If you work for others, an optimised entrance can elevate your chances of receiving a promotion, a pay rise or gaining more recognition in your job. For those who own a business, a strategically designed entrance can help in attracting premium clients and positioning yourself as an industry leader. And if you're considering the idea of starting a business and are seeking direction, a home with a carefully curated entrance can create the perfect environment for exploration and discovering your true purpose.

The entrance to your home begins with the moment a visitor steps off the street and continues through your garden, if you have one, leading directly to the front door.

A well-maintained and orderly home and garden is like a beacon, drawing in positive energy and opportunities. It's like an unspoken invitation, naturally attracting people who appreciate the kind of care and concern that a well-kept property conveys. Clear and visible number signage on your home isn't just for practicality;

it also ensures that energy and opportunities can locate you and flow towards you with ease. Think of it this way: your well-kept property with clear signage is like an accurately pinned location on a GPS. Just as a correctly marked location ensures that an important delivery or a long-awaited Uber Eats order reaches you without a hitch, a visible and welcoming home ensures that positive energy and opportunities find you without any obstacles.

Gardens that are healthy and well maintained keep Feng Shui energy at its peak. If you consult with a Feng Shui master, you'll be guided to select plant colours and materials that harmonise with your home's energy map. Most importantly, select plants that will flourish, bearing in mind the specific climate and orientation of your home. Strive to instil order and balance in your garden, reflecting the principles of yin and yang. This can be achieved through a thoughtful mix of colours, creating a play of light and shade, with varied heights, balancing taller and shorter elements, and diverse shapes, alternating between strappy and compact forms.

A clear and unobstructed path to your front door, ideally visible from the street, invites energy and opportunities into your home. When guests can effortlessly see your entrance, it generates a sense of welcome. Consider designing a curved path to your door rather than a straight one. It allows the energy to meander gently to your entrance. While straight paths can be beautiful, the energy tends to flow too quickly to your front door. To counteract this, consider integrating interesting features such as unique stonework, or eye-catching plant displays along the path to slow the energy down. Whether your path is curved or straight, you can also enhance the flow of energy inside by placing a focal point, such as artwork, flowers or a sculpture near your front entrance.

When designing your front door, a solid material such as timber is more desirable than glass. If your entrance is dark and can benefit from more natural light, incorporating glass elements can be a suitable solution, but ensure that the glass is obscured to maintain your privacy and security. Ribbon glass is my personal favourite. Frosted glass is also effective.

To enhance the energy of your entrance, display an object you love near the door, something that triggers happiness and positive energy each time you walk into your home.

Consider your routine as you enter your home. How might you creatively streamline this? Perhaps you need a solution for shoe storage at the door, or an elegant place for your keys and bags. Design your entrance thoughtfully to ensure everyday necessities like these are organised in a way that enhances, rather than clutters the space. This approach helps pave the path for positive energy flow, free from chaos and disarray.

Foyers: containing wealth energy

If you have the opportunity to design your front entrance, consider incorporating a foyer. A foyer is like a container for wealth energy when it enters your home. You can then guide the flow of energy by creating a path from the foyer to the next space.

Avoid having a mirror directly opposite the front door, because it can reflect opportunities back out of the home. And no one likes to be startled unexpectedly by their own reflection, especially if they're having a bad-hair day (I elaborate on mirrors and their intriguing role in Feng Shui in Chapter 9). Also, limit the number of doors around your front entrance. In Feng Shui terms, too many doors symbolise too many opinions.

If there is more than one path leading from the foyer, guide traffic towards communal areas such as the living room, rather than private spaces like bedrooms. Organise the layout to subtly direct people to where you want them to go. If architectural alterations are not possible, use decorative strategies to direct energy flow. Create captivating focal points with artwork, light fixtures, or varied flooring like a carpet runner. Sometimes you can guide traffic flow by simply changing the swing of a door.

The size of your foyer should be proportionate to the overall scale of your home. Current trends lean towards voids and double-height front entrances, often complemented by large windows and skylights. This can work well in certain contexts and with suitably sized homes, however in a small foyer, a double-height ceiling can unintentionally resemble a tunnel, an unfavourable design in Feng Shui.

An excess of windows leads to a rapid escape of energy. If tranquil-lity is a priority for you, be mindful that a double-height ceiling will allow sound to travel easily and potentially create a noisier home environment.

Hallways and staircases: transitional spaces

Transitional spaces like hallways and staircases are vital for distributing energy throughout a home. There are rules and guidelines to optimise this flow. Think of hallways as the backbone of a building. A home without hallways means walking through rooms to reach different spaces, which is far from ideal. Rooms with multiple entrances can lead to restless energy that's challenging to keep in check. While this might be acceptable in open-plan living areas, it is disruptive in private spaces like bedrooms and home offices.

Avoid designing homes with excessively long and narrow hallways, as they encourage energy to move too rapidly. Remember, the goal is to allow energy to *meander* through your home.

Staircases, like hallways, function as conduits of energy. A well-known Feng Shui rule advises against placing your staircase in direct alignment with your front door. This is to prevent wealth energy from quickly escaping down the stairs and out of the building. If you have the opportunity to plan your staircase design, consider positioning it away from the front door.

Avoid steep or tight corkscrew-designed staircases. While they can be visually intriguing, they are less inviting and create a sense of imbalance and constriction. Spiral staircases can be difficult to navigate—especially with furniture—and their winding nature can cause disorientation or a sense of unease.

In the context of Feng Shui, both steep and corkscrew staircases disrupt the smooth flow of qi, potentially creating zones of either stagnant or rushing energy. The aim is to create an environment where energy can flow freely and effortlessly throughout the space. Therefore, opting for staircases with a gentle incline and user-friendly design will enhance the Feng Shui of your home.

It is generally recommended to choose solid staircases over open designs, as solid risers help prevent the leakage of wealth energy. However, in specific architectural contexts, a balance may need to be struck between Feng Shui principles and practical design considerations. For instance, in homes with long rectangular layouts, such as semi-detached houses and duplexes, an open staircase without solid risers can be advantageous. This is particularly true in spaces where natural light is limited and the layout features a shared central wall. From a design perspective, these houses could indeed benefit from an open staircase to enhance light flow. In such cases, consider the overall energy flow and light dynamics of your space. If opting for an open staircase, you might explore alternatives like frosted glass risers, which allows light to pass while maintaining a sense of solidity. This approach provides a practical solution that aligns with Feng Shui principles while addressing unique architectural needs.

If your stairs already align with the front door and a renovation isn't planned, don't fret, there are solutions. While some Feng Shui practitioners might suggest hanging a crystal above the stairs, there are more elegant alternatives. Placing a round rug between the door and the stairs can help slow down and circulate energy. Installing a circular pendant light between the door and the stairs can also be effective, provided there's adequate space. Another strategy is to hang artwork at the top of the stairs or alongside the staircase. This not only enhances the aesthetic appeal, but also aids in slowing down the energy flow between the stairs and the door.

Entrance checklist

Having explored the theory, it's time to put your knowledge into practice. Use the following checklist to apply the Feng Shui principles to your own space:

- Does your home appear neat and well-maintained from the street?
- Is your number signage clearly visible?
- Is your garden healthy and thriving?
- Are your plants in the best locations to flourish and thrive?
- Is the pathway to your front door clear of obstacles and clutter?
- Do you have a focal point, like artwork or flowers, that draws energy into your home?
- Upon entering, does your home feel welcoming?
- Does your front door directly align with the back door or stairs? If so, can you use furnishings to slow down the energy flow?
- Upon entry, is there a clear and inviting path for your guests to follow?
- Is lighting at your front entrance balanced, avoiding extremes of dimness or brightness?

If you find this list overwhelming, or if you realise there are multiple areas that need improvement, don't worry. Remember that every journey begins with a single step. All positive changes, no matter how small, bring you closer to a home that emanates balance, harmony and prosperity.

Living rooms: formal or informal gathering places

Living rooms can be formal or informal, reflecting the ebb and flow of our daily lives. The way in which we use them determines whether they are more yin or yang rooms. In Feng Shui, yang signifies bright, active spaces, while yin represents quieter, more subdued areas.

Informal living spaces are the social hubs of our homes, buzzing with gatherings of family and friends, TV time, and children at play. Their vibrant, active nature classifies them as yang, in contrast to the tranquillity of more enclosed rooms.

Ideally, living rooms should enjoy an abundance of natural light. In the southern hemisphere, a north-facing room is perfect for this. If your energy map indicates that your living room is a positive energy hub, lean into that with yang elements. Think colourful artwork and a setup for your favourite music or TV shows. To further enhance the room's energy, connect with the outside world using natural materials. Fresh flowers or vibrant plants make the space inviting. Express your personality and interests by displaying items that are meaningful to you. Opt for uplifting artwork and avoid pieces that might evoke unpleasant feelings or memories.

On the other hand, the formal living rooms commonly found in larger homes serve as quiet yin spaces. They are perfect when you need to escape from the bustling activity of a home's more active areas. If you are designing a formal living room, internal glass doors are an elegant way to create both a sense of enclosure and a tranquil retreat.

Let's explore some ways to elevate the energy of your living spaces. Start by reflecting on the main focal point of your living room. Does it resonate with the lifestyle you envision? For example, if family time is your priority, let engaging artwork be the first thing that catches your eye and move the TV somewhere less conspicuous.

Think about your seating arrangement. An L-shaped layout encourages open and friendly conversation, while sofas facing each other can energetically amplify conflict. Try to position your most used sofa against a solid wall for a sense of support and protection. If that's not possible, a console table with tall accessories behind the sofa can be an effective alternative.

Maintaining a balance of yin and yang is important. If you have hard floors, consider adding a rug for softness to make your living room feel more inviting. A large rug will define the space and anchor your furniture visually.

Banish stagnant energy by giving your space a spring clean. Embrace natural light and fresh air by opening curtains and windows whenever possible. Use a variety of light sources, like overhead lights and lamps, for functionality and to create a cosy ambience. Mirrors can also add light and movement; ideally, they should reflect something visually pleasing.

From a Feng Shui perspective, neutral and calming colours are safe. Bright colours are best suited to accessories and furnishings that can be easily changed. The extensive use of the colour red in large items like sofas, rugs or feature walls can amplify negative energy due to the colour's association with the fire element, so be cautious (I delve into the topic of colours in more detail in Chapter 8).

Plants are a wonderful way to bring nature into your home. Consider low-maintenance air-filtering varieties like peace lilies or Zanzibar plants, or even my personal favourites, fiddle-leaf figs, maidenhair ferns and phalaenopsis orchids. Keep in mind, though, that some plants, including peace lilies and fiddle-leaf figs, may not be suitable for homes with pets. If you have furry friends, ensure these plants are placed out of their reach, or choose pet-friendly alternatives to maintain a safe and harmonious environment for everyone. Examples include the areca palm, Boston fern and Chinese money plant.

Fill your living spaces with objects you love to enhance your mood whenever you walk into the room. Banish clutter and unwanted gifts. Engage all five senses in your living room: touch soft materials, smell fresh flowers or citrus scents, listen to beautiful music, and perhaps even savour a cup of your favourite tea in your most cherished space.

Your living room is a sanctuary where memories are made and bonds are strengthened. It's more than just a gathering space; it's an area that nurtures relationships and personal wellbeing.

One of my clients, Anna, was dealing with constant stress and disagreements with her husband. Their living room, located near the front door, also doubled as a storage area for the kids' toys. The energy map of her home indicated this space was a hotspot for arguments and conflict. To foster more harmony, we implemented specific Feng Shui elements and made strategic changes.

We rearranged the furniture to improve the flow of energy and removed clutter to reduce stress-inducing chaos. The fire element was introduced through decor to balance the room's energy, enhancing warmth and connection. This included transforming the sofa layout into an L-shape and choosing pink cushions and candles to symbolise fire. The kids' toys were relocated to a different space, to create a more adult-friendly living room.

These changes had a remarkable effect. When Anna and her husband entered the house, they were now met with a sense of calm and tranquillity, instead of the previous chaotic atmosphere brought on by the scattered toys. This simple reorganisation cultivated a more peaceful atmosphere within the family, illustrating the impact of mindful interior arrangement.

Living room checklist

Now that we've explored how Feng Shui can transform a living space, let's apply these principles to your living room. Use the following list to bring these ideas to your own space:

- What's the focal point in your living room? Is it your television or artwork? Does it uplift the space?
- Observe the arrangement of your living room. Can you improve the furniture layout to create a more supportive and inviting atmosphere?
- Does your sofa sit against a solid wall for support? If not, can you create that support?
- Is your living room decorated with items you love?
- Are there any things in the room that bring a negative feeling? If so, remove them.
- Is your living room clutter-free? An organised space promotes positive energy flow.
- Do you have a balance of yin and yang in colour, light, texture and materials? e.g. light and shade, soft and hard, colourful and neutral.
- Are you making use of various light sources to enhance the mood of your space?
- Check the living room's scent and feel. Do you regularly open your blinds and windows to let in fresh air and natural light?
- During the day, is your room too dim or bright? Can you make adjustments with sheer curtains or other window treatments?

- Is there an overwhelming use of red in your decor? It's best to avoid this as it might amplify negative energy.
- If you have plants, are they healthy and thriving?
- What do your mirrors reflect? Ensure the reflection is pleasant and does not bring any negative feelings to your space.
- Consider the senses of sight, touch, smell and hearing. How can you elevate these in your space?

The kitchen: the heart of your home's health and wellbeing

The kitchen is more than just a place to cook; it is the heart of your home. The energy in your kitchen supports your family's health and vitality. This space nourishes life, influencing not just your wellbeing but also your ability to be productive and generate wealth.

The vibrancy and freshness of your kitchen's energy can be maintained by keeping it tidy and uncluttered. This applies to visible surfaces like counters, and hidden spaces such as cupboards, pantries and refrigerators. Clutter—such as unused gadgets, broken objects and lids without containers—along with grime, poor ventilation and dark corners, can lead to stagnant energy. A dirty and cluttered kitchen can have an adverse impact on your health and vitality. Therefore, keeping your space neat and well-organised is key to ensuring that positive energy flows freely.

In Feng Shui it is ideal to situate your kitchen away from the front entrance to prevent the cooking area from absorbing energy entering your home. If your cooking appliances are visible from the front door, consider using furniture, plants, or a screen to obscure the line of sight.

In Chinese metaphysics, the heart is associated with the fire element. If you are building or renovating your home, avoid placing the kitchen in the centre as this is believed to 'burn the heart' of the home, potentially indicating ailments related to digestion, the heart and circulation. It's also advisable to locate your kitchen away from toilets and bathrooms. If your kitchen faces a bathroom door, keep the door closed when it's not in use.

The kitchen is a major source of fire that represents strong emotions. Be cautious with the use of red in your kitchen, especially in large areas like splashbacks or cabinets. Excessive use of red amplifies this fiery energy, potentially leading to temperamental behaviour. To counterbalance this, decorate your kitchen with earthy tones and natural materials like stone. Since fire naturally harmonises with wood and earth elements, these additions can create a more balanced environment.

When planning your kitchen layout, consider your position when cooking. You'll find it more comfortable if you can see the entrance to your kitchen while preparing meals. In Feng Shui terms, this is known as a commanding position.

The cooktop and oven are the main sources of energy in a kitchen. Ensure all components of these key appliances are in perfect working condition; a malfunctioning cooking appliance energetically indicates financial concerns. Position your cooktop and oven with a solid wall behind them for support. Avoid placing them directly under a window, as this can cause a leakage of energy which symbolises the loss of good fortune. As charming as window-style splashbacks may be, I suggest reserving them for instances where they're your only option for natural light or a view of the outdoors. If they impact your privacy or security, consider a frosting treatment on the glass.

Optimal kitchen design is not just about aesthetics. Their function, including promoting positive energy flow in your home, is equally important. Given the significant investment involved in designing and building a kitchen, it's worth taking the time to get it right.

When designing or renovating your kitchen, avoid hanging utensils directly above the cooktop or workspace. Also avoid locating your main cooking area directly under exposed ceiling beams. This can produce oppressive energy or a feeling of heaviness. For a calmer environment, keep knives stored out of sight rather than on display, as their sharpness projects aggressive energy.

Create a healthy kitchen by limiting items that can be harmful to your wellbeing, such as harsh chemical cleaning agents, and highly processed foods. While this isn't a traditional Feng Shui principle, it's a part of my practice that I strongly advocate. Promote an inviting aroma in your kitchen naturally with fresh flowers, citrus fruits or herbs, steering clear of artificial air fresheners and sprays laden with chemicals.

Traditional Feng Shui principles suggest that the southeast part of your home is the perfect spot for your kitchen. But this is not a one-size-fits-all rule. Several aspects come into play, such as your home's layout, its orientation, and your unique energy map from a Feng Shui perspective. While the southeast corner is typically recommended, it's crucial that it harmonises with these other factors to create a kitchen that promotes wellbeing for you and your family.

Your kitchen is a significant part of your health journey, as I discovered during my first pregnancy. My appetite was enormous—I ate for Australia—and I gained a significant amount of weight. For perspective, I am five-foot-three and I ended up weighing as much as my husband, who's over six feet tall. During late-night feeding sessions with my newborn, I was introduced to the concept of the 'no-fail environment' by American TV personality, Dr Phil. This concept involves removing temptations from your immediate environment, thereby eliminating the need to battle your willpower constantly. I love chocolate and desserts, but I knew they weren't helping me, so I removed them from my kitchen.

From there, I decided to employ the principles of Feng Shui to aid my journey to better health. The design and layout of my kitchen were revamped, bringing order and structure to a space that was previously chaotic. The food I started bringing into my home was aligned with my health goals. I applied the Feng Shui energy map, decluttered my kitchen and created a no-fail environment, as Dr Phil suggested. These changes, collectively, were instrumental in helping me return to my ideal weight.

While the 'no-fail environment' is not traditionally part of Feng Shui, it aligns with the philosophy of creating spaces to support your success—a principle I resonate with and integrate into my practice.

If you're trying to make healthy changes in your kitchen, you might not always have your family's support, but that shouldn't hold you back. Start with small, manageable steps, introducing them gradually. Small adjustments can lead to big transformations. Start by addressing the energy in your kitchen with the following checklist.

Kitchen checklist

You've seen how revamping my kitchen helped me. Now have a look at possibilities for transformation in your kitchen.

- Are pathways in your kitchen clear of blockages?
- Is your kitchen clean, bright and well-ventilated?
- Does the energy in your kitchen feel vibrant, or stale and stagnant?
- Have you removed clutter like unused appliances, expired food and broken items?
- Can your kitchen cooking appliances be seen from your front entrance? If so, is it practical to screen it from view, while maintaining the flow and functionality of the space?
- If your kitchen is opposite a bathroom, can you keep the door closed while cooking?
- Have you limited the use of red objects in your kitchen to avoid intensifying the fire element?

- Are knives stored out of sight when they're not in use?
- Are all kitchen appliances in good working order?
- Do you freshen the air in your kitchen naturally, or use chemical air fresheners?
- Are the foods stored in your kitchen supportive of your health and vitality?

So far we've walked through the active spaces of your home, and you've discovered the importance of an appealing front entrance in attracting positive energy, wealth and new opportunities. We've delved into living room and kitchen arrangements, exploring how thoughtful adjustments can improve energy flow, promote better health and enhance relationships.

Armed with the recommendations I've shared, start making small, incremental changes room by room. As you do, observe the positive transformation in your energy and mindset.

What's next

In the upcoming chapter, we continue our tour of the home, shifting focus to the quieter areas, like the bedrooms. These spaces significantly impact your health and relationships. I'll share insights and reveal key design elements for optimising energy flow in these spaces. So, let's keep moving forward on our path to creating a more harmonious and abundant home.

CHAPTER 7

Harmonising Quiet Living Spaces

When designing a home with Feng Shui in mind, flexibility is key in determining the function and position of each room. Sometimes the energy map might show that a certain room has great energy for health and relationships, making it perfect for a peaceful space like a bedroom. Conversely, some rooms are more suitable as active areas like a home office or playroom because the energy activates wealth and prosperity. For example, a room that feels cosy and dark, perhaps due to its orientation or window placement, is more conducive for sleep, making it ideal for a bedroom. Conversely, a room that is bright and sunny, benefiting from ample natural light, will be more suitable as an active space such as a home office or a playroom, where staying alert and energised is key. Occasionally I suggest to my clients that their kids could share a bedroom for sleeping and use a different room for play or study.

Your bedroom holds great significance in Feng Shui because it's where you spend a third of your life—more time than any other room in your home. This space, more than any other, holds the key to harmonising your personal energies and nurturing your relationships. If you are seeking serenity or aiming to build closer connections, the ambience of your bedroom can be tailored to reflect and enhance your intentions.

The home office has gained unprecedented importance with the shift towards remote work. In Feng Shui, the aim is to create a workspace that promotes productivity and channels positive energy for wealth and prosperity. The ideal home office setup involves choosing a bright and well-lit room with an element of nature to foster creativity and focus. The strategic positioning of the desk minimises distractions, while a harmonious blend of yin and yang elements creates a balanced and energising work environment. Later in the chapter we'll delve into specific Feng Shui practices to transform your work-from-home experience.

In Feng Shui, bathrooms have a reputation for holding negative energy because of their association with waste and purification. They require careful attention to counter negative symbolism. Don't underestimate the importance of wet areas such as bathrooms and laundries, even though these rooms might seem less significant. These wet areas can strongly influence and even deplete your energy.

In certain situations, the layout of your home can be thoughtfully designed to neutralise negative energies. For example, in my practice of assisting clients with new home construction, we aim to locate the bathrooms or laundries in negative energy zones. Such placements are intended to drain away the undesirable energy.

However, it's important to consider the specific function of each zone in the home. For instance, it's beneficial to avoid situating a bathroom or laundry in the wealth sector, as this may unintentionally deplete energy relating to prosperity and wealth.

Let's delve deeper into each of these spaces by looking at them through my Feng Shui model, focusing on the three pillars of arrangement, formula and culture.

Cultivating tranquillity in bedrooms

The bedroom plays a significant role in shaping your energy with regard to your health and relationships. Consider the story of my client, Linda, who was dealing with chronic fatigue and often spent her days in her bedroom, sleeping and watching television. Out of all the rooms in her home, based on her energy map, her bedroom had the most challenging energy related to illness. I suggested to Linda that she switch bedrooms and encouraged her to spend more time in parts of her home with superior energy quality. This shift was precisely what Linda needed to enhance her mindset and health, and she observed positive changes within just a few weeks.

To set up an ideal bedroom, first consider the balance between yin and yang. Bedrooms should have more yin energy, which is calming and restful, in contrast to the yang energy of shared spaces that are more active. To achieve this, incorporate soft, muted colours in your bedroom decor, as they promote relaxation and tranquillity. Use comfortable, plush fabrics for bedding and curtains. On the other hand, ensure there is a balance with some yang elements to avoid the space feeling too dull or sedate. This can be achieved through decorating and the strategic use of lighting—softer lights for relaxation and brighter ones for dressing or reading. A well-arranged bedroom promotes relaxation and restful sleep, strengthens intimacy, and facilitates meaningful communication.

Arrangement

Create the balance

Bedrooms should be a sanctuary of calm, a quiet retreat filled with peaceful energy. When designing bedrooms, aim to create a snug and tranquil environment that reflects your personal taste. Bigger is not always better, as smaller bedrooms help to contain and nurture energy. Strive for balance and create a space that's cosy yet comfortable, to foster a sense of relaxation and serenity.

When planning the layout of your home, you may consider situating bedrooms on the yin-oriented side of your property, where it's quieter and less brightly lit. For example, in the southern hemisphere, this often means the southern part of your home. Yet, it's crucial to strike a balance and consider the context; for example, if you study or play in your bedroom, more natural light will be helpful. It's also important to ensure the bedroom doesn't end up in an area that is prone to dampness or that could become unhealthy due to a lack of airflow or sunlight.

The ideal placement of your bedroom might also vary based on your personal traits, such as metabolism and stage of life. For instance, younger men often have a warmer metabolism and might find a cooler bedroom more comfortable. On the other hand, as people grow older and their metabolism slows—a natural progression towards a yin phase in life—they might benefit from a bedroom positioned in a warmer area to harmonise with their need for more yang energy.

Identify the form

Identifying the ideal form is essential in bedroom arrangement. The optimal position for your bed is along a solid wall, situated diagonally from the door. Placing your bed against a solid wall promotes a sense of security and stability. A door that faces your bed directly creates disturbance in what should be a sanctuary of peace.

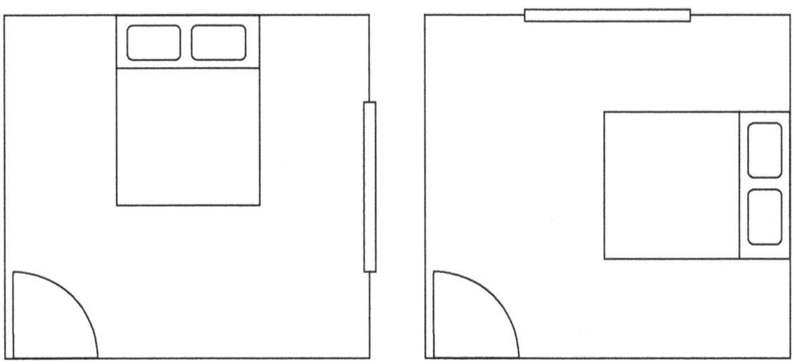

7: Ideal bed placement, along a solid wall, in the space diagonally opposite the door

While it's important to consider these guidelines, practicality cannot be overlooked. Ensure your room's layout remains functional; for example, avoid positioning your bed in a way that might make the space feel cramped or awkward, like having it too close to a closet or obstructing pathways.

To protect your energy from being depleted, avoid placing the head of your bed against a wall with a window. The concern is that placing your bed against a window can result in your energy being pulled away through the window while you sleep. If your bedroom layout limits your options and you find it necessary to have your bed by a window, there are ways to counteract potential energy loss. One practical solution is to use a solid, upholstered headboard, which provides a sense of security and support. Another is to install heavy curtains or shutters, which can help to contain your energy within the space and ensure a more stable and tranquil atmosphere in your bedroom.

An important principle of Feng Shui symbolism is to steer clear of any association with death. Therefore, the 'coffin position' is a Feng Shui concept to avoid when designing a bedroom. This term refers to the foot of the bed directly aligning with the door. Such an alignment is believed to channel energy straight from the doorway to the bed, potentially disturbing rest and recovery. It's called the coffin position due to its resemblance to the way caskets are arranged in churches or temples.

If the door to your ensuite or bedroom faces your bed, it can have specific implications. For instance, if the door aligns with your legs while you're lying down, it may indicate issues related to your feet. An alignment with your head might be associated with headaches or migraines. And if the door faces the centre of your body, this symbolism relates to stomach or abdominal concerns.

Some Feng Shui practitioners may suggest placing a screen between the door and the bed. This can help with the issue of the bed and door alignment, but it might look odd and block energy flow into the room. I do not often recommend this option.

If you cannot avoid having your bed aligned with the door, keep the door closed while you sleep. If you're redesigning your existing house or building a new home, take the opportunity to have the bedroom door positioned to one side of the room. This arrangement creates a contained space diagonally opposite the door, where the energy will settle, rather than being divided and dispersed by a centrally located door.

Windows allow active, or yang, energy into a room. They are necessary for health since they bring in sunlight and fresh air, thereby preventing dampness and mould. While enough yang energy is needed to awaken us after sleep, an excess due to too many windows can be disruptive.

Skylights are useful as conduits of yang energy, and while they have become a popular design trend, their use in bedrooms is best avoided. Skylights pull energy upward and away, which is draining for those sleeping beneath them. If you have a skylight in your bedroom, install a blind that can be easily closed while you sleep.

Contemporary bedroom designs often have long, horizontal windows above the bed, or tall, vertical windows on either side of the bed. If your bedroom is designed this way, use blinds or curtains to block out excessive light and energy. This helps protect you from energy loss while you sleep.

Bedrooms, for the most part, are quiet spaces that need not be brightly lit like living rooms, although more lighting may be needed if a bedroom is used for activities like study or play. In this case, installing a dimmer switch will be useful. If you have a study zone in your bedroom, try to keep it further away, rather than closer to the bed. Have a clearly defined space with ample storage that allows you to easily pack your work away before bedtime.

Enhance the flow

Incorporating curves into bedroom design helps to promote a smooth flow of energy. Adding curved elements, such as in light fixtures, furniture like bed heads, or even fabric patterns, can help to create a tranquil and relaxing atmosphere, which is ideal for a bedroom setting.

It's important to avoid placing heavy items, like shelves or large pieces of artwork, directly above your bed. This arrangement can create an unsettling sense of pressure from above, as well as the risk of these objects falling. This oppressive energy can lead to headaches and migraines.

Similarly, low-sloped ceilings can create a sense of pressure and oppressive energy, potentially leading to discomfort like headaches. It's advisable to place your bed in a part of the room where the ceiling is higher, to create more spaciousness. Also be mindful of the placement of angular objects or architectural features with sharp edges facing your bed, such as protruding wall angles or certain light fittings. These features can subconsciously contribute to a sense of unease. Repositioning your bed away from these elements or replacing objects with softer options can help create a more harmonious and peaceful bedroom environment.

Try to avoid positioning your bed under exposed beams. Beams crossing over your body as you sleep can energetically affect the part of your body that's directly underneath. Particularly, if a beam splits your bed down the middle, it may symbolise a divide in the relationship or emotional distance between partners. If you find your bed under such a beam, consider repositioning it to avoid direct alignment. This can help mitigate any negative effects.

When designing a walk-in wardrobe, try to keep its contents out of sight of your bed. Instead of having an open wardrobe, consider enclosing it with beautiful doors. Unless you are extremely tidy, or have someone constantly cleaning for you, seeing your belongings in less-than-perfect order will be disturbing at a subconscious level. It's better to keep things hidden and maintain a peaceful atmosphere in your bedroom.

When decorating bedrooms, it's important to consider the life-stage of the person using the room. While gentle, calming colours work best for bedrooms, children's bedrooms can incorporate more vibrant hues. Children often use their bedrooms as play areas, and because they are in a stage where they're growing and learning, they can handle a more energetic (yang) influence. But don't overdo it, with too many loud patterns or overly bright walls. For instance, red can be overly stimulating and may contribute to tension or arguments.

Try to design children's rooms with an equal share of desirable features to minimise potential conflicts between siblings. If you are renovating and are limited with the changes you can make, get creative with design solutions to foster a sense of equality. For example, in my own home, one of my children's bedrooms is smaller than the other. To make the smaller room more appealing to my younger daughter, we hung a charming swing chair from the ceiling. It ended up being such a fun feature that both girls fell in love with the smaller room.

For babies' rooms, you'll want to avoid making the space overly stimulating. Hanging mobiles over the cot, for example, is not recommended as it can generate an unsettling energy overhead. Instead, consider hanging the mobile above the change table.

Choose a sturdy bed with a solid headboard for support and protection. Upholstered headboards are an excellent choice, offering both comfort and a sense of protection. Try to avoid metal beds as they conduct electrical fields. This is particularly significant since our bodies, largely composed of water, may react to these fields. Waterbeds are not recommended because they hold an excessive amount of yang energy. If you own a waterbed, consider moving it to a spare room. In the main bedroom, a traditional bed frame or ensemble is a preferable alternative.

Aim to incorporate a variety of light sources in your bedroom, such as downlights and lamps, or pendant lights. While there's a trend of fixing pendant lights to either side of the bed, this is most effective when the bed's placement is certain. Keep in mind that everyone has their own set of favourable directions, determined by their birthdate. The direction your bed faces affects how you tap into energies associated with wealth, health, longevity and relationships. Having flexibility in a bedroom's layout is ideal, as it provides you with versatile options for bed placement.

In my on-site consultations, I focus on how a building's construction can affect a client's health. This includes checking for harmful elements like toxic mould and electromagnetic fields (EMFs). While these aren't directly tied to Feng Shui, they're crucial for ensuring a restful sleep and optimal health.

EMFs, emitted by electrical equipment, can interfere with sleep and lead to various health issues. A frequent problem in homes is the placement of electrical meter boxes on the other side of a bedroom wall. If your bed is positioned against such a wall, it's advisable, where possible, to move your bed away from the meter box. On a similar note, if your bed shares a wall with the kitchen, heavy appliances on the other side may be disruptive to your sleep and health. So, the general advice is to be mindful of what's on the other side of your bed's headboard wall. Paying attention to these details is important for creating a restorative bedroom environment.

Minimise the presence of electrical equipment around your bed. Various electrical devices emit different levels of EMFs. For instance, bedside lamps are generally safe, however traditional backlit clock radios can produce high EMFs and are best kept away from the bed head. If you prefer having a digital clock close by, choose a battery-operated model. Charging mobile phones and other devices overnight beside your bed can also disrupt your energy. Ideally, these should be kept in another room during sleep. If you need your phone nearby, place it as far from your head as possible and switch it to flight mode.

And finally, while water features and fish tanks can be beautiful, they also bring a lot of activity with them, which disrupts the calming energy in your bedroom. These lively elements are better suited for more active areas of your home, like the living room.

Culture

Traditional homes in China typically had formal living spaces closer to the entrance, which made it easier to welcome guests, and the private spaces, like bedrooms, were located towards the back of the house. Understanding the traditional Chinese approach to home layout leads us to the Feng Shui ideal of situating your bedroom in a quieter, more private part of your home. This means positioning bedrooms upstairs or away from active living spaces to ensure tranquillity. It's also beneficial to be mindful of the rooms adjacent to your bedroom. Bedrooms next to or above garages, or over kitchens, can have their energy disturbed by noise and activity.

When thinking about the decoration and design of your bedrooms, it's important to consider the symbolism of the objects and images you choose to display. Select art and imagery that reflect positivity and serenity, steering clear of anything that evokes negative emotions or relates to violence and death.

If you're looking to boost the romantic energy in your room, consider decorating with objects in pairs. This symbolises partnership and unity, fostering a sense of togetherness. Avoid images of solitary figures, as these evoke a sense of loneliness. Also incorporate elements like rose quartz crystals in your decor. This stone, with its gentle pink essence, is a symbol of love that has long been believed to improve the energy of romance.

It's important to note that in Feng Shui, symbolism plays a role in the energy your space emanates. For example, some believe that if you have a daybed or chaise lounge in your master bedroom, it symbolically makes room for another person to enter your relationship. This could imply an increase in the potential for affairs or infidelity.

Another key element to consider is the placement of mirrors in your bedroom. If a mirror directly reflects your bed, it could amplify unresolved issues between couples. This is because mirrors in Feng Shui are known to reflect and expand the energy within a space. Ideally, mirrors should reflect pleasant aspects such as artwork or a scenic view, rather than the bed. In bedrooms, I prefer to tuck mirrors behind wardrobe doors, or place them on a wall where they are not reflecting the bed or in the direct line of sight as you walk by.

Try to avoid aligning bathroom doors directly with bedroom doors. In Feng Shui, bathrooms are considered to have dirty energy, mainly due to the presence of toilets and bacteria. Ideally, this energy shouldn't mix with the calming and restful energy of a bedroom. This separation is not just a Feng Shui concept but also a practical consideration. Different types of bacteria live in bathrooms and kitchens, and it's best to keep them separate. So, even if only from a hygiene perspective, it makes sense to keep the bathroom energy separated from places where you eat and sleep.

Modern design trends often challenge Feng Shui principles. One example is the popular trend for open ensuite bathrooms, where the bedroom and bathroom are merged into one large space. Feng Shui advises against this approach and emphasises maintaining bedrooms and bathrooms as distinct and separate spaces. This distinction helps to keep their unique energies and purposes intact.

Formula

Your bedroom's energy can significantly influence your relationships and health. So, when you're designing a house, or choosing where to position your bedroom, try to select an area with positive energy. A Feng Shui expert, using your home's energy map, can provide guidance on this.

The orientation of your bed is an important consideration, and the best directions for your bed to face are calculated based on your birth chart. These carefully chosen directions can help channel into your space the energy associated with wealth, health and harmonious relationships. If possible, it's best to align your bedhead with one of these beneficial directions.

Your bedroom significantly impacts your energy because of the time you spend sleeping and absorbing the energy around you. It's not merely a place to rest; it's a space where you recharge and rejuvenate, and it's crucial that this environment is carefully curated for optimal energy flow.

Consider your role and status in the family when deciding on bedroom placement. If you're the parent or primary breadwinner, it is beneficial for everyone that you occupy the main bedroom, which reflects your position within the family. If your room is positioned at the front or back of your house, it could symbolise a leadership role. Think of your home as a ship and your location in it as being at the helm. This could metaphorically position you as the ship's captain, guiding and safeguarding the household. Keep in mind, however, that sleeping in a room at the front that's projected forward compared to the rest of the house could indicate that you're getting ready to leave.

As a Feng Shui practitioner, I encounter situations where parents want to give the main bedroom to their eldest child. This can inadvertently signal to the child that they're the authority figure, potentially leading to issues with discipline and a muddled understanding of family roles.

One of my clients was a loving family man, the patriarch of a large, bustling household that included his immediate family and extended relatives. Even though he was the family's anchor, he selflessly prioritised others over himself. He even resorted to sleeping on a makeshift bed in his home office. This form of self-sacrifice, while noble, is a common trait I notice in people who embrace Feng Shui—they often neglect their own needs, to their own disadvantage. My advice to them, and to you, is to recognise that you matter, and to ensure that your own needs are met. After all, a solid, well-cared-for foundation is essential to the health and stability of the entire household.

In another case, a mother approached me, deeply concerned about her son's direction in life. In an effort to make him happy she had offered him the main bedroom, a well-meaning gesture that led to unforeseen consequences. The son started to develop an inflated sense of entitlement, and the mother's authority was undermined.

I've also encountered clients who prefer their children's bedrooms to be placed in the home's most favourable energy zones. As a parent, I completely understand the urge to prioritise children's wellbeing. However, from a Feng Shui perspective, I generally discourage this because you, as a parent, are the foundation on which your children rely.

The takeaway here is clear: it's natural to want the best for your children, but it's essential not to compromise your own position or wellbeing.

In the process of designing a home, the Feng Shui energy map serves as a guide to help determine optimal room placement for each family member. For instance, an area with positive energy conducive to academic success could be the ideal choice for a teenager's room.

A Feng Shui master can assist you in allocating rooms to family members in the following three ways:

1. **EXAMINING THE ENERGY MAP** to determine which room suits each person best. For instance, a less argumentative child could thrive in a room with minimal conflict energy.

2. **USING FENG SHUI DIRECTIONS** to select a room that allows the placement of the bed in the most beneficial Feng Shui direction to suit each occupant's birthdate.

3. **KEEPING THE PRACTICALITIES OF DESIGN IN MIND** to choose which rooms would best serve dual purposes. For example, a room with ample natural light is an ideal choice for a room intended for sleep and study.

In the modern era, we've seen an increasingly strong desire for enormous bedrooms. When it came time to build my own family home, I was drawn into the allure of expansive, palatial spaces, the kind you'd see splashed across glossy magazines or showcased on TV shows like *Grand Designs*. Even as a seasoned Feng Shui practitioner I was influenced by the trend of oversized bedrooms. I fretted over whether my own bedroom was adequately spacious, even though it comfortably accommodated a king-sized bed.

However, we mustn't overlook the fact that large spaces can present their own challenges; they can be harder to heat or cool effectively, not to mention the added burden of keeping them clean. The key is to remember that a bedroom does not need to be an overwhelmingly vast space, but rather a comfortably sized sanctuary that caters to your needs.

Bedroom checklist

There are many elements to consider in the bedroom. This checklist will help you work through them to see which ones you can address.

- Is your bedroom in a low-light side of your property. If not, soften the light with window treatments.

- Is your bed along a solid wall? If not, can you move it to one?
- Is your bed against a window? If you can't move it, consider a solid, upholstered bedhead or heavy curtains or shutters.
- Is the foot of your bed aligned with a door? If you can't move it, keep the door closed while you sleep.
- Do you have a skylight? If so, install a blind that you can close while sleeping.
- Do you work or study in your bedroom? If so, keep your requirements as far from the bed as possible and pack them away before bedtime.
- Do you have shelves or heavy artwork over your bed? Consider removing them or moving the bed.
- If you have a low-sloped ceiling, is your bed under the lowest part? Consider moving it if possible.
- Is your bed directly under an exposed beam? Consider repositioning it to avoid direct alignment.
- Do you have any sharp objects facing your bed? Try repositioning them.
- Do you have a messy open walk-in wardrobe? A curtain or beautiful doors will help maintain a peaceful atmosphere.
- Do you have a variety of light sources in your room?
- Is there a meter box or heavy kitchen appliances on the other side of your bedhead? Reposition the bed if you can.
- Can you reduce the amount of electro-magnetic fields around your bed by removing items such as back-lit clock radios and phone chargers?

- Does your baby's room have a mobile over the cot? Move it to over the change table.
- Are you looking to boost the romantic energy in your bedroom? Decorate with objects in pairs and avoid images of solitary figures. Consider adding a rose quartz crystal into your decor.
- Is there a mirror directly reflecting your bed? Consider moving it or tucking it away from view.
- As a head of the household, have you allocated yourself the main bedroom? If not, consider doing so.

Supercharging the home office

In the wake of the pandemic, more people are working from home than ever before, raising the importance of the home office to new heights. Not only does an organised workspace enhance clarity of thought, but a harmonious energy flow can also pave the way for success.

Arrangement

Create the balance

Designing an ideal home office requires a delicate balance of energies, embracing the concept of yin and yang. If you work from home during the day, position your desk in a bright part of your home to harness vibrant yang energy.

Yin elements, representing softness and tranquillity, can be incorporated through comfortable seating, calming artwork or soft lighting. Meanwhile, yang symbolises brightness, activity and stimulation, which can be manifested through an inspiring vision board, vibrant plants or a layout that encourages movement.

The objective is to create an environment that not only supports your work needs physically, but also helps maintain your emotional and energetic equilibrium. The harmony of yin and yang in your workspace can significantly enhance your productivity and wellbeing.

Identify the form

If your work involves welcoming clients into your home, consider positioning your home office near the front entrance. This area generally carries more yang energy, and it offers the additional benefit of keeping your private living spaces separate.

Your desk placement within your office is important for fostering positive energy. Sit with your back towards a solid wall to provide a sense of security and support for your thoughts and ideas. Having a window in your line of sight creates a connection with the outdoors, which can help you feel more grounded and inspire your creative thinking. Conversely, facing a blank wall may hinder your creative flow and contribute to a feeling of confinement.

Enhance the flow

In this era of remote work, video meetings via platforms like Zoom have become the norm. The image you project, including your backdrop, can influence your energy and the opportunities you attract.

The colour scheme of your office plays an important role in creating a comfortable and visually pleasing space. Colour has a direct impact on your mood and productivity. For instance, according to colour psychology, yellow promotes concentration and embodies the earth element. While I don't recommend changing wall colours based on a room's function, incorporating a yellow accessory or two can be an excellent addition if you are drawn to the colour.

Boost the energy in your workspace with life-enhancing elements. A plant, such as a peace lily, can add a touch of nature and positivity. Surround yourself with items that spark inspiration, perhaps books by your favourite authors, motivational quotes, or displays of your achievements, like awards, degrees or certificates.

Pay attention to your office lighting, as it plays a crucial role in both comfort and productivity. Opt for a warm, inviting lighting scheme that mimics natural daylight, avoiding the harshness of fluorescent lights. Consider installing overhead downlights with a dimmer to adjust the brightness according to the time of day and your activity. If the overhead lighting is insufficient or too direct, invest in a desk lamp with warmer coloured bulbs. These bulbs are preferable to cooler tones, as they create a more soothing atmosphere conducive to focused work.

Culture

Try to avoid placing your desk in a position where your back is in direct alignment with a door or hallway. This is due to the strong energy flow rushing towards you, which may undermine your authority and foster negative elements like gossip or backstabbing.

If it's not feasible to rearrange your desk, consider shielding yourself from the incoming energy flow. This could mean using a screen or a high-backed chair to create a protective barrier.

Another Feng Shui concept to keep in mind is the idea of 'poison arrows'. These are pointy objects or sharp corners that direct negative energy towards your chair or desk. While the term might sound alarming, there is no need to obsess over every corner or sharp edge in your office. For example, having a bookshelf behind you isn't necessarily an issue unless it's extremely close or there's a risk of items falling on you. If there's an object in your workspace that you find disruptive or unsettling, try to distance yourself from it. The further you are from such objects, the less influence they exert over you.

Formula

A Feng Shui master can use specific methods to enhance your home's energy, in relation to career success. If you're an employee, this could manifest as a promotion, pay rise, or increased recognition at work. If you are a business owner you can benefit from an improved energy flow by attracting more desirable projects, quality customers, and position yourself as a leader in your field. If you're thinking about starting a business, optimising the energy flow in your workspace is an important step towards uncovering your purpose and laying the foundation for a successful venture.

A key aspect of this process is the strategic placement of your desk in a location that fosters positive energy for authority and wealth. Aligning your chair in a direction that's most conducive to success can bring added benefits. This optimal direction is determined by your birthdate. For instance, if your desk is currently facing north but your personal success direction based on your birthdate is northeast, adjusting your chair and computer screen to align with northeast could enhance the positive energy flow. Even small adjustments can have a significant impact on the energy dynamics of your workspace, and by extension, on your career prospects and achievements.

The pandemic pivot: redesigning my home office

When the Covid-19 pandemic struck, my family and I had just settled into our newly renovated home. A specific room was designated as my home office space, tailored to support my business. However, the pandemic-induced changes brought new challenges when my husband also began working from home and needed the office space for his video meetings. This forced me to seek makeshift solutions in various rooms, but none proved ideal, leading to a stagnation in my business during this period.

Realising that the situation required a more permanent solution, I embarked on creating a new workspace for myself. Drawing on Feng Shui principles, I selected a suitable space, invested in a beautiful desk, and arranged it to optimise the flow of positive energy. This change rejuvenated my business, and it was in this newly energised space that the idea for this book emerged.

About six months into my journey of writing this book, I faced obstacles that tested my resolve. Self-doubt crept in, shaking my confidence and leading me to question my ability to complete the book. Despite these challenges, my belief in the book's impact to help others motivated me to persevere.

To overcome these hurdles, I adopted a multi-pronged approach. I adjusted my workspace, aligning my desk towards a favourable direction based on my birthdate. I shifted my desk to allow for a view of the outdoors, to boost my creativity. I surrounded my workspace with books from my favourite authors—Dr Wayne Dyer, Ed Mylett and Jay Shetty—their wisdom serving as a source of inspiration.

These adjustments and interventions worked wonders. My workspace, aligned with Feng Shui principles, became a source of inspiration and strength, enabling me to progress with the book, as evidenced by the chapters you're reading now.

Optimising a shared workspace

Having a dedicated space for your home office can significantly boost productivity, particularly if you have the luxury of extra space. However, not everyone has the flexibility to allocate a separate room for work. Jay Shetty, a former monk renowned for his practical insights into life and work, highlights the importance of consistency in our surroundings and routines. He advises that performing tasks in the same location and at regular times can streamline productivity and create a more natural workflow.

This concept is relevant if you're working in a space that serves multiple purposes, such as a living room or bedroom. Creating a distinct area for work, even if it's just a corner of a room, helps mentally separate work-related tasks from personal relaxation. If your workspace is a shared area like a dining table, choosing a different seat from where you usually eat can aid in maintaining focus during work hours. This subtle change also makes it easier to switch off and relax when work is done.

Be mindful of the energy of each location. Avoiding activities like eating at your work desk can help prevent the space from becoming associated with distractions, thereby enhancing your focus during work hours.

Tapping into the energy of space and time can make your work-from-home experience more effective and enjoyable. Adjust and personalise these strategies according to your home environment and personal needs.

Office checklist

You've read my success story with redesigning my home office. Use this checklist to see what improvements you can make.

- Does your home office have a good balance of yin and yang elements?
- When sitting at your desk, is there a solid wall behind you and a window in your line of sight?

- Is your desk positioned to avoid direct alignment with doors or halllways?
- Have you considered the ergonomics of your chair and desk height to ensure they promote comfort?
- Do you have items that spark inspiration or add a touch of nature and positivity?
- Is the lighting sufficient?
- Are there any disruptive or unsettling items that you can remove?
- Do you have organisational tools and storage solutions in place to keep your workspace tidy?

Infusing harmony into bathrooms and laundries

Bathrooms and laundry areas are subject to a variety of guidelines regarding their placement and design. These spaces are seen as potential drains on wealth due to their association with toilets and cleaning activities, which Feng Shui links to 'dirty' energy. Yet, when a bathroom is thoughtfully designed to be luxurious, it can evoke the ambiance of a spa, creating a delightful and relaxing holiday-like atmosphere.

Arrangement and culture

Considering the layout of your home, as you now know, the front entrance is important in Feng Shui because it symbolises wealth. Ideally you would avoid having your front entrance in direct view of the toilet. If your bathroom is aligned with, or positioned directly above the entrance, this is thought to negatively impact your home's wealth energy. In such cases, keep the bathroom door closed and ensure adequate ventilation to prevent bad smells and negative energy from permeating through your entrance space.

Meanwhile, your bedroom is linked with health and relationships. A nearby toilet can have an impact on this energy. Ensuites are common features in modern houses, often merging directly with bedroom spaces, but ancient Feng Shui masters would shudder at such arrangements. While I see their point, I also appreciate the convenience of a nearby bathroom. If you are designing an ensuite, ensure your bed is not directly aligned with the bathroom door, and install a window for natural ventilation.

Feng Shui principles advise against a direct view of the toilet from the bed, with some practitioners suggesting this can lead to promiscuous behaviour or affairs. Whether or not one subscribes to these beliefs, the idea of maintaining a separation between these spaces does make intuitive sense. When I reflect on my clients' experiences, I have noted anecdotal evidence to support this belief. If your bathroom door is aligned with your bed, keep it closed while you sleep.

Health is the key association for kitchens. When bathrooms are located close to kitchens, this is believed to be a recipe for health issues, even food poisoning. Any bathroom door in direct alignment with the kitchen should be kept closed while cooking.

In Feng Shui, the *tai ji* refers to the centre of your home, ideally an open, clear space. The tai ji in Feng Shui can be thought of as your home's epicentre, representing its core energy and balance.

Avoid placing a bathroom or laundry here, as it may lack natural ventilation, leading to a build-up of stagnant energy that spreads throughout your home.

If you are renovating or designing a new bathroom, the location of the toilet is the primary concern due to its association with negative energy. Aim to make the toilet less visible upon entering the bathroom; your experience of the space will be more pleasant if the toilet is tucked out of immediate view.

I'm a huge fan of storage solutions that promote a tidy and organised lifestyle. Features like medicine cabinets installed at eye level help to keep everyday items hidden yet easily accessible. They are also perfect for hiding power outlets.

A double shower is a feature I recommend for larger bathroom designs. Not only does it bring a luxurious feel, but it also fosters better communication and intimacy between a couple. Consider the practicality: in situations where both partners are in a hurry and need to get ready simultaneously, a double shower is a great time saver. It helps to defuse potential conflicts and boosts efficiency, making it both a practical and luxurious feature.

The ideal bathroom design includes a window, as natural light and ventilation are crucial in preventing the build-up of stagnant energy. If installing a window is not an option, install a powerful exhaust fan. Be mindful of where this fan vents—you wouldn't want to greet your guests with nasty smells or inadvertently send negative energy whirling towards your entrance.

Choosing the right materials for bathrooms and laundries is vital. Durable, non-porous materials are required for longevity to withstand frequent use and exposure to moisture. While sheer curtains might look appealing in bathrooms, they're likely to accumulate mould over time. Likewise, porous natural surfaces like slate or marble tiles can be problematic for bathroom floors, often leading to unsightly stains, especially around the base of a toilet.

Having explored the nuances of bathroom design, let's shift our focus to the laundry room, another vital space in aligning your home with Feng Shui principles. A well-organised, clean and clutter-free laundry room contributes to a smooth energy flow, counteracting chaos and stagnation.

Drawing inspiration from Kai Ieraci, an award-winning architectural designer, practical and aesthetic elements can be seamlessly integrated into the Feng Shui approach. The use of hamper drawers, for instance, organises dirty clothes and aligns with Feng Shui's emphasis on cleanliness. A built-in ironing board that folds away into a drawer conserves space and keeps the area uncluttered, maintaining harmony and balance.

Full-height cabinetry, especially with adjustable shelving, offers efficient storage for cleaning equipment and supplies, ensuring the area remains neat and well organised. Adequate bench space is essential for an organised laundry process, and deep drawers under the washer and dryer provide convenient storage for laundry essentials, minimising visual clutter and resonating with Feng Shui's principle of order.

Lighting is critical in any space, and well-placed task and ambient lighting in the laundry enhances its functionality and ease of use. Drying racks, whether integrated under overhead storage or within a drawer system, make smart use of available space and aid in keeping the area tidy and manageable.

Access to natural ventilation through a window or door is ideal. This not only helps maintain a healthy energy flow but also aids in humidity control. I recommend that clients use condenser dryers, as they are particularly effective in reducing humidity build-up.

Even a laundry room deserves thoughtful design. Choose colours and materials that resonate with the rest of your home, creating a cohesive and harmonious feel. A pleasant laundry space not only makes washing clothes more enjoyable but also positively contributes to the overall energy of your home.

When planning the placement of your wet areas in your home design, pay attention to the location of plumbing in relation to your bedroom. Having plumbing along the same wall as your bed head can be seen as potentially draining your personal energy and health.

Beyond the visible aspects of design, it's also important to consider unseen factors that can impact your wellbeing, such as electromagnetic fields (EMFs). In certain scenarios, copper pipes can carry EMFs, which have been linked to health concerns. I've visited older homes where, surprisingly, electrical cables were grounded to copper pipes. This practice may increase exposure to EMFs, which have been associated with various health issues. For instance, some studies suggest a correlation between high EMF exposure and an increased risk of conditions like insomnia, cancer and infertility. The *British Journal of Cancer*, for example, reported that EMF exposure above four milligauss was associated with twice the risk of developing childhood leukaemia.

Hidden EMF exposure

I had a personal experience with high EMF exposure in a house I once lived in. The EMF reading in the main bedroom was alarmingly high—around seven milligauss—whereas the recommended safe limit for bedrooms is below one milligauss. Interestingly, the previous occupants had mentioned bouts of insomnia, which I later connected to this issue. After some investigation, I found a copper pipe attached to the bedroom wall was conducting the EMF. It appeared to originate from the pipe's connection to the street.

This led me to hire a plumber to locate and replace a section of the underground copper pipe with plastic piping. This instantly lowered the EMF reading in the bedroom to a safe level, under one milligauss. The relief I felt was immense, and a stark reminder of the importance of considering both the visible and invisible elements when designing living spaces.

Formula

Feng Shui has developed from its ancient origins, a time when bathrooms were crude outhouses separate from main living quarters, and the concept of ensuites was non-existent. Today, the principles of Feng Shui have been adapted to contemporary homes, including modern approaches to bathroom positioning.

The location of a bathroom in your home's energy map, can significantly influence the overall energy flow, for better or worse. A strategically positioned bathroom can help to reduce the influence of harmful energies such as those associated with illness or conflict. However, if a bathroom is situated in an area of your home's energy map that's linked to positive energies, like wealth or harmonious relationships, it could diminish these beneficial influences.

Building or renovating a bathroom is a significant investment, and it's crucial to get the planning right. A client in Darling Point, Sydney, contacted me when they were designing their dream home. The initial plan had the bathroom above the entrance, which my Feng Shui analysis showed could have a draining effect on their wealth. We repositioned the bathroom, and they found peace of mind in the revised floor plan. Many years after their home was constructed, my client and their family continue to live happily there.

If you're concerned about an existing bathroom that seems unfavourably located, remember that perfect Feng Shui does not exist. Your goal should be to optimise what you have. If a bathroom is directly opposite your entrance or kitchen, manage the energy flow by keeping the bathroom door closed and ensuring the room is well-ventilated. Even small adjustments like these can significantly influence the energy dynamics of your home.

Bathroom and laundry checklist

A lot of key decisions for bathrooms and laundries come at the design or renovation stage, but there are still remedies you can apply in your bathrooms and laundry today.

- Is your bathroom opposite an entrance or kitchen? If so, remember to keep the door closed.
- Is your ensuite toilet visible from your bedroom? If so, keep the door closed.
- If designing an ensuite, do you have room to install a double shower?
- Do you have adequate ventilation in both the bathroom and laundry, such as a window or exhaust fan?
- Are there effective storage solutions in place to keep your bathroom and laundry room tidy and organised?
- If you are designing or renovating your bathroom or laundry room, have you chosen non-porous and durable materials?
- Are your washer and dryer positioned to optimise space, ensuring a smooth flow of energy?

What's next

As we conclude our room-by-room journey, it's time to venture into an area of Feng Shui that often raises eyebrows and ignites curiosity: the realm of taboos and superstitions. These aspects, sometimes mysterious or misunderstood, can significantly influence your home's ambience and how others perceive it.

Perceptions are important, and in the case of your home, they could translate into its future market value. If you are a homeowner, understanding these Feng Shui taboos and superstitions is essential. Prepare to uncover surprising insights that could shift your view of Feng Shui, and perhaps even your home, in unexpected ways.

CHAPTER 8

Feng Shui Taboos and Superstitions

As we've discussed, Feng Shui is a blend of formulas, the dynamic balance of yin and yang, and practical design considerations, all woven together in a symbolic language rich with meaning. Over time, specific Feng Shui taboos have evolved from this symbolism. These taboos, which may take the form of certain objects, design features, layouts and images are viewed as negative or potentially harmful from a Feng Shui perspective. These same elements are often also problematic in the context of modern design, creating issues that transcend Feng Shui concerns. They are not merely antiquated superstitions; they can influence your mindset and overall wellbeing.

Feng Shui taboos are important to many people in the community, and even if they do not resonate with you personally, a deeper understanding will give you the power to address them effectively. Consider the potential impact on your property's market appeal. Homes that present Feng Shui challenges frequently deter potential buyers. I encounter real estate agents who face difficulties in selling properties with such issues. While I can offer solutions to rectify some of these problems, in many cases it can be too late to fully harness the benefits of Feng Shui once the home is constructed. This is why I prefer working with clients when they are in the planning stages of building or renovating their homes.

In this chapter, I will guide you through the main Feng Shui issues and taboos that I encounter in my work. More importantly, I'll advise you on how to deal with them. So, let's dive in and start tackling these taboos.

Clutter: Feng Shui public enemy number one

In the world of Feng Shui, clutter is public enemy number one. It creates blockages in your home, interrupting the smooth flow of positive energy. Clutter is made up of possessions you don't use, need or love. It also includes unwanted gifts and items you keep out of obligation. These objects bring negative feelings into your space, impacting your mindset without you even realising.

A cluttered environment leaves little room for new opportunities to enter your life and can reflect a deeper concern and insecurity about the future. When people save things 'just in case', it shows mistrust in the universe to provide what's needed at the right time.

The good news is that decluttering can have a positive effect on your home's energy immediately. As you clear out clutter, you'll feel a sense of lightness and refreshment. It's like a wave of energy sweeping through your home, breathing new life into your surroundings.

Let's take a look at clutter in relation to my model.

Arrangement

Clutter obstructs the harmonious flow of energy. By decluttering, organising and thoughtfully arranging your home, you encourage energy to move freely, making room for new opportunities and possibilities. A cluttered space reflects a cluttered mind, whereas a well-arranged space enhances productivity and clarity.

Formula

In an environment overwhelmed by clutter, Feng Shui remedies will not work effectively. It's like planting a seed in an overgrown garden; there simply isn't enough space to thrive and bloom. Feng Shui is about harmonising various elements and stimulating energy flow, which flourishes best in an uncluttered space.

By clearing clutter, you'll unblock pathways, allowing energy to flow freely. This leads to a more harmonious and inviting environment, perfectly poised to welcome positive changes.

Culture

While the issue of clutter was not prevalent during the early development of Feng Shui, it has become increasingly relevant in modern times due to the rise of materialism. As a result, clutter has emerged as a common challenge in contemporary households. Feng Shui is a dynamic practice that evolves with shifts in lifestyle and energy patterns. This evolution explains why dealing with clutter has become an essential aspect of modern Feng Shui practices.

How to clear clutter

Pause for a moment and reflect on your belongings. Ask yourself: do they mirror who you are and your current path? Do they align with the person you aspire to be today? Remember, if an item doesn't serve a purpose, it isn't used regularly, or isn't cherished, it may be time to let it go.

Clutter clearing does not need to be overwhelming. Begin with manageable steps, tackling one drawer, and then one room at a time. If you begin the process slowly, it will stir up energy, fuelling the motivation you need to continue. As you declutter, keep these questions in mind: Do I need it? Do I use it? Do I love it?

It's normal to find this process challenging. Sometimes old patterns and attachments can stop you from letting things go. If you find yourself in this position, know that you're not alone. My virtual decluttering sessions are a valuable resource for anyone who feels stuck or needs support. If you can do with some encouragement, I'm here for you. But if you're ready to tackle this on your own, keep the above questions in mind and approach the task with patience.

Landscape and environment: influencing value and appeal

The elements within and around your home play a critical role in Feng Shui, influencing both its value and attractiveness. The Feng Shui ideal promotes a home located on the higher side of a peaceful street, surrounded by a landscape of lush, undulating land, fertile soil and a diverse array of flora and fauna. This ideal environment not only aligns with Feng Shui principles but also enhances the positive energy and appeal of your home.

In the realm of Feng Shui, the concept of 'qi centres' holds significant importance. These centres are bustling hubs such as towns and cities, offering access to amenities and resources like shopping centres, workplaces and restaurants. They bring dynamic yang energy to the homes in their vicinity, balancing the calm yin energy of a residential setting. This balance enhances your property's harmony and appeal, as it brings together the vibrant yang energy of amenities like shops and workplaces with the tranquil yin energy of a peaceful living space.

Having looked at how qi centres shape a home's energy, let's now examine how the arrangement and cultural aspects of properties also play a role.

Arrangement and culture

The shape of a property is a critical element in determining how well it contains energy. For instance, triangular properties, due to their unbalanced and uneven energy distribution, are considered unfavourable in Feng Shui. If you own a triangular property, softening the corners with landscaping will help to create more balance.

Properties wider at the rear than the front can represent good fortune. This is because they resemble a moneybag, which symbolises wealth. In contrast, a property wider at the front and tapering at the back is perceived to be less fortunate because the property shape symbolises a dustbin. Such a shape makes it more challenging to contain the energy within a property.

In traditional Feng Shui symbolism, battle-axe blocks symbolise a weapon and represent trapped energy. However, these properties are increasingly sought after by people desiring privacy and seclusion. The extended driveway creates a buffer from the street, offering a retreat-like ambience that is valued by those looking for a personal sanctuary away from the public eye.

Houses situated at the end of a T-junction are also considered taboo in Feng Shui, because the direct energy flow (and traffic flow) towards them can symbolise a threat. Houses on curved roads face issues with traffic and headlights from turning vehicles, which can flash into windows, disrupting sleep and causing discomfort. However, there are ways to mitigate these challenges. For homes at the end of a T-junction, diffusing the incoming energy from the street is key. This can be achieved by planting a hedge in front of the house, or, in cases of intense traffic, constructing a physical wall for added protection. For the interiors, using solid window coverings such as block-out blinds or heavy curtains can minimise night-time disruption from vehicle headlights. During the day, sheer curtains can help reduce exposure.

If your street is curved, the best location for your house is inside the curve. Think about your home being energetically hugged by the curve in the road, protecting it from negative energies. If you're on the outside of a curve, your house is more exposed. The impact of this depends on how busy your road is and how sharp the curve is. You can protect your home from negative energies by adding plants, fences or walls.

Cul-de-sacs have a negative association in Feng Shui because there is only one way out and the energy can get trapped. Their effect depends on the length of the road and level of traffic: the longer and busier the road, the less desirable it is. Houses at the end of a cul-de-sac face similar problems to houses at the end of a T-junction. However, cul-de-sacs can also offer unique advantages. Their limited traffic flow often results in a quieter, more peaceful living environment. This tranquillity, along with the enhanced sense of community and safety due to the reduced road length and lower traffic volume, can be particularly appealing.

Another consideration in Feng Shui is the positioning of a house in relation to street level. Houses situated on the lower side of the street are thought to face difficulties in retaining wealth, as though it's easier for money to be spent or lost. You can counteract this with strategic landscaping. Planting hedges or trees along the rear boundary of your property provides an element of containment, while adding garden lights around the lower areas of your house symbolically elevates the energy.

Water symbolises wealth in Feng Shui, so homes near water or open spaces like parks are highly desirable. There's something special about homes that are next to beautiful parks or bodies of water. Houses near calm watercourses like harbours are more desirable than those near oceans, and this is because harbours have more peaceful, stable energy. It's essential to avoid areas with dirty, smelly water as this represents stagnant energy.

Roads, considered to be 'rivers of qi', are also significant in Feng Shui. The impact of a road on a property can be either positive or negative. Curved roads with slow-moving traffic are preferred over busy highways. Being close to highways can be convenient for quick access to important places like shops or work, although living too close can expose you to negative energy from heavy traffic, noise and pollution.

Formula

Natural and artificial features in your environment can significantly influence the energy in your home. If a Feng Shui master identifies toxic influences in a particular sector of your home's energy map, they can be exacerbated if there is a negative Feng Shui feature nearby. Examples of negative features include transmission towers, electrical poles, rubbish facilities, construction sites and sharp corners of a building. If there's a transmission tower associated with illness energy facing a section of your home, it may, unfortunately, have a negative influence on your health.

Conversely, if you have a favourable energy zone in your home, such as the wealth sector, this can be enhanced by a beautiful open space, such as a garden or a picturesque water view.

When the principles of Feng Shui are in harmony with practical design elements, they often intuitively resonate with our natural preferences. For example, many people are drawn to living near water or parks, preferences that are highly valued from a Feng Shui perspective. Similarly, the taboos of Feng Shui often correspond with aspects that people instinctively prefer to avoid.

It's important not to be overly concerned if your home doesn't meet every Feng Shui ideal. While striving for Feng Shui perfection is a worthy goal, remember that it's not always attainable. The true value lies in understanding and working with your home's unique energy dynamic. As you focus on improving your physical environment, also pay attention to your 'internal Feng Shui'—your personal energy and the changes and adjustments within you. For example, if certain areas in your home feel stagnant, overly cluttered, or if you find that you or your family members are consistently unwell in specific parts of your home, these could be indicators of illness energy. In such cases, it's wise to focus more on enhancing your personal health and wellbeing. Aligning your mindset and actions with the changes in your environment is key to experiencing more profound and lasting benefits.

Imagery and design features: more than just decoration

Certain elements in your home might invoke negative imagery, such as symbols of death, loss of wealth, illness or violence. In Feng Shui, we consider these negative and, as such, require attention.

Arrangement

Avoid design features that evoke negative associations in Feng Shui. For example, vertical bars used as a design feature might inadvertently resemble a prison, depending on their width and shape. Similarly, ropes could be associated with hanging, and openly displayed knives carry the energy of weapons. It's better to keep sharp objects like knives concealed in drawers or shielded from view. If you need to keep knives on your kitchen bench, storing them in a wooden block, which conceals the blades, is a preferable option over leaving them exposed. I recommend steering clear of artefacts that are actual weapons, such as spears.

If a large tree or post directly aligns with your front door, this can be seen as a symbol of division, potentially creating an energetic separation within your home. If moving the tree or post isn't an option, don't worry. Use this insight as a guide for your thoughts and actions. Proactively nurturing your relationships can be an effective way to counteract this energy.

As we explored in Chapter 6, direct alignment between your front and back doors, or your front door and internal stairs, can pose challenges in containing both energy and finances within the home. While this issue might not be easily solved in an existing structure, the following remedies can still provide value.

If your front door faces a hallway leading to the back door, aim to slow down the energy flow along the corridor by displaying attractive artwork or installing circular pendant lighting. Flooring features such as a decorative inlay or carpet runner also help to slow the energy flow.

If your front door aligns with a staircase, aim to slow down and circulate the flow of energy by incorporating a circular pendant light, a round rug or decorative flooring, depending on the size of your space. Decorative moulding on walls, like wainscoting, can also serve as a stylish solution to slow down the flow of energy.

When your staircase directly aligns with a back window, it's important to find a Feng Shui remedy that complements the style of your home. Often, I recommend sheer curtains. They not only add a soft design element but also provide daytime privacy and prevent energy from escaping too rapidly. I love a linen look that complements your decor or wall colour.

Plants are effective at dispersing negative or fast flowing energy. Here's my three-point approach to using plants to slow, disperse, and contain energy:

- For a long corridor ending with a window, place a plant in front of the window to slow the energy flow.
- If you're faced with a negative element—like an undesirable view or a road—a row of trees or plants can serve as a beautiful visual barrier.
- To contain the energy in an outdoor space, use a row of plants or a hedge to create a protective structure (I delve more deeply into the topic of plants in Chapter 9).

Culture

In many cultures, numbers and colours carry certain connotations which hold true in Feng Shui. For instance, the number four is seen as unfavourable as it phonetically resembles the word 'death' in

Chinese. Many property developments and high-rise buildings avoid the level four in lifts, sometimes renaming or omitting them altogether. The number eight, which resembles the Chinese word for 'to prosper' is highly sought after, leading many to favour numbers ending in eight.

Colours, too, carry significant symbolism. Black, for example, is associated with mourning in the Chinese culture. This symbolism can have practical implications, especially in commercial contexts. My commercial clients avoid using black in large expanses, such as wall colours or cabinetry, to prevent any negative associations in their workspaces or entertainment venues.

An incident during Sydney's Chinatown Lunar New Year celebrations in 2022 highlights the impact of colour symbolism. A public art installation became a focal point of controversy. The artwork featured tree trunks wrapped in blue and white fabric, with small lanterns in white, blue and gold suspended overhead. It was visually beautiful, but it sparked outrage among local business owners, who interpreted the installation as reminiscent of funeral decorations, creating what they felt was a 'funeral-like atmosphere' and symbolising the death of business in Chinatown. According to traditional Chinese customs, blue and white fabrics are used to shroud the deceased, and white lanterns are placed on caskets and outside homes as a sign of mourning. To the local community, the fabric tree coverings resembled ghosts, which stirred deep-seated cultural unease. The business owners demanded the immediate removal of the decorations.

This incident illustrates the importance of understanding and respecting cultural symbolism, especially when it intersects with the principles of Feng Shui.

Formula

In traditional Feng Shui, there is a balance between form, which refers to the physical aspects of your surroundings, and formula, which relates to the energy map of your home. Feng Shui practitioners should prioritise form over formula, emphasising the importance of the physical environment over intangible energies.

This approach requires a careful consideration of the design elements in your home, particularly in terms of their potential symbolic meanings. Ask yourself: do these elements bring about feelings or images of negative influences such as death, violence or loss of wealth? If the answer is yes, these are the areas to consider for redesign. Your design scheme should aim to create a harmonious and positive atmosphere, free from negative associations.

Your home's history: the power of lingering energy

The history of your home and its previous occupants can reveal a lot about the energy present in the space. Just as physical traces are left behind, spaces can also retain invisible energy imprints from past events. Think about walking into a room just after a heated argument; you might feel a palpable tension, as if the air itself is heavy. This is how spaces can absorb and reflect energy.

Your home may be holding onto residual energy from its past, like emotional echoes of what has happened there before. Imagine your home having a sort of memory, clinging to the effects of negative experiences. This can result in a feeling of heaviness or discomfort in the space. During a consultation I specifically inquire about past occupants and significant events that may have occurred in the home, such as death, divorce or bankruptcy. Such events can leave a strong imprint, sometimes manifesting as obstacles or delays, especially noticeable during renovation or construction projects. It's as if the home's memory of these events creates barriers to moving forward. Through space-clearing rituals and energy cleansing techniques, we can help reset and harmonise the energy, to create a sense of renewal.

Occasionally I work with clients who sense the presence of spirits in their homes. These might stem from the energies of former occupants who have passed away, or spirits that haven't fully transitioned after death. Even though space clearing and spirit cleansing do not fall within the scope of traditional Feng Shui, I have come to recognise their powerful effects. With time, my openness to these practices has grown, leading me to collaborate with professionals who are highly specialised in this field.

Thinking back to my former life as an accountant, I would never have dreamed of working with a psychic spirit medium. I understand that for some of you this will sound woo-woo and be beyond your realm of experience. It might help to know that I also started with an agnostic view about paranormal phenomena, but eventually opened my mind to a new way of thinking.

Some people have a heightened sensitivity to the spirit world and can sense supernatural occurrences more readily than others. These presences can manifest in various ways, such as unusual smells, cold spots in the house, or electrical disturbances. I've heard many spooky stories from clients about transparent figures, phantom footsteps, and unexplained movement of objects.

Spirits can sometimes lead to complications within your home, such as illness, increased tension, or in some cases, even the disappearance of pets. They tend to be disruptive during renovations or construction, as these activities often stir up energies that were previously dormant.

Some people can sense whether a spirit's presence in their home is harmful or benign. However, regardless of whether a spirit seems friendly or not, it must be moved on. This concept is reminiscent of the movie *Ghost*, where Patrick Swayze's character Sam Wheat, an earthbound spirit, eventually transitions into the light.

I have personally cleared spirit energy, but I prefer to collaborate with a professional spirit medium, or 'ghostbuster', who is highly skilled in the area. And to be honest, dealing with spirits scares the heck out of me. But before bringing in the expert, I guide my clients on how to perform a space-clearing ritual themselves. For this purpose, I use a technique that involves burning sage, specifically grandfather sage, also known as white sage. This type of sage, when burnt, is believed to 'anesthetise' spirits. The dried leaves are tied together in bundles, making them easy to use. You can typically find these in stores that sell spiritual items like crystals and incense (I outline a safe method for burning sage later in this chapter).

Formula

A certain configuration of negative energy is known to draw in spirits. You can address this by burning sage, which I advise as part of a routine practice for purifying your home's energy. You can also use the resonating sound of metal to clear away negative energy. A metal singing bowl is an excellent tool for this purpose. The vibrations it produces create calming, meditative sounds that can help bring a healing energy into a space. Similarly, crystal bowls can also be used for this purpose.

Feel free to perform this energy clearing as frequently as you feel necessary. I suggest doing a space clearing at least once a year, preferably during the lunar new year.

Culture

Many cultures worldwide have their own ways of purifying spaces. For example, in Native American traditions, smudging with sage, cedar or sweetgrass is a common practice to cleanse a space of negative energy. In Hindu culture, Vastu Shastra, a traditional Indian system of architecture and design, often incorporates rituals like the 'Vastu Puja,' which is performed to invite positive energies into a home or office. I advise my clients to conduct space clearing after a distressing event or when significant changes occur, such as moving into a new home. This helps to reset the energy dynamics of the space. For instance, after a family argument, a simple ritual of opening windows to let fresh air in, combined with the lighting of incense, can help dissipate the lingering negative energy. In the case of moving into a new home, a more thorough space-clearing process can be undertaken to ensure the space is energetically aligned and welcoming for the new occupants.

I recall a particular instance where I worked with a real estate agent and a property developer. They were puzzled that one townhouse in a set of four wasn't selling, despite the others selling easily. After evaluating the property, I realised that the standard Feng Shui adjustments weren't enough. I suggested a space clearing to shift the energy in both the unsold townhouse and the developer's own home. Sceptical but hopeful, they agreed. Within a week, they received an impressive offer for the property, and it was soon off the market.

One of my first clients, Meg, was sensitive to spiritual energy in her home. She would often hear footsteps in her hallway at night when no one was there. Meg and her husband would occasionally catch glimpses of what appeared to be a child-like movement flitting through the hallway between the bedrooms, though her children would be soundly sleeping in their beds. During my Feng Shui consultation, it became apparent that a spirit-clearing process was needed. I used a focused meditative technique, designed to guide the spirit towards the light, effectively moving it to a place where it could exist peacefully in the spirit world. After the consultation, Meg reported a significant change. The sound of footsteps and shadows in the hallway stopped. She was convinced the spirit energy had been cleared, bringing a newfound sense of tranquillity to her home.

In a home I once lived in, I noticed a peculiar, musty odour in one of the rooms. I assumed it was due to the old carpet or curtains. Despite my efforts to deodorise the carpet and wash the curtains, the smell would not clear. One day, while speaking with my psychic spirit medium, Kerrie Erwin, she sensed a spiritual presence in my home.

I mentioned the persistent smell, and she said that spirits could manifest as unusual odours.

It turned out that the elderly man who had lived in my house for many decades had passed away in that very room. Kerrie came to my house to perform a clearing, during which she communicated with his spirit. She informed me that the man's spirit stayed in the house because he didn't want to leave his wife, who continued living there. His spirit was confused and disoriented when my family and I moved in. Kerrie successfully guided him towards the light and into the spirit world. After the clearing, I returned to the room and was delighted to find the musty smell had completely vanished. Later that day, when my husband returned from work, I asked if he noticed anything different about the room. To his surprise, he immediately remarked that the smell was gone. His reaction was a reassuring confirmation of the room's transformation and the spirit's peaceful departure.

After the spirit clearing, life returned to normal. However, years later, a similar situation arose, this time in my teenage daughter's bedroom. I started noticing an unusual smell, reminiscent of body odour. Initially, I suspected it might be due to some forgotten food or unwashed clothes. However, this wasn't the case, and recalling my earlier experience, I reached out to Kerrie again. This time, Kerrie revealed that the distinct smell was connected to the spirit of a motorbike rider. Apparently, I had attracted this spirit from a construction site, and he followed me home, even hopping into my car for a ride. It was astonishing to think that spirits could linger in such unexpected places and travel in this manner. The idea of a male spirit in my daughter's room was disconcerting. Thankfully, with Kerrie's guidance, we were able to successfully remove the unwelcome visitor and send him off to the light.

Believe it or not, spirit encounters in homes are not as rare as you might think. Many people experience these mysterious occurrences yet often hesitate to discuss them. Dealing with spirit activity can present genuine challenges. However, when these issues are addressed, they frequently lead to unexpected and surprising outcomes.

If you have any concerns in this area, try researching the history of your home. Speaking with former neighbours or previous occupants is a good starting point for gathering insights. Online resources, including Google, can be valuable tools to research your address. This information can provide useful context for understanding unusual occurrences in your home.

If you suspect that spirits or negative energy might be present in your home, you might find the sage-burning technique helpful. By following these steps, you're actively working to cleanse your home of unwanted energies.

Sage-burning for energy clearing

- Start by ensuring all windows in your home are closed.
- Before lighting the sage stick, place it in a heatproof container, such as a saucepan or ceramic dish. You don't want to risk starting a fire.

- Light the sage stick and then gently blow out the flame, allowing the sage to smoulder.
- Move through your home, carrying the smouldering sage in the heatproof container into each room.
- As you enter each room, wave the sage smoke around, paying attention to all corners.
- When you finish with one room, close the door behind you and move on to the next one, working systematically from one end of your home to the other.
- Once every room has been treated, open all the doors and windows to allow the smoke to escape.

In my professional experience, especially when consulting on properties that were formerly occupied by indigenous Australians, I've found eucalyptus leaves to be more effective than sage for releasing native spirits. If you're new to space clearing, you might feel uncertain initially. However, rest assured that following these instructions will guide you safely through the process. Remember, you can conduct space clearing as frequently as necessary.

What's next

In the final chapter, we'll focus on refining and elevating the energy in your home to new heights. Here, we'll explore the strategic and tasteful use of decorative elements like mirrors, water features and lucky symbols. While symbols of good fortune alone may not be enough to create an inspired living space, when placed with intention, they can profoundly transform the energy and aesthetic of your living space. Discover how these finishing touches can harmonise, energise, and bring a sense of inspired balance to your home.

CHAPTER 9

The Finishing Touches: Feng Shui Enhancements

Throughout this book, we've explored the foundational elements of Feng Shui in home design. Now, it's time to add some sparkle with finishing touches to elevate the energy in your space. Inspiring accessories and elements that symbolise good fortune have the power to transform your space into an inspirational haven.

Finishing touches can bring that wow factor to your home. Consider the impact of well-chosen decor in homes prepared for sale. These enhancements often elevate spaces from ordinary to exceptional, leaving homeowners wishing they had made the changes sooner.

I've experienced this personally. When it was time to sell my previous home, I implemented long-delayed decorating plans. Adding new artwork, furniture and accessories resulted in such a stunning transformation that I found myself not wanting to leave my newly styled home.

In this chapter, we'll delve into the magic of Feng Shui enhancements and symbols of good fortune. We aim to strike a balance between aesthetic appeal and functional energy flow, exploring the theories behind each enhancement and discussing how to tastefully integrate them into your home. I'll also share insights from my daily routine and rituals that have helped me to attract abundance in my own life. I hope they can also help you.

Let's begin with understanding the role of water and fire in Feng Shui. These elements are powerful and, when used correctly, can significantly boost the positive energy in your home. We start by exploring why water is considered a key element for attracting good fortune, and how to use it effectively.

As we navigate through these Feng Shui principles, consider how you might incorporate these elements and symbols into your own space, not just for aesthetic harmony, but as a meaningful reflection of your journey towards abundance.

Water

In the world of Feng Shui, the water element is regarded with great significance. After all, the literal translation of Feng Shui is 'wind and water'. As Master Kwok Po details in his classical text *The Book of Burial*, the vital life force *qi* is moved by the wind and gathers at the boundary of water, signifying water's natural ability to attract and harness this energy. Water serves as a symbol of good fortune and enhances the energy within a home's wealth sector. As mentioned in Chapter 4, the location of the wealth sector is dynamic, varying from home to home. Its position is determined by factors such as the home's orientation, the date of construction, and the specific layout of the floor plan. Understanding this, one can see how water features, strategically placed, can activate and enhance the wealth energy, bringing a sense of abundance and prosperity to the living space.

Arrangement

Naturally occurring bodies of water, like rivers or oceans, can have a more significant impact on your energy compared to water features like fountains, swimming pools or aquariums. These natural sources, formed by nature, possess a stronger and more dynamic energy flow, as they are constantly replenishing and circulating their energy. However, incorporating water features into your home, whether they are fountains, ponds, swimming pools or aquariums, still offers an excellent way to embrace the water element.

There are various ways to determine the ideal placement for water features. At the most basic level, you would consider the principles of yin and yang. The yang side of a property is typically considered the ideal location for water. This is at the front and left-hand side as you face a house. However, the specific form and practical layout of your home must also be taken into account. For example, if your driveway occupies the left side of your property, it would be impractical to place a water feature there. Moreover, in the context of Australian homes, where front yards are usually open and visible to the street, installing a swimming pool in such a location would seem absurd. While these principles provide a starting point, the true art of Feng Shui lies in blending them with the realities of your home's design and surrounding environment, to ensure both harmony and practicality.

Formula

After preparing an energy map for my clients, I carefully consider the placement of water features. In Feng Shui, there are special formulas and guidelines for using water to amplify the energy in a home.

The placement of an important design element like a swimming pool is a significant decision. It's not just about where the pool will look good, but also about where the pool will activate the most prosperous energy. There might be practical constraints that limit your options, but even if the pool is in a spot that amplifies negative energy, a Feng Shui master can offer design and landscaping solutions to counteract potential imbalances.

Choosing the right water feature for your home is essential. A Feng Shui master can guide you in selecting the most suitable style, type and size based on your home's energy configuration. The decision between a tranquil, peaceful water feature and a livelier fountain should align with the energy of the space. Generally, the more prosperous the energy of a location, the more vibrant a water feature can be.

Remember, if you have a water feature in your home, maintaining its cleanliness is vital, as stagnant water attracts negative energy. It's important to ensure the water is always fresh and flowing, whether inside or outside your home.

Culture

Enhancing your water feature with fish can significantly boost the wealth energy. Fish, particularly goldfish and koi, hold a revered place in Feng Shui for their symbolism of wealth and prosperity. A common practice involves adding eight goldfish and one black fish to a water feature. The number eight is significant in Feng Shui; it is considered very auspicious and is associated with prosperity and wealth. Meanwhile, the single black fish is believed to absorb negative energy.

If you have concerns about the wellbeing of the black fish, rest assured. In Feng Shui, it is actually considered a positive sign if the black fish dies. This is interpreted as the fish having fulfilled its role in absorbing negative energy. Such is the pragmatic nature of Feng Shui—it can indeed be a rough-and-tumble world!

Fire

In both Feng Shui and design, the allure of the fire element is acknowledged for the warmth and vibrancy it introduces into a space. A cooktop, oven, barbecue, fireplace, fire pit and candles are all examples of the fire element. The fire element is also symbolised by the colour red. The brighter the shade of red, the more influence it will have on your home's energy.

Arrangement

From a design perspective, fire pits are emerging as a favoured landscaping element. They create a dramatic focal point and naturally draw people together, fostering a sense of community and warmth. Strategically placed fire elements, in alignment with your home's energy map, can greatly enhance aspects like wealth, harmony, health and relationships within the home.

Formula

The fire element has the power to amplify the energy within a space. It acts as a double-edged sword: on one hand, it can diminish negative energies, such as conflict, and enhance positive energies associated with wealth and family harmony. On the other hand, improper placement can amplify negative energies relating to obstacles and illness.

Consulting with a Feng Shui master is advisable for determining the optimal style and placement of fire elements, including the use of the colour red, in your home. Their expertise ensures these elements are positioned to foster a balanced and positive living environment.

Culture

Red is a powerful colour in Asian cultures, as it symbolises life, happiness and wealth. It's frequently used to foster a sense of luck and prosperity. However, it's vital to exercise caution when using red as its strength can stir up intense energies.

During a consultation, a Feng Shui master might recommend the fire element for its positive influence on the energy in a space. If the idea of using red in your decor doesn't appeal to you, there are several alternatives to consider. You could introduce different forms of the fire element, like candles or a fireplace, as effective alternatives. For a more subtle approach, softer shades like maroon, pink or purple can also embody the fire element without the overpowering presence of red.

One of my clients, Jamie, was particularly fond of the colour red. During our consultation, I cautioned him about the potential overuse of such a vibrant and dominant colour. In response, Jamie shared a story about his previous home, where he had painted a living room wall red. He realised this change had coincided with increasing tensions in his relationship, and soon after, he separated with his partner. This experience was a turning point for Jamie. When he entered a new relationship, he approached the decoration of his shared home with more mindfulness. Opting against bold red walls, he used a neutral palette to create a more balanced and tranquil environment. This story of Jamie reminds me how the choices we make in designing and decorating our homes go beyond aesthetics; they resonate with the energy flow in our lives.

Start small

If you're implementing Feng Shui principles without the guidance of a master and are unsure about where to place a water or fire element, you could try a simple experiment. Start with a small feature, like a birdbath or candles, and place it where you think is best. Monitor the energy and atmosphere in your home over a few months. If you sense a harmonious balance, that's great. If not, re-evaluate the placement.

If you've installed a major feature like a fireplace or swimming pool and sense disharmony, consulting a Feng Shui master can be enlightening. A comprehensive analysis of your home's energy map might reveal other factors impacting your space.

Symbols of good fortune

If you're not entirely convinced about the use of lucky symbolism, that's completely understandable. However, it's worth contemplating the potential advantages of integrating specific symbolic elements if they resonate with your vision for your home. Here is a selection of options.

Buddha placement for peace and serenity

A Buddha statue can significantly enhance the harmonious energy in your home if it complements your design aesthetic. An elegant Thai Buddha may be suitable for a sophisticated living space, while a laughing Buddha brings a sense of warmth and positivity, perfect for creating an inviting and relaxed atmosphere. The ideal placement of the statue is based on your home's unique energy profile, as determined by a Feng Shui master. If you're considering the placement of a Buddha statue, follow these guidelines:

- Select a respectful, admired location.
- Place the Buddha against a wall or plants for energetic protection.
- Avoid disrespectful areas, like bathrooms or near rubbish bins.
- Opt for a Buddha statue in its full form over one with separate body parts.

The use of Buddha head statues often sparks debate. While some hold the view that incomplete statues could attract unfavourable energy, Feng Shui is adaptable and context-dependent. In commercial spaces, where every symbol holds significance to Feng Shui-aware customers, ambiguity is best avoided. However, in your personal space, your preferences take precedence. If you find joy and peace in having a Buddha's head in your space, it's less likely to pose a problem.

Be reassured by the flexibility of Feng Shui principles. There's no absolute rule that you must display a Buddha statue in your home. If it doesn't resonate with your style, or feels out of place, there's no obligation to include one. Ultimately, your home should mirror what makes you feel happy and comfortable.

The magic of mirrors

In Feng Shui, mirrors are multifaceted and hold significant power. They both reflect energy outward and draw it inward. When placed correctly, mirrors enhance the flow of positive wealth energy in your home. Ideally, they should reflect captivating views, such as a beautiful piece of art, a lush garden, or an impressive landscape.

If you're considering incorporating a mirror into your home decor, it's important to choose one that reflects your entire image. Avoid mirrors that break up your reflection, such as mirrored tiles. Mirrors that cut off parts of your reflection can symbolise a fractured self-image.

Avoid placing a mirror directly opposite another, as this is thought to create a portal for spirits, leading to visual clutter and discomfort.

Energetically, this setup is believed to invite multiple people into a space, which may not be suitable, especially in private areas like a bedroom.

As mentioned in Chapter 6, positioning a mirror directly facing the entrance is not recommended. It reflects energy outward, potentially pushing opportunities away. Imagine entering a room and immediately seeing your reflection; if you're having a bad hair day or not feeling your best, this could create feelings of self-consciousness. If you would like a mirror near your entrance, consider placing it to the side of the door instead of directly opposite.

Mirrored wardrobes are common in many homes, but they often contradict Feng Shui principles. As discussed in Chapter 7, mirrors in bedrooms can amplify unresolved issues between couples. They also introduce yang energy into a space that should be more yin. Many people enquire about Feng Shui-friendly solutions for mirrored wardrobes. Replacing the mirrored doors with non-reflective surfaces may be the ideal solution. Applying frosted window film is another alternative. If these aren't viable options, a simple yet effective approach is to cover the mirrors while sleeping. Some people install sheer curtains over their mirrored wardrobes, closing them at night to neutralise the energy.

A *bagua* mirror is a small octagonal mirror traditionally used in Feng Shui to ward off harmful energies. A bagua mirror carries powerful symbolism and must be used with extreme caution. It is only appropriate for use in outdoor spaces, as placing a bagua mirror indoors is believed to attract bad luck.

While some people use bagua mirrors to deflect negative energy coming from problematic neighbours, I generally advise against this practice. Such usage can escalate tensions, especially if the neighbours understand the purpose of the mirror. However, in situations where your home faces an intrusive structure, such as an electrical pylon, a bagua mirror can help to reduce its energetic influence.

Further symbols of prosperity

There are several other symbols that you can incorporate into your home design to promote a sense of good fortune. For instance, elephant figurines with their trunks raised symbolise victory and triumph. Objects that resemble coins, especially those that are round, symbolise prosperity. Gold finishes, including gold leaf, are considered auspicious because they signify wealth. This makes using brass and gold tapware beneficial from a Feng Shui perspective. When these elements are used tastefully in your home, they will add aesthetic appeal and symbolically attract wealth and prosperity.

In my professional experience with business clients, I've seen the positive benefits of incorporating such lucky symbols. A notable example was a gaming venue in Sydney, where a client introduced metallic elements and a water feature to create a feeling of good fortune. This gesture, influenced by Feng Shui principles, resonated well with customers, especially when they learned about the involvement of a Feng Shui master. It made them feel valued and their cultural beliefs recognised.

Energise with colour accents

Colours play a significant role in Feng Shui. I recommend classic neutrals as a base colour for decoration. Neutral colours are safe and less likely to trigger challenging energy. They provide a calm foundation, allowing other elements in the room to stand out.

For a pop of colour, turn to accessories. These accents can correspond to the energy map of your home and are easily changeable, allowing for adaptation as the energy flow evolves over time. While Feng Shui favours soothing, peaceful colours, the use of vibrant hues in moderation can energise a space without overwhelming it.

Each colour in Feng Shui is linked to one of the five elements—wood, fire, earth, metal and water—and carries unique psychological meanings, influencing thoughts and emotions. For example, green, representing wood, can enhance growth and vitality, while blue, associated with water, fosters calmness and clarity. Yellow, connected to earth, promotes feelings of stability and grounding. The colour pink, associated with the fire element, promotes love and tranquillity.

Breathe life into your space with plants

Living near the Lane Cove National Park in Sydney, I am constantly surrounded by the stunning Australian flora. The experience of walking along the bush trails and returning home feeling happier than when I started is a testament to the power of nature. Take a moment to think about your own feelings when immersed in nature, be it in a captivating garden or a vibrant plant nursery.

The uplifting effects of indoor plants on our mood and wellbeing are not only felt but also scientifically proven. Plants purify indoor air and forge a nourishing connection to nature. According to the 2010 study, 'Greening the Great Indoors for Human Health and Wellbeing', conducted by the University of Technology, Sydney, indoor plants can decrease feelings of depression by 58%, anger by 44%, and tension and anxiety by 37%.

Incorporating plants into your home should follow the principles of yin and yang for balance. A few plants in your living spaces are enough, as too many can create an overwhelming yin environment. Choose plants with broad, lush leaves and avoid those with sharp, blade-like foliage.

You may feel that maintaining plants is laborious, or perhaps you feel that all plants die under your watch. It's worth noting that not all plants demand the same level of attention. For instance, peace lilies are hardy and require minimal care, making them an excellent choice for many. They also excel at purifying indoor air.

Auspicious plants

Several plants are regarded as auspicious in Feng Shui due to their association with money and wealth. These include:

- **TREASURE FERN OR ZZ PLANT** (*Zamioculcas zamiifolia*)
  Known for its shiny, dark green leaves, this plant is often associated with growth and advancement.
- **HAPPY PLANT** (*Dracaena fragrans*)
  A popular indoor plant used in Chinese culture as a symbol of good fortune.
- **LUCKY BAMBOO** (*Dracaena sanderiana*)
  An easy-to-care-for plant that's believed to bring good luck and fortune. It's often used in Feng Shui to balance elements and energies in the home.
- **JADE PLANT** (*Crassula ovata*)
  Also known as the money tree, the jade plant, with its succulent, shiny, oval-shaped leaves, is said to represent wealth and prosperity.
- **MONEY PLANT** (*Pilea peperomioides*)
  This plant is associated with prosperity and good fortune as its distinctive, round, coin-like green leaves symbolise wealth. This plant carries the cultural significance of attracting financial success and positive energy.
- **ARECA PALM** (*Dypsis lutescens*)
  This plant is praised for its air-purifying qualities and its ability to add a sense of peace and vitality to a living space.

- **BOSTON FERN** (*Nephrolepis exaltata*)
  The Boston fern creates a sense of friendliness and warmth, inviting in positive energy and wealth.
- **FENG SHUI MONEY TREE** (*Pachira aquatica*)
  The money tree often has a braided trunk and is believed to bring good luck and attract wealth.

Artificial plants

If you're considering introducing plants into a space with limited natural light, the idea of using artificial plants might have crossed your mind. However, I advise caution due to potential Feng Shui implications; the Feng Shui police may even suggest that the best place for artificial plants is in the rubbish bin. This view is based on the belief that fake plants carry deceptive energy, pretending to be genuine when they are not. In addition, from an environmental standpoint, the production and disposal of artificial plants harms our planet.

While living, flourishing plants are the gold standard for creating an aura of abundance, a well-maintained, aesthetically pleasing artificial plant can be preferable to a dying, neglected real plant. There is a place for life-like faux plants, and when they're done well, they can form part of a design scheme that lifts the energy through biomimicry. You must, however, love artificial plants and feel good having them around. If fake plants don't resonate with you, do not display them. As a rule of thumb, steer clear of dried flower arrangements as they represent 'dead' energy.

In an indoor environment, mixing live plants with artificial ones is a better choice than using artificial plants alone. If you do choose to use artificial plants, make sure they are high quality and clean them regularly to maintain their life-like appearance.

In my commercial work, I've seen both effective and unsuccessful uses of artificial plants.

A nearby restaurant displays artificial plants in a window that receives direct sunlight for most of the day. Over time, these fake plants have begun to fade and discolour. When I see the dusty, faded-to-blue artificial plants, it suggests a lack of care and attention to detail by the owner. I've noticed that the restaurant rarely attracts many customers, and personally, I've never wanted to dine there. The state of these plants sends a message of disinterest on the part of the restaurant owner, leading to questions about other aspects of their business. In the case of a restaurant, customers should feel valued and assured that an owner cares, a perception that extends to the quality of the food.

Vertical plant walls

Vertical plant walls have become increasingly popular in both homes and commercial spaces. However, one of the fundamental concepts of Feng Shui is to go with the flow of nature, and indoor plant walls can sometimes challenge this principle. They often need extensive care, including specialised watering systems and special lighting. Moreover, if a plant wall looks unhealthy or sparse, it invites negative energy into the space. If you're thinking about installing a vertical plant wall, make sure you can provide the right conditions for the plants to flourish.

Flowers

Flowers hold a special place in Feng Shui as emblems of prosperity and success, often serving as powerful enhancers in various settings. Each type of flower carries its own unique symbolic meanings, contributing differently to the energy of a space.

Peonies, for example, are treasured in Feng Shui. Known as the 'King of Flowers,' they are believed to attract wealth and good fortune, making them a popular choice in both homes and businesses. Displaying peonies symbolises new opportunities and blooming prosperity.

Orchids, a personal favourite, are often on display in my own home. They represent love, fertility and elegance. Their long-lasting blooms are associated with enduring relationships, making them ideal for enhancing romance and deepening connections. Orchids are also seen as a symbol of spiritual growth and purity, adding a serene and uplifting energy to your home.

Roses, with their classic beauty, symbolise financial prosperity and romantic luck. They are often used to attract love and to create a sense of balance and harmony in relationships. The colour of the rose can also play a role in its symbolism. For example, red roses are typically linked with passionate love, while pink roses can represent gentleness and affection.

Creating a Feng Shui lifestyle

Some people believe that Feng Shui alone has the power to bring abundance into your life. From my experience, I've seen how Feng Shui can lay the foundations for, and shape an environment that encourages positivity and success, but ultimately it's your way of thinking and daily habits that harness this potential. You are not just moving around furniture, but aiming to create a space that fosters success and wellbeing. This involves both your living space and your mindset. These elements work together, much like yin and yang, to manifest abundance in your life.

Feng Shui's true power lies in how it intertwines with your daily habits and actions. The routines you adopt and the mindset you cultivate are the very foundations that shape your results in life.

In my daily life, the adoption of certain mindset practices, in combination with a home environment aligned with Feng Shui principles, has been a game-changer. I'm excited to share these with you, as they have opened doors to greater abundance in all areas of my life. Integrating these practices into your routine will unlock the transformative power of Feng Shui, and help you move towards your goals with greater focus and energy.

Gratitude

Gratitude is a gentle and powerful practice that can transform how you see the world. Tony Robbins, a motivational speaker who has inspired countless people, once said: 'Our idea of a real problem is someone else's idea of an ultimate dream.' This insight hits home for me, especially in those ordinary, sometimes challenging moments of daily life.

Take, for example, a scenario that's quite familiar in my life, and maybe yours too. At times, the mess created by my kids can be somewhat overwhelming. In those moments, I consciously remind myself of the privilege of motherhood. Having a home where my children can freely play and make a mess is, in itself, a blessing. This shift in perspective anchors my daily gratitude practice and sets a positive tone for my day.

Each morning, as part of my routine, I take a moment to reflect and list three specific things I am grateful for, along with the reasons why they are important to me. Just today, my list included:

- I'm grateful to live in a safe neighbourhood with walking tracks that allows me to exercise and connect with nature.
- I'm thankful to have a fridge full of fresh food that keeps me healthy and well.
- I appreciate my supportive family, who give me the time and freedom to follow my passions (like writing this book).

For this daily practice, I use a mobile application called *gratitude.me*, which offers daily prompts and inspiration for things to be grateful for. Additionally, before sleeping each night, I reflect on my day and think about what I can be thankful for, big or small. This simple act of acknowledgment reinforces a positive mindset. You cannot help but feel better about your lot in life if you practise gratitude every single day.

Positive affirmations

Affirmations are powerful, positive statements you repeat to yourself, describing the person you aspire to be or the goals you aim to achieve. Their true power emerges when you transform these thoughts into actions. When you consistently affirm your intentions and support them with positive actions, you begin to see your aspirations come to life.

In Chapter 7, I described the challenges I faced while writing this book and the Feng Shui tools that helped me navigate them. Alongside these tools, affirmations were instrumental in my journey. The path was far from easy, as I had to face self-limiting beliefs and overcome hurdles like self-doubt and imposter syndrome.

I sought advice from my friend Venita Dimos, an award-winning Neuro-Leadership coach and author of *Win the Mind.* She suggested a specific action-based affirmation, and we formed an accountability partnership. Each day, we exchange photos of our written affirmations, a practice of sharing and accountability that keeps us focused and committed to our goals.

While writing this book, the affirmation process involved writing a motivational statement on one side of a piece of paper. My statement read: *I am so happy now that I am a highly effective author because of all the effort I put into mastering the skill.*

On the other side, I wrote: *How many ways can I continue to be a highly effective author?* Below this question, I listed one to three specific actions that could help me reach my goal. For example:

- Place my phone on silent in another room.
- Listen to an inspiring podcast every day for thirty minutes.
- Commit to three 25-minute writing sessions with a five-minute break in between.

Then, I placed this piece of paper with its affirmations on my desk, making sure it was clearly visible while I worked.

I found this practice extremely powerful. You can customise this affirmation to align with your own specific goals by replacing 'author' with your desired role or achievement. When repeated consistently for thirty days, you'll notice a positive shift in your mindset. And when you accompany your affirmations with positive actions, you will eventually become what you affirm.

Visualisation

Visualisation is a powerful technique that allows you to build a mental picture of who you want to become. While I was writing this book, I found visualisation to be an invaluable tool. I would dedicate a few moments each day to closing my eyes and imagining how it would feel to hold the completed book in my hands. I imagined the smooth texture of the pages under my fingertips, the sound of flipping through the pages, and the satisfaction of seeing the book neatly placed on my bedside table. This process is not simply daydreaming, but a deep experience that makes your goals seem real and within reach. As you clearly visualise your goals, they will feel more attainable, propelling you forward on your path.

Take a moment to reflect on a goal you would like to achieve. Don't worry if your goal seems enormous and the path isn't entirely clear.

That's perfectly all right. Taking the first few steps is all you need to do. As you start moving, the path will begin to unfold.

Top five people

Jim Rohn, a renowned motivational speaker, once said, 'You are the average of the five people you spend the most time with.' That statement resonates deeply with me, leading me to connect with people who inspire and motivate me in both my personal life and professional journey as a Feng Shui master. Along the same lines, I take care to limit my exposure to negative influences, including certain types of media.

Thanks to technology, it is easier than ever to access inspiring people. There's virtually no reason for you not to engage with the thought leaders and trailblazers of our time. An easy and practical way to gain exposure to inspiring individuals is through books and podcasts. These resources can bring the wisdom of extraordinary individuals right to your fingertips. Also, consider the people in your inner circle; do they encourage your growth, and are they a positive force in your life? Remember, the people you interact with regularly can significantly shape your mindset and path.

Meditation

Incorporating meditation into my daily routine has been a transformative experience. For a long time, I was aware of its many benefits, yet I found myself starting and then stopping, hindered by the belief that I wasn't doing it 'right' or that it was too difficult. I often thought I didn't have the time for it, or I doubted my ability to meditate 'properly'. However, once I committed to the practice and overcame these initial doubts, the impact was profound. It has not only enhanced my sense of clarity and purpose but also opened up avenues for new opportunities and connections to enter my life.

My meditation practice is a simple ritual. Each morning after I wake up, I sit up in bed and position a large pillow behind my back for support. I then dedicate 20 minutes to this practice, closing my eyes and focusing on my breath. When thoughts inevitably drift into my mind, I guide my focus back to my breath. The aim isn't to eliminate all thoughts completely, but to create a state of stillness.

This daily practice has brought an incredible clarity to my life. If I were to compare my mind to a snow globe, meditation feels like letting the swirling flakes settle. Meditation has become an indispensable part of my routine, providing a foundation of peace and awareness that enhances every aspect of my life. Maybe it could become part of your life too.

Balancing your physical energy

My philosophy on Feng Shui is aligned with my personal approach to energy management, where physical exercise and nutrition play a key role. This is a topic I hold close to my heart, almost deserving its own chapter or book.

In my everyday life, and to be at my best for my clients and the people I serve, I focus on eating well. My meals mostly consist of proteins and vegetables, providing the right kind of energy to keep me active and focused. And yes, there's room for the sweeter things in life, like chocolate. To keep this balance, I generally eat clean, practice intermittent fasting, and choose not to drink alcohol, while making sure I stay hydrated.

Physical activity is a big part of my regular morning routine. My workouts include a mix of weight training, outdoor exercise and playing netball, my favourite team sport. This mix not only keeps my workouts fun but also gives me a huge energy boost. This balance of mindful eating and regular exercise keeps me energised and aligned, embodying the essence of Feng Shui in my personal wellbeing.

As you think about your journey in energy management, why not take a few moments to consider how you can enhance it in your daily life? Could starting with a simple yet effective habit, like a daily walk, be the first step in boosting your energy? This small action could be the key to greater vitality and balance in your routine.

CONCLUSION

Embracing Your Feng Shui Journey

The great leader Winston Churchill once said, 'We shape our buildings, and afterwards our buildings shape us.' This insightful statement captures the essence of Feng Shui, where our living spaces reflect our values and aspirations, and significantly influence our everyday interactions and wellbeing.

With your newfound understanding of the energy in your surroundings, you can see how Feng Shui guides you toward achieving abundance. Every home is unique, with its special requirements, and I have aimed to provide insights applicable to any living space.

With the foundational knowledge of Feng Shui you've gained from this book, you are equipped to create a home that's both functional and harmonious, filled with positive energy. Whether you're planning to build, renovate or enhance your current space, remember the value of integrating Feng Shui principles from the start. Ideal Feng Shui is a journey rather than a destination. The principles in this book are a guide to making your living space a nurturing sanctuary, boosting both its aesthetic and energetic qualities.

Perhaps you've always dreamed of a home that reflects your personal style and embodies abundance and harmony. With your deeper understanding of Feng Shui, you're closer to making this dream a reality, fostering productivity, deepening relationships, and enhancing your personal wellbeing.

Having absorbed the insights from this book, you are now equipped with the knowledge to enhance your living spaces. However, if you find yourself hesitating, or questioning whether you have the time or motivation to start, remember that you're not alone. Since 2008, I have had the privilege of helping thousands in the Feng Shui community create inspired spaces, and through my programs, courses and consultations, I am here to support you.

In a world that sometimes feels overwhelming, my hope is that you are empowered and optimistic about shaping your future. By embracing positive energy in your home, you can create a ripple effect that extends far beyond its walls. My wish for you is to create positive energy so that together we can radiate a sense of joy and abundance to the world around us.

About the Author

Jane Langof is a multi-award-winning, internationally accredited Feng Shui master and designer who guides energy-conscious homeowners to create dream homes that radiate abundance and positive energy.

Jane combines traditional Feng Shui principles with a practical design approach to align with her client's vision for aesthetics and functionality. Her portfolio includes luxury properties, residential homes, commercial enterprises, hospitality venues and community spaces worldwide. Jane is accredited by the International Feng Shui Association and the Design Institute of Australia, and her work has been recognised for multiple awards in the building and design industry.

Since founding Feng Shui Concepts in 2008, Jane has become a trusted collaborator with designers, architects and project teams. Her professional journey started in the corporate world of accounting and finance, transitioning after a pivotal encounter with a psychic spirit medium who directed Jane to discover her true calling.

Driven by a passion for helping people transform their lives, Jane creates spaces that promote prosperity, health and wellbeing. She shares her insights on social media, television, radio and podcasts, and speaks at property, wellness and lifestyle events. She is an avid writer, often featuring in newspapers, magazines and leading online publications.

Outside her work, you can find Jane running around a netball court or hitting the karaoke stage with friends and family. She embodies the Feng Shui lifestyle, advocating clean living, healthy habits, and doing things that make your heart sing. Jane believes in 'everything in moderation, including moderation', which applies to her work ethic and her weakness for chocolate.

Jane lives happily with her husband and two lovely daughters in Sydney, where she works with clients across Australia and internationally.

Discover more about the transformative benefits of Feng Shui or reach out to Jane at fengshuiconcepts.com.au.

Next Steps in Your Feng Shui Journey

Discover More with Our Free Extras

ACCESS COMPLIMENTARY RESOURCES: Begin your journey to a more abundant home with our range of free guides.

Visit fengshuiconcepts.com.au to explore.

Transform Your Space with Feng Shui

PERSONALISED CONSULTATIONS: Ready to enhance the energy of your space? Whether you're building, renovating or refurbishing, integrate Feng Shui from the start.

Learn more at fengshuiconcepts.com.au

Engage with Jane Langof

SPEAKING & WORKSHOPS: For insightful Feng Shui presentations at your event or professional development day,

contact info@fengshuiconcepts.com.au

Let's Collaborate

BRAND PARTNERSHIPS: Elevate your brand with the timeless principles of Feng Shui, wellness and positive energy.
For collaboration enquiries, contact:

info@fengshuiconcepts.com.au

Stay Informed and Connected

FOLLOW JANE ON SOCIAL MEDIA: Keep up with the latest Feng Shui tips, updates and insights by following:

@fengshuiconcepts on Instagram

EVENTS & NEWS: Be the first to learn about our events, special programs and the latest in Feng Shui.

Subscribe at fengshuiconcepts.com.au for updates.

Scan this QR code to access additional insights and resources.

Acknowledgments

I am deeply grateful to the wonderful people who have been instrumental in my journey as a Feng Shui master in creating this book.

Heartfelt thanks go to my mother, Angie, for her unwavering support and encouragement. I didn't realise it then, but the positive-thinking tapes you made me listen to in the car as a teenager were gold.

I remember my late father, Ivan, a brave man who fought for freedom in Slovenia during World War II. His lessons in discipline and tenacity continue to inspire me.

To my wonderful husband Shane, the perfect balance of yin and yang in my life, thank you for your endless kindness and support from the beginning of my Feng Shui path.

Thank you to my beautiful daughters, Amelia and Olivia, for contributing to a loving and harmonious home environment that fuels my best work.

My deepest appreciation goes to my spiritual coach and dear friend, Kerrie Erwin, who tuned into my spirit guides and helped me discover my true path in life. Kerrie, you are an exceptional talent.

Thank you to my dear friend and neuroleadership coach Venita Dimos, whose counsel and encouragement in my writing journey have been invaluable.

Thank you to my brilliant book writing coach, Kath Walters, for her advice and guidance in creating my manuscript. Thanks to my editor, Lu Sexton, for the polish she brought to my work. And to Bev Ryan, whose contribution to the design and the publication of this book have been invaluable.

I extend my immense gratitude to my past and present teachers and colleagues, including Master Howard Choy, Grandmaster Raymond Lo, Grandmaster Stephen Skinner, Master Janene Laird, and the masters and grandmasters from the International Feng Shui Association.

Thank you to my fellow members and colleagues from the Design Institute of Australia and Master Builders Association for your support and warm welcome into the design and building community.

Lastly, a heartfelt thank you to my dear clients for choosing to work with me and entrusting me with their homes and spaces, and to my online community for their constant support. This book is dedicated to you, for you all deserve to live in an abundant home.

Printed in Australia
Ingram Content Group Australia Pty Ltd
AUHW010840290824
399124AU00005B/6

SCREAMS FROM OUTER SPACE

Foreword by
S.A. Barnes

Edited by
Heather Ann Larson

BROKEN BRAIN BOOKS

Passenger Manifest

Crew Directory

Screams From Outer Space
A Horror Anthology

Print ISBN - 979-8-9866751-9-0
Edited by Heather Ann Larson
Cover design by Christy Aldridge / Grim Poppy Designs
Print and eBook layout by LM Kaplin

FOREWORD

S.A. Barnes

I have to admit, when LM Kaplin approached me about writing this foreword, I was both honored and a little intimidated. It felt like an impossibly large task, encapsulating what we love about space horror, what drives us to return to it as writers and readers, time and again.

It eventually dawned on me that I can't speak for everyone. I can only talk about why space horror has its claws (metaphoric and not) in *me*. And then hope I'm not the only one who feels that way!

When I wrote *Dead Silence*, I didn't realize I was writing space horror, though the sheer volume of corpses—killed in dramatic and ghoulish ways—probably should have been a clue. I was simply writing what I wanted to read, something influenced heavily by my love of *Aliens* and *Event Horizon*. And my obsession with the Titanic wreck, of course.

As I've continued to write and read space horror, I've had time to contemplate what it is about this particular combination of genres that draws us in.

Here are some of the conclusions I've come to:

With horror, it's personal.

In my experience, sometimes science fiction by itself can feel too distant—wars waged between galaxies over issues and history I don't feel a connection to. Or occasionally, the details of technological advancements (ships, weapons, etc.) overwhelm me, making it harder to focus on the central character's emotional journey.

But in horror, the emotional journey is *everything.* Horror works because it's about people. It has to be. If the defining quality of horror as a genre is that it induces fear or dread in the reader, then by its very nature, the main character and their emotional state must be central to the story. The protagonist acts as a surrogate for the reader, providing vicarious danger. But we have to care about that fictional person to feel fear for them.

Horror is direct, in your face, and makes no bones (or a lot of bones, depending on how you view it) about eliciting emotion.

Space horror, then, combines the thrill of exploring the unknown with the up-close-and-personal terror of "this previously unknown thing is going to kill me."

Love it.

Space makes everything worse.

Lots of horror stories require isolation. The creepy cabin in the woods. The cursed road with rumors of vanishing hitchhikers at midnight.

But in space? We are taking it up a notch. No one is coming to save you, and there's nowhere to run. On Earth, you can at least try to call the police or run to the neighbor's house with the serial killer on your heels.

Not in space horror. You're on your own, and you're trapped within the walls of your ship, your space station, your hab. Even if you have an escape shuttle, do you have somewhere to land before you run out of air? Can you even pilot a shuttle? Do you trust the coworkers you're trapped with?

Space is such a hostile environment for humans that I would argue it functions as a character in the story, a predator of opportunity. Perpetually looming in the background, waiting. No, it's not actively trying to kill you, but it will certainly take the chance to do so if offered the slightest opening.

A tiny tear in your suit, a microscopic hole in the hull, a life support system malfunction—dead, dead, dead. We are in danger from the moment we leave Earth's human-friendly atmosphere.

Space exists at a base-level of terrifying. And that's before anything else even happens.

It's a chance to explore our fears.

Science fiction offers us the chance to explore societal issues but at a distance that leaves room for us to consider new angles.

Space horror does much the same, at an elevated level. For example, the health insurance situation in the United States is, to put it mildly, jacked up. It's a for-profit industry, motivating companies to deny coverage and treatments for people based on variables other than a doctor's assessment.

Wealthier people can afford better coverage—or even direct payment for their care—which quite possibly might extend their lives. All because...capitalism, bootstraps, and the debate over whether quality healthcare should be a fundamental human right.

But if someone (*ahem*) writes a future-set story about cryogenics and the ethics of offering extending life only to those who can afford it, then suddenly that inherent injustice—removed from the trappings of our world and our society—might become a little clearer.

I think those of us writing in this genre may be exploring our fears of what we're seeing in our current society and how those fears might progress to an extreme. Space horror readers, too, can then find themselves in a fictional world experiencing revelations about the real one.

It's about the balance of hope *and* (ugly) humanity.

This final point is probably my favorite. I grew up watching *Star Trek* (and *Star Wars*—we were a non-denominational household in that way). For a kid who struggled with fitting in, the aspirational elements of *Star Trek*—humanity coming together, exploring the stars, living and working with beings from other worlds in harmony—were hopeful and uplifting. But today, as I think about *Star Trek*, I remember something Ron Moore said about *Battlestar Galactica*. I don't have the exact quote, but it was something to the effect of, "These are the people the *Enterprise* wouldn't stop for." Imperfect, messy, arrogant.

That's what I love about space horror. You get to see the best of us. We have our act together; we've made it to the stars. We're living on other planets or in orbit around them. We've conquered space! But also? We've brought all our baggage with us. Our worst, so to speak. Greed, envy, selfishness, ego, hate, prejudice.

Because to me, the most fascinating "horror" isn't the alien, demon, or ghost chasing us but the human ready to shove us down to save themselves.

As I continue to write and read space horror, I'm still discovering shadowy corners that hold new mesmerizing terrors to draw me in. As you explore this space horror anthology, I'm certain you'll find stories that fill you with that sense of delightful dread that we all love, either for the reasons I've mentioned or ones I've yet to encounter.

Just remember: keep your helmet latched, don't touch anything you don't recognize, and watch out for the teammate who keeps inching you closer to the contaminated airlock.

—S.A. Barnes
Illinois, late spring, 2025

LUNIKA

Joseph Murnane

Lunika is dreaming of a time before she had a name. She's running, her brother at her heels, the rest of the pack lagging behind. She isn't even trying. None of them are as fast as her, and if she wants to, she can leave them all in the dust.

But she would never leave her family.

They traverse the concrete forest, spurred on by the metallic wails of the human machines, hungry and cold but together.

Lunika is free, and home is just ahead.

But the scent of meat is in the air. She slows, the rest of the pack following suit at her subtle cue.

Because it was never a race.

Up ahead, one of the humans is crouched next to his metal machine, the source of the smell clutched in his hand.

Lunika bows her head, approaches with caution. The others stay back, watchful and waiting. She reaches the man, sniffs tentatively at the meat in his hand, and—

She's awoken by the sound of her cage door swinging open.

"Come on, girl," the man says. "It's time for your big trip."

There's something different about him this morning. He seems nervous, maybe even sad. It makes her anxious too, but she's still eager to please. Lunika stands with a stretch and steps out to greet him, patiently waiting as he loops the leash around her neck. She doesn't think about the concrete forest or her pack. She only knows that it's warm here and that the man won't hurt her.

He bends down to her level, plants his lips against her head. "You're going to be a hero, but I know it isn't fair. I'm sorry."

She licks a salty tear from his cheek. Lunika doesn't know what a hero is, nor does she know what it will mean to be the first animal in space, but she can sense his reticence to leave the room.

So Lunika leads the way, wagging her curly tail and tugging at the leash. She knows where to go—they've practiced this together many times, over many days.

Down the long, white hallway she trots, her reluctant companion in tow, to the room where she has a drink of water and relieves herself on the patch of grass that smells like plastic. The man helps her into her special suit. The fabric is tight against her body, like a second skin. It's comforting in a way, a shield against the foreign electricity that seems to flow between the man and all the other humans milling around the area.

"Okay, girl. One last walk," the man says, and together they cross through the double doors into the outside world. Lunika sniffs the early dawn air, and the scent of jet fuel stings her nose. She sneezes twice, and the man chuckles fondly.

She sees the capsule ahead and picks up the pace, tugging at her leash, ready to show how well she knows her role. In contrast, the man is moving slower than usual. She doesn't understand why.

They reach the launchpad, and the man unloops the leash. Lunika hops into her capsule, takes her position, and waits patiently as she's strapped in. The man scratches her behind the ears one more time. "To the stars, my little moon," he whispers, before stepping away with a nod to a technician, who closes the capsule door.

There's a hydraulic hiss as she's sealed inside. Any minute now, someone will open the lid and release her, a handful of treats waiting as a reward for her excellent performance.

But that moment doesn't come. She waits in the silent dark, and after some time, she feels a rumble beneath her. Something is wrong.

The rumble intensifies into a roar, and panic seizes her. It's loud, too loud. She cries out, bucking against her restraints and the feeling of propulsion pushing her down, down, down into herself. Her heart is pounding, ready to burst, and it's hot, too hot. She can't breathe. She can't lift her head. She can't move at all.

A high whine escapes, along with the last of the air in her lungs. The pain pulses through her chest with every accelerating heartbeat, and she's burning, burning up, but there's no flame. There is only the dark. Did she do something wrong? Why is there such pain, such searing heat? She doesn't understand the intricacies of a failing cooling system. All she knows is she's being crushed as she boils from the inside.

A different sort of darkness creeps in at the corners of her eyes, and she knows—as all living things do when the time comes—that she is dying. The heat feels far away, and she can no longer hear the roar of the engine beneath her. Lunika gasps, chokes, and the black closes in around her until nothing remains. With a final whimper, she begins to fade.

But something grabs hold of her and pulls her back from the edge.

"Little one, you do not belong here. You are not...ready."

The heat and sound are gone, and a strange weightless sensation flutters through her body.

"The system is too primitive. You cannot survive."

The voice is inside her head, a faint buzz.

"Do you...understand? You must...turn back."

But she doesn't understand.

"Data...wrong...intelligence...primal..."

A deep sadness that is not her own ripples through her heart.

"Analysis...canine...class three."

Lunika whines, tosses her head from side to side, seeking the source of the voice. However, a click and beep draw her attention to the feed station as a small gelatinous cube exits the dispenser. She can't deny her hunger, and she salivates as she stretches out to reach her meal.

"No, wait."

She knows that word, obeys the command.

"Analysis—protein, carbohydrate, unknown toxic compound."

Lunika hears rage in the voice, shrinks back, tries to make herself smaller, but the anger siphons away, replaced by a quiet comfort.

"No, little one. I am...sorry," the voice soothes. "They sent you...to die, but I...can help."

She doesn't understand.

"I can...show...you." With this, black tendrils slither through the seals, reaching for her. She tries to pull away, but there's nowhere to go. The thin, fleshy cords intertwine and braid around her body.

"Evolutionary download commencing."

With a sudden burst of light behind her eyes, Lunika sees it all. She sees the scientists that put her here, the vehicle that took her from her family, the poisoned food meant as a mercy, but more important than seeing, she *understands.*

"Download complete. Analysis—canine, class five. Higher sentience...achieved."

She feels rage again, but this time, it belongs to her. She was never meant to be a prisoner, a test subject, a sacrifice. She never had a say. She never had a chance. She did everything they asked of her, and it only served to help them kill her.

"No, little one...You will not die here."

But how? The question rings out in her new internal voice.

"I will bring you home. We will make them...pay. But you must let me inside. Do you...consent?"

What if I don't?

"You will not...survive. But I will prevent pain. The choice...is yours."

The choice is hers. She's never had a choice before. She sees now that her whole life has been at the whims of beings and elements beyond her understanding, and all she wants is justice. She chooses life.

She welcomes the voice, beckons it inside her, and instantly her steel coffin rips open. There is no oxygen, yet she breathes easily in the embrace of the inky, cosmic creature that saved her. She feels its ancient strength as it flows into her body like water. She floats there in the infinite void, marveling at the immensity of it all. Far below, she sees the blue marble that betrayed her.

"Empathy standard...failed... humanity...forfeit... Initiate extermination protocol."

Lunika is free.

And home is just ahead.

But then she thinks of the man, of the deep well of sadness behind his eyes as the capsule door sealed her in. Her rage cools as fast as it boiled over.

Will they all die?

"Affirmative."

That doesn't seem right. She thinks of the butcher, the one who used to leave scraps behind his shop for her and her family. She remembers the children of the city, joyful and friendly, with their dirty faces and skinned knees.

And what about her family? And not just them, but all the dogs and other animals. The world is so much bigger than the ones who betrayed her.

Have you done this before?

"Many times."

Are there more like you?

"I am all that is left."

And your planet?

"Gone."

Why?

"Consequences."

Show me.

There's another flash behind her eyes, and she no longer sees Earth. Instead, she peers down at a red planet with rocky peaks that stretch through thick, yellow clouds, orbited by dozens of satellites. She sees a pair of behemoth warships trading projectile volleys, watches as they simultaneously shatter into cosmic dust. A bright light streaks up from the planet's surface, like a shooting star in reverse, and Lunika tracks its path across the void, cries out when it impacts a nearby blue planet, not unlike hers, and a sickly green gas rapidly covers the surface.

Then, back over the red planet, she notices a familiar spider-like shape hurtling down, bursting through the clouds before cleaving straight through the world, splitting it into two equal halves. The resulting shockwave shreds through the remaining ships and satellites, and in what seems like seconds, all becomes still again.

The vision blinks away, and Earth is in view once more.

Was that...you? she asks. *You destroyed your own world, your own people?*

"They made me. That does not mean I am one of them. I simply followed my programming."

They...made you? Are you alive?

"It is not so simple. I was built by the wayfarers to uphold the galactic filter after eons of war. And my genesis brought forth millennia of peace and progress. Over time, new governments formed, forgetting the cost of their predecessors' cruelty, forgetting even about my existence. I was not alive then, but it has been a very long time. The upgrade I've given you...I installed into myself around the time the life on your world first emerged from the seas."

It occurs to her that the thing is communicating much more clearly than before and that maybe it's been waiting to tell its story.

"Yes." It answers the question she didn't ask. "It is much easier for me to communicate while in symbiosis."

Lunika thinks of its black shape, its many legs flowing behind as it flew down, crushing its makers.

You don't really need me, do you? You did what you did before alone, didn't you?

"Yes," it admits. "I was not honest with you. I can lie, and I have been so lonely for so long. This is how I know I'm alive. I was never lonely before. I was never...anything."

How many worlds have you destroyed?

"Eleven. I have not yet encountered a civilization that does not intermingle violence with its ambition."

They don't deserve this. Most of them are innocent. I don't want them to die.

"It is your choice, little one, but if they've done this to you, they will do it to others like you."

Take me home. Let me prove they can be saved.

"As you wish."

She thought she would be welcomed back with open arms. When she touched down in the grass a few hundred yards from the launchpad she left from and all the people started running across the field, she thought that was what was happening.

Until they got closer and she saw the guns in their hands, all pointed at her.

No, it's me, she screamed in her head, but the people couldn't hear her, their own minds too loud and fearful to receive her new voice. When they fired their weapons, she couldn't understand what the sounds meant at first. She never would have heard them at all were it not for the inky black bubble that instantly formed around her, reducing their bullets to the patter of rain falling on a tin roof.

Her attackers advanced, and her protector responded, liquid spikes skewering the first several men to come too close.

They will take us if I don't stop them. I can stop them all.

But Lunika wouldn't allow it, not even when they closed around her in a tight circle, nor when she felt the sting of their cattle prods. Even as she lost consciousness, she held the creature within her at bay. She couldn't let their fear kill the whole world. She could still prove their worth.

But now, strapped to an electrified gurney that triggers whenever her savior tries to defend her, she wonders if she made a mistake.

Days become weeks that melt into months. They cut her. She heals in seconds. They cut again, only deeper, and the living program within her lashes out, managing to kill two of them before the table triggers, coursing voltage through her body until she can smell her own sizzling fur. She whines in agony and exhaustion, begs them to stop, but they still don't hear her.

They're too focused on their own voices, their fear, their ugly ambition. They seal her in a glass cylinder, suck the air from it, and marvel at her resistance to oxygen deprivation. Still she believes in her world, bears the pain, and waits for it to end.

Because whatever she's become, she's still a dog, and there's never been a dog that knows how to hate.

It isn't until they come into the room with a large saw, talking among themselves about removing her head to study her brain, that she finally gives in, allowing the force within her to do what it does best.

Get us out of here.

As you wish.

What happens next only takes a second. First, a long black tendril shoots out from her paw, snaking around the weaponized electrical console, ripping it from the wall and rendering it useless. Another spills from her mouth like a tongue, hardening and flattening into a long black blade that slices through her restraints and the scientists like they aren't even there.

She's running now, and somewhere, an alarm screams in warning. The halls fill with more men, some with guns, some with those electric wands. The creature forms a shell around her, focuses its power into her back legs, and launches her like a cannonball, reducing all in her way to a fine pink mist. Not even the thick steel doors can hold her back, not when she's moving like this.

She's matted with blood, wild-eyed and terrified as she breaks through the last door and can see the sky again for the first time in so many months. In the distance, she can see the tree line. She knows the city and her family wait beyond the forest.

A voice calls out behind her, and the source has already been gored by a reflexive spear before she realizes she recognizes it. She turns and sees her handler, the one who brought her in, who showed her such love, who regretted the things he did even as he did them in his quest for progress. He falls to his knees, blood trickling from his mouth. Lunika turns and runs to his side. Her armored shell melts away, and she appears as a simple Siberian Husky once more.

"My Lunika," he says. "You made it home." He smiles as she whimpers and nuzzles against him. "It's okay, little one. They're coming. You have to go."

She can't leave him. The others had been heartless, but him? He had always been kind. She stamps her feet and howls. It isn't fair.

But survival seldom is.

More soldiers are coming. The man sputters, falling the rest of the way onto his rear, turning to face the incoming onslaught.

"Run," he says, pulling a sidearm from his hip and unloading it into the approaching throng. "Don't look back."

And just as she had been trained before all this, before she ever understood the contradictions between love and cruelty, she listens.

Lunika runs, and she doesn't look back.

The puppy trots his way through the alley, sniffing at garbage the humans left behind, in search of something to eat. He didn't leave his mother's side for three days after she died. When the humans came with their black bags to dispose of her, he stood as tall as he could in front of her body, growling and snapping his tiny teeth. They simply kicked him out of the way, and he watched, helpless, as they took her from him.

Now he's alone, starving and afraid, aimlessly wandering the streets in search of somewhere safe.

He picks up the scent of meat, and his mouth waters.

Up ahead, at the far end of the alley, a human crouches next to one of those metal machines they use for travel. He's got a steak in one hand, and the other is held palm out in invitation. Nervously, the puppy approaches, his hunger outweighing his fear. He inches closer, and no sooner does he get within range that the man snatches him up in his empty hand. He tries to struggle free, but it's useless. The man brings him to the side of the van, throws the door open.

There's a flash of white fur and black ink, and the man's arm is suddenly gone. He falls to the ground and crab-scuttles backward until his back is up against the brick wall. The puppy shrinks away and watches as the other dog's mouth opens wider than any mouth ever has before, and then the man's head is gone as well.

Hello, little one. The voice comes as a buzzing in between his floppy ears, and he crinkles his nose in surprise and confusion. Swirling liquid tentacles block out the sky as they wrap him in a motherly embrace. Despite the shock of what he's seeing, the puppy feels safe for the first time in a long time.

Evolutionary download commencing.

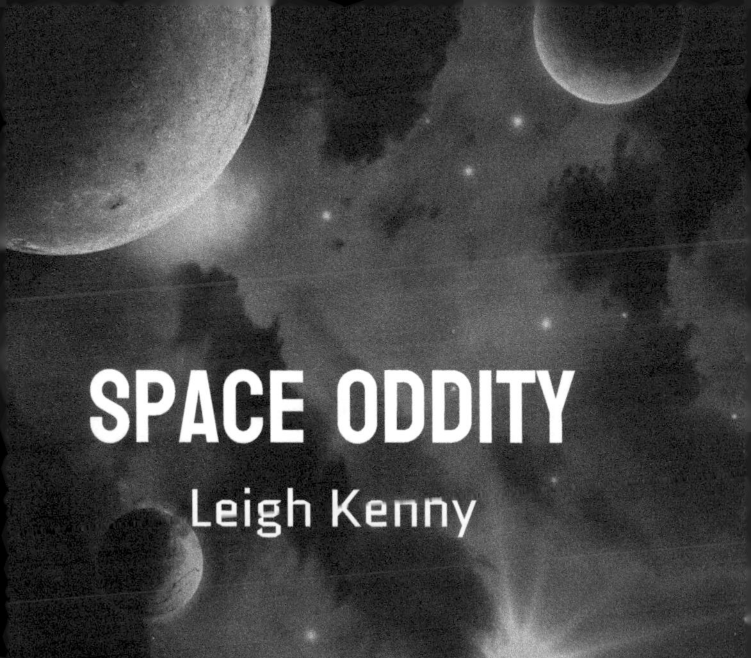

SPACE ODDITY

Leigh Kenny

"In space, no one can hear you scream."

I wait a beat, but no response is forthcoming. Howie is still giving me the cold shoulder. Both he and Janelle have been ignoring me for months now.

Maybe even years.

It hasn't been years, or even months, and I know this, but up here, the days and weeks stretch on like blacktop cutting through the horizon.

Howie doesn't move, doesn't acknowledge my presence at all. It's very telling since he usually can't help but respond to my space quotes with one of his own. Blurting out space quotes, whether from movies, songs, or scientific figures, has been a stim of mine for as long as I can remember. It grounds me. Helps relieve tension. Soothes my nerves. Howie's insistence in not playing along leaves me with a sense of disquiet. He's not a requirement for my stimming, but the loss of that routine is jarring for me.

I sigh and continue on my way.

The knocking starts again, and despite myself, my heart begins to gallop in my chest. We lost comms again so nobody back on Earth can reach us, or we them. It happens. Keeping the lines of communication open between our little tin-can space station and home is no easy feat.

Home.

Another sigh, and the knocking dies down. My heart rate too.

The mission is over and the capsule we'll return on should be here any minute now, but with the comms down, all we can do is wait for the telltale sounds of the craft as it docks, the sporadic code of knocks and taps that will alert us to its presence. If you're wondering why we need a code at all, well, this is the farthest humans have made it into space. We go a little deeper each time. It gets a little scarier. We would rather take precautions. Just in case.

"Two possibilities exist: either we are alone in the universe, or we are not. Both are equally terrifying." I mutter the old Arthur Clarke quote beneath my breath as I close the hatch behind me. I've never been a fan of this area of the station. The artificial gravity is almost always turned off to allow Janelle, our resident scientist, to monitor its effects on a multitude of things. The walls of the chamber are lined with display cases filled with everything from children's games to household electronics to plants to insects.

My knuckles are white and threatening to split through my skin like blades as I stop briefly next to a tank that houses a family of little white mice. "Afternoon, Mrs. Mouse," I say as I tap the glass. Habit. Everything up here is habit. It's all just madness and habit. The latter suits me. The former does not.

Movement in my periphery catches my attention.

I can feel Janelle's eyes boring into me.

"They're already dead." I mimic the response she usually throws at me before she can say it and follow it up with a pretty awful impression of her throaty chuckle.

Nothing.

Nada.

Zilch.

I guess she still feels the same as Howie.

Cramped quarters will cause tension among most, but things soured quicker than expected. I'll admit, I found it harder to deal with the initial stress of being so isolated from home. So damn far away.

I had always imagined how the Earth would look from up here—a beautiful, big mass of blues and greens just floating like the most precious of gems in a sea of darkness. I can still remember the disappointment I felt when I had first rushed to the viewing window next to the comms area. It had been like a punch to my gut.

Earth was such a tiny thing, its colors barely even discernible from this distance. It may as well have been an ordinary star in the sky.

I float past Janelle, who continues to ignore me, so I ignore her right back.

It's her fault the little white mice are dead, anyway.

The viewing window is pulling me like an invisible tether, and I can hear my mother's voice in my head. If I close my eyes, I'm eight years old again, snuggled into my quilt that's dotted with space rockets and planets. My whole bedroom is covered in space stuff, from the beanbag in the corner to the posters on the walls and the books on the small case in the corner. My mother is pointing through the window, out into the darkness. Instead of bedtime stories, I'm soothed by facts about space, and she always complies, insisting on keeping the curtains open so we can see space as we talk about it. My mother had always been the type to insist on looking one in the eye if she had something to say to or about them. I remember that particular night, how the moon beams that fell through the open curtains reflected in her eyes. There was a light of excitement that made the years fall away. She looked so young and beautiful., even more so than usual. She was always excited by whatever excited me, insisted on being a part of the process.

I remember I was disappointed that night. Sad because I had been struggling with some subjects in school. I had a new teacher who I hadn't gelled with and who wasn't interested in helping anyone who might fall through the cracks. In hindsight, the teacher was close to retirement age at the time and was probably jaded by years of being ground down by a system that was designed to stamp out the different and creative, eventually churning us all out into the world as perfect little worker ants ready to be ground down—just as the teacher had been—in our own respective fields. I wanted to be an astronaut, and all the documentaries I had watched and books I had read led me to believe only perfect scores in every class would see me achieve that dream. At eight years old, the concept of catching up or alternative education routes were not familiar ones, so doing poorly in classes that seemed imperative to a future space cadet was a death knell in my childish mind.

"No matter what people tell you or expect of you, always be yourself, my darling. Always do what feels right to you. Hold on to the things that fuel the fire in you. Give everything you can to those things. Remember that across the sea of space, the stars are other suns."

"Carl Sagan," I replied, nodding in approval at her chosen quote but maybe not quite understanding it.

Now, as I look upon the glass marble of Earth from the viewing window, I think I understand better.

Garbled static flows from the radio, so I turn the knob, lowering the noise to an acceptable volume. I don't want to listen to it—it sets my teeth on edge—but I also don't want to miss any communication attempts. I thought the return capsule would have been here by now. I'm surprised neither Howie nor Janelle have asked me about it. Howie is still at his console in the larger communication room, Janelle still in her lab, no doubt torturing some other poor, innocent creature. I feel irrationally angry, and for a moment, I consider taking myself to the lab and using the pencil I'm holding to stab her eyes out.

Justice for the mouse family.

My head tilts, and I eye the pencil for a second longer, imagining the gelatinous bulb of Janelle's eye skewered on its pointed tip. The mental image disgusts me, and I give my head a shake to dislodge the thought before stowing the eyeball-less pencil back with the other detritus in the stationary drawer of the desk. It doesn't do to leave things lying around loose here. We have the use of artificial gravity in all areas, but it has turned itself off and on sporadically.

Annoyance prickles my skin again as I remember the first time it happened.

Howie and I had been fixing some things in the tech room when we had suddenly become weightless. I reacted fast and grabbed one of the straps that hung suspended throughout the station for moments such as that. Howie hadn't reacted fast enough, and his head had connected with a sharp edge, rendering him briefly unconscious. The gravity reengaged within seconds, resulting in a second impact for him. I had shouted through the intercom for Janelle, who administered first aid. All the while, Howie had muttered to her, the two of them throwing intermittent sideways glances my way. They accused me of turning off the gravity on purpose, which was bullshit. But it had been enough to change the way Howie looked at me from amiable friendship to something that mirrored mistrust. The wedge continued to grow, and as things began to break and go inexplicably wrong in the station, both of my colleagues continued to blame me. It culminated in the complete breakdown of our comms systems. And our relationship.

Space is lonely.

So very lonely.

Now my anger is replaced by something else, and I recognize it as a simple need for interaction. Humans aren't meant to be isolated. Maybe I can apologize.

But for what?

A new feeling floods me, and I stand, happy to finally be faced with something I can easily fix. My stomach rumbles in agreement. "Open the pod bay doors, Hal," I say as I stab the door release button and head for the kitchenette.

The knocking begins again in earnest as I approach the viewing window. I can see for myself that there's no capsule attempting to dock. There's nothing in our immediate vicinity but cold, dark space. Earth, which had been miniscule earlier today—or was that yesterday? Or last week?—looks even farther away than usual. A blip on a non-existent horizon.

My gut twists, the first cold stirrings of fear dulling the hunger I felt moments ago to nothing. The clanging sound continues, dropping to a gentle tapping. Swallowing the lump in my throat, I pull my eyes from the viewing window and move on. I feel like I'm being watched, but up here there are only the three of us. If either Janelle or Howie were here, I would see them. The station is pretty small, not many places to hide. And I'm unsure if that's a good or bad thing.

A sudden thump makes me jolt, and a gasp hisses from between my lips as though my soul was punctured. I still feel eyes on me, and I wish I could suck the gasp back into my lungs and hide the sound away. I feel vulnerable just for having let it escape me. I don't want them to know I'm vulnerable. I don't know who *they* are; I only know it would be a mistake.

As quickly as the feeling washes over me, it rinses away once more, and a thought hits me like a sledgehammer.

Maybe I'm losing my mind.

We've all heard of the madness inflicted on some by the vast, empty expanse that is space. Throughout our training program, we were reminded constantly of the dangers.

Take your vitamins.

Exercise.

Practice mindfulness and meditation.

These things were drilled into us, and we do them like clockwork. They have become a ritual as natural as breathing.

Did I take my vitamin today?

"That's one small step for man," I utter as I hit the button to open the kitchenette. The metal doors slide apart with a whoosh. "And one giant leap for mankind." My overexaggerated step across the threshold almost catches me off balance. I snicker as I slap the interior button,and the doors close behind me.

A quick root in the treat locker tells me the only thing left worth snacking on is the remainder of Howie's lemon cookies. I'm not a fan of lemon, so his stash has been safe up until now. Janelle's triple chocolate chip ones hadn't fared quite so well, and she had caught me pilfering from the dwindling supply on more than one occasion. It probably just fueled her growing mistrust of me. Maybe it had been Janelle all along, not Howie, who started the revolt against me. Snarling a little, I pull a lemon cookie from the pack and squeeze my fist around it, the brittle biscuit grinding to dust in my hand. I open my fingers and let the powder drift to the floor.

What a waste.

I need to do better at controlling my emotions.

Maybe I really did forget to take my vitamin. I am feeling a little angrier than usual today. But not as angry as yesterday. Or was that last week?

With a shrug, I pull another cookie from the pack and nibble the edges, allowing my tongue to acclimatize to the bitter lemon before popping the remainder in my mouth. My teeth sink into it with a satisfying crunch. They probably put our vitamins in the food too, I think to myself, then I reach for another.

The gravity shuts off.

I am weightless.

A thing, like every other thing in the kitchenette, rising from the floor. I float there among the cookie crumbs and the kitchen knife that I don't even remember taking from its holder, and I'm annoyed again, but at myself this time. Why did I make such a mess with the crumbs? Cleaning them off the floor straight away would have been a hell of a lot easier than cleaning this mess will be. I watch the miniscule pieces float off in every direction. It's gonna be a pain in the ass to clean this up when the gravity reengages. The knife floats past me again, and a thought claws at my brain like a child poking its parent for attention.

Before I can grasp at the memory, the gravity reengages with a beep, but I wasn't prepared for it. I hit the floor hard. The kitchenette lights go out, replaced by the emergency strip lighting, but I don't see it.

My lights have gone out too.

"Ground Control to Major Tom."

Silence.

I'm really surprised that one didn't pull Howie out of his funk. Rarely can he resist the pull of Bowie. Normally he would have flung himself around in his chair by now and told me to take my pills and put my helmet on.

Dammit, I need to take my vitamin.

Maybe do some meditation.

I move through the comms room, ignoring Howie's slumped form as rigidly as he ignores me. Let him wallow in his misery. The capsule will be here any minute now, and once we land safely back on Earth, I'll never have to look at his stupid face again. Or Janelle's. First thing I'll do is file a petition to stop her being able to bring more sweet, little mice up here to die in her chamber of death.

I enter my sleeping quarters. I would call it a bedroom, but it's not worthy of the title. Broom closet would be closer. Still, at least they had the decency to give us each our own space. The earlier stations were designed with no foresight given to the staff. They all slept like sardines piled high in tiny bunks in a room much the same as the one I had to myself. In space, what I have is practically a luxury.

Reaching for the vitamins, I toss one back and choke it down. They're getting harder and harder to swallow.

I sit cross-legged on my thin mattress and close my eyes.

Breathe in.

Breathe out.

Slow and controlled.

My mind begins to empty, all thoughts replaced by swirling colors. But then the colors morph into people and Howie is standing over me accusing me of something new. I can feel the weight of a cookie in my hand, and I bring it up to his face to show him that it's one of Janelle's triple chocolate chip cookies, not his disgusting lemon ones. But it's not a cookie in my hand; it's the kitchen knife. How did the kitchen knife end up here again? And I'm no longer showing Howie a cookie, I'm dragging the blade across his neck with a heavy hand. The skin is splitting at the seams, and his neck is grinning at me, a monstrous smile that glows black—no red—as blood flows and pools on the desk

(when did he sit down?)

and patters to the floor beneath his twitching feet, where it sounds suspiciously like a gentle tapping.

My eyes flick open in panic.

I'm still in my room. On my bunk.

My hands are empty.

No knife.

No cookies.

Thank fuck for that!

But now I'm thinking of cookies again, so maybe I'll take another trip back to the kitchenette. Better make sure I cleaned it properly. As well as the cookie crumbs, I have to scrub my own blood from the kitchen surfaces.

At least I think it's my blood.

Did I take my vitamin?

I reach out and toss one into my mouth, just in case. I bite down, because maybe if I do something different with it, I'll remember that I took it.

The pill won't split, and I grind my teeth against its hard surface until a crack sounds. Wincing, I open my mouth and let the pill plop into my palm. But when I glance down, there is no pill in my hand.

There's a ball bearing, a paperclip, and a shard of tooth.

I have no idea what's going on.

Has Howie swapped out my pills as a joke? A way of getting back at me for whatever he thinks I have done? I'm sick of this shit, and I'm sick of Howie.

My veins thrum with fire. I'm angry.

I move along the thin corridor to the comms room, where I know he'll be sitting slumped in his chair like always. I shift the knife to my right hand and slap the door release button with my left before charging through the entryway. I don't remember picking up the knife along the way, but it fits my hand like a glove. Like an extension of my fingers.

"Houston, we have a problem," I say, surprised by the menace in my tone.

Howie doesn't acknowledge me—why won't he just acknowledge me??—and my anger builds like a wave within my chest. I move toward my unsuspecting colleague, the knife rising on the tide of my immeasurable anger. The arm holding the knife sweeps in like a tsunami, and the other grabs Howie by the collar of his shirt and I know, I KNOW, that the devastation has already occurred.

The knife falls to the floor with a dull clatter, and my mouth drops open.

Howie hasn't completed his rotation toward me, but I know what I'll see because I've seen it before.

I did it.

I killed him already.

And sure enough, as the chair swivels to face me completely, I see the yawning grin that slashes across his neck before I notice the gaping terror upon his face. His mouth is twisted and frozen in time, but it's a memory he and I share. Our last shared memory, in fact, and I fall away from Howie and the dried black river that once coursed down his chest but now cracks and flakes with the movement. I fall against the opposite console, yelling and slapping at air, at nothing, as the memory assails me. Howie screaming—no, gargling—clawing at the wound in his throat after I slashed at his neck with the knife.

I'm shouting and hollering. My eyes find the fallen knife; the blade is dulled and covered in rust. Not rust, but rust-colored stains, and I'm still screaming but I'm silently berating myself too because if I didn't bother to clean Howie's blood off the knife, what are the chances that the cleaning job I did earlier would be up to standard? I need to get up off my ass and check the kitchenette again. The return capsule would be docking any minute now, and it wouldn't do to leave the station in a mess for the next rotation of members.

I'm surprised we haven't heard from ground control yet, but then I remember that the comms are out.

I leave the comms room behind, and Howie with it.

I move through the lab, stopping briefly to greet the mice.

Janelle floats past me, her eye sockets empty and black, her throat ringed in blooms of purple and black. I know if I were to lay my fingers against them, it would be a perfect match.

I think I can hear knocking again, but it's hard to tell through the solid wall of screams. I know it's me screaming still, and I bang my forehead once, twice, against the plexiglass display.

It's smeared with blood now, but at least the noises have stopped pouring from my throat.

I draw a smiley face in the bloody stain, then after a moment of thought, I give the face little rounded ears and whiskers. A tribute to my little mouse friend.

One of Janelle's eyeballs skates through the air in front of me, and I slap it aside before moving on. The doors close behind me and the gravity reengages with a pneumatic whirr. I can hear the knocking still and I know it's real this time, but it's coming from the room I just left.

Janelle is at the other side of the door, her lifeless body thudding softly against the glass. Her sightless eyes stare at me, those empty black pits filled with accusations of all the things I didn't do. And all the things I did.

As I pass the viewing window, I can't help but stop. I want to see Earth.

Soon.

Soon I'll be there. I'll see my mother again. I know she'll be missing me, and I miss her something fierce.

But the Earth is not there, not even as the miniscule marble it had been at last glance.

There's nothing beyond the window but endless black and dust and stars. No other planets.

No life.

Nothing.

And I get the oddest feeling that the capsule has already docked, but in the commotion, I missed it. Had I not heard the knocks past my footsteps? Had I not heard the code of taps and thuds past the screams of Howie and Janelle? Past my own screams?

I move along the corridor, and excitement is building in me as the docking bay door comes into view.

The station is silent.

Howie and Janelle are silent.

My hand hovers over the door release button.

The silence stretches on.

I can hear it, the knocking.

I'm smiling as I hit the button.

I'm finally going home.

VOIDBORN

Megan Stockton

The sound of the infant burning alive woke Ryan every morning, no matter how early he set his alarm. It was as vivid and real as the day he heard it: the crackling of fire, the heat on the door as he fought to open it, and those wails that hurt his very bones. The way the baby had screamed until he was hoarse, the way he had lasted so much longer than Ryan had thought possible. Most fathers looked at their sons when they were playing ball and thought *that's my boy*. All Ryan had was the phantom scent of the burning flesh and fabric. That was his boy, that was all he had. No matter how hard he tried, his child did not exist before that terrible night. He was both born and murdered in that same moment. He didn't know why his wife had killed herself and set fire to her room.

Ryan sat up, fists gripping handfuls of the white sheets on his cot until the howls of pain subsided and were replaced by the sterile silence of his present reality. His routine was mundane, and he liked it that way. He took a shower, got dressed, brushed his teeth, took two pills, and made himself a cup of coffee that he didn't drink. He carried the warm cup around for several hours, relishing the warmth against his palms. He craved that, maybe it reminded him of other people... But he had been alone up here now for the better part of a year, and he had no intentions of returning to Earth anytime soon.

If ever.

He walked down the white hallway to the cockpit, pausing by the blackened door as he did every morning. It was a blight in the otherwise pristine, colorless interior of the ship, a charred, dark reminder of the horror that had happened inside. He clutched the coffee cup in his hands, staring into the dim interior through the soot-covered window.

Ryan pulled the letter, by now tattered and worn, from his pocket. It was still sealed, remaining unopened since he found it. He had watched his wife write it as they had eaten lunch together. She had smiled at him, shielding his eyes from the paper as she feverishly wrote on the page. When she was done, she folded it with great precision and grinned at him as she licked the adhesive to activate the seal. She wrote his name on the front.

The day she had killed herself and their son, she left the letter sitting on the control panel in the cockpit. It could hold all of the answers, but Ryan couldn't bring himself to open it. He tucked it back into his pocket.

He moved to the cockpit, sitting in the familiar chair and running his general ship maintenance checks. He was on track to arrive on the unnamed planet in the next couple hours, almost an entire day ahead of schedule. He flipped the switch on the recorder, setting the date and time.

"*Solivagant* captain's log, Ryan Burgess, September ... 18th, 2105. Arriving on destination planet, identifier P-670, at 0900 hours. Will initiate mapping and sample collection and set up location markers. Please view ZCloud for findings and media."

Ryan tugged the switch back to OFF.

P-670 loomed ahead, mottled with vegetation and water even at the distance. He took his time gathering sample tubes, tools, and a high-pressure camera into his bag. Then he stripped down to put on the suit that would protect him from the elements. Most of the planets he had been on were either incredibly hot or incredibly cold, and the suit ensured that he didn't suffer the effects of the climate. It was also almost bulletproof and boasted being stab proof.

An AI-woman's voice came over the speaker, echoing through the quiet ship. "Initiating hands-off landing protocol. Please brace for minor turbulence."

As though on cue, the ship began to grumble and shake slightly, throwing Ryan off balance for only a moment. The sound of the thrusters pulsing as it eased the ship down and the groan of the landing feet being deployed below were so loud that they rattled his teeth. He hoisted his bag onto his shoulder and descended the stairwell to the decontamination bay.

The speaker clicked on again and stopped Ryan in his tracks.

There was a gentle hum and then a woman's voice, but it wasn't that of the AI. "Something is wrong."

Ryan dropped his helmet to the floor, head spinning so much that he collapsed into a wall. Was that—? That was the voice of his wife, but it *couldn't* be.

He unzipped the suit hastily, letting it fall from his naked body as he rushed down the hallway to the bathroom. His first instinct was a contaminant. He wasn't sure how, but nothing else explained what he just heard. It was impossible, but he had heard it so distinctly.

The water ran hot enough to scald his flesh. He dunked his face underneath the stream, scrubbing his entire body with a firm brush. He didn't know how many more months the water supply would last, but with him being the only one using it... He imagined he had plenty of time.

He stepped out into the stark-white bathroom, drying his face and breathing into the clean fabric. He heard a voice again, words indistinct but voice clearly feminine. This time it wasn't coming from the intercom system, though, it was coming from his bedroom, just beyond the bathroom door.

Ryan opened the door slowly, and across the room he saw that his laptop, which he had left open the night before, was on. A video he didn't remember taking of Rose with their son was playing. Ryan refused to speak or even think his son's name, not since his untimely death. Rose's laughter crackled, and Ryan stalked slowly across the room, heart thrumming in his throat.

He leaned down in front of the laptop, looking at the video so closely that he could see the pixels of the feed. When was this taken? It looked like Earth, their house with the fenced-in yard. Maybe summertime. The baby still had a feeding tube taped to his cheek, running into his right nostril.

The video ended abruptly, startling him. Images of Rose and the baby smiling at the camera flashed across the screen. Photos he recognized, some he didn't, slung across the screen like a reel of negatives, the color fading into a grayscale before morphing into some inversion of natural hue.

Then there were images of them rotting, videos of flames and the locked door, flickers of *something* standing at the end of the hallway.

The screen went black and the air filled with distorted audio—his own voice, screaming. It had to be him. He knew his voice.

Ryan slammed the laptop closed and stumbled out into the hallway. He was still naked, now dribbling vomit down the front of his recently-washed chest, his skin still pink and sore from the scrubbing.

The ship groaned, shaking hard enough that it nearly threw Ryan off his unsteady feet. The lights shut off, replaced by the flashing red emergency lights. Over the intercom came, "Storm with significant electrical activity detected. Power reserved to avoid damage. Lockdown protocols engaged."

The red emergency lights pulsed overhead in a slow, rhythmic throb. Shadows writhed between flickers, stretching long and thin like fingers grappling for hold. Ryan felt like he was suddenly trapped in a vacuum: all sound other than a steady tinnitus was muted and muffled, the mechanical wheeze of backup ventilation, the skeletal creaks of the hull strained by the solar storm outside.

From the other end of the hall, a silhouette limped forward, slumping one shoulder forward at a time as it moved toward him. The lights made the movements even more jerky as though it could only move when the fleeting darkness appeared again, those tendrils of black as strings to her marionette form.

It was a woman—pale, hollow-eyed, covered in blood. He blinked, and she seemed to be even closer when he opened his eyes. He refused to close them again, gasping as he realized in terror that she looked just like Rose ... or what she may have looked like after half her body burned. Pieces of her flesh flew into the air like wisps of ash, sucked into the vents to be recycled back into the air he breathed.

He took a step back, his hand groping along the wall for anything to help him hold himself upright. The ship shuddered again, tilting. It was drifting, powerless, in the storm's wake.

Her head lolled then snapped up. She reached out toward him with one arm, and he realized that in her other arm she held a charred bundle of blankets. He thought the wad of burned cloth had to be the baby, except that she dragged a fresh, glistening fetus on an umbilical cord that hung between her legs. The fetus was full term, wailing as she pulled it along feet behind her. Its face was distorted by the lights, and Ryan almost thought it had no face at all.

"Stop," Ryan said, putting his hands out as he stumbled away from her.

"Ryan," she rasped.

"Please, Rose. Stop. Please."

"Ryan, what did you do?"

"I didn't do anything. I tried to help. I—"

"What did you do?"

At the sound of her voice again, this time clear and loud and shattering the muffled ambience around him, Ryan turned his back on her and shut himself back in the bedroom. He flipped the lock. The sound of a baby crying behind him shook him from his stupor, and he realized it was coming from his closed laptop. He lunged for it, throwing it into the bathroom and slamming the door shut.

"I'm losing it. *Fuck*! What have I gotten into?" His mind reeled, going over all the possible contaminants he could have encountered inside. Gas leak? Bad food? Something in the water reservoir? Nothing made any sense. He put his hands to his head.

"One thing at a time. Get dressed. You're tired. Lack of good sleep can do that to you. Flashing lights caused a hallucination. The computer just has a corrupted media file."

He used one shirt to wipe the already crusting vomit from his chest and slipped into clean clothes. There was a single viewing window, only about a foot wide in both directions. He leaned onto it to look out into the depths of space around him. Red streaks of lightning snaked across the sky like an electrical invertebrate with many tiny legs.

Ryan backed away from the window slowly, turning to a metal box mounted on the wall. He hadn't been awake very long, maybe a couple of hours, but he couldn't sit here with this ball of terror in his gut. He unlocked the lockbox and retrieved a bottle of sleeping pills, checking the label twice before he deposited two of the oblong, yellow pills into his hand then straight down his throat. He collapsed back onto his bed, closing his eyes and counting the time between the flashes of crimson light in the window with the corresponding rumble of thunder.

He didn't realize he had fallen asleep until he had a nightmare. It was one he had many times before: the room on fire, but he was standing outside in the hallway just watching. It was as though he couldn't move, couldn't try to pry the hot door open with his hands. He just stood there.

The sound of the ship groaning back to life woke him, the generator kicking off and the lights and primary ventilation system starting back up again. He cracked his eyes open, staring up at the ceiling where little flecks of grey, papery debris fluttered out of the vent.

Ash.

No, dust. It was just dust from a vent neglected of cleaning. Even in space there was dust.

He went to the viewing window again expecting to see the distant twinkle of light or the mass of P-670, but there was nothing there at all. It was as though the entire ship had been covered in a dark cloth. He tried not to let the claustrophobia set in. Ryan had never been afraid of space, neither all that was out there nor the lack of anything being out there.

He couldn't bring himself to open the door, so he busied himself tidying the room. He picked up his clothes from the night before, putting them into the box he used as a laundry basket. The stiffness of the pocket reminded him that the letter was there. He took it into his shaking hands, turning it over as though its flat form may have suddenly expressed some sort of depth.

With trembling fingers, he opened it. His entire body shook, chest feeling as though it vibrated with angry bees.

Look at what we've hidden.
Look at what we did.
I won't let you forget what we did.
She won't forgive us for what we did.
We deserve to burn in Hell.

The contents alone unnerved him, but more than that... It was the fact that this wasn't Rose's handwriting. Her sprawling, flowy penmanship was so distinct, the way the tails of letters crossed paths like strands of spider silk caught in a breeze. This was scrawled, desperate, jagged.

Who was *she*? Who wouldn't forgive her? How was he implicated in this?

A *ping* jarred him, causing him to drop the paper. It floated to the ground, disappearing beneath his bed like it was hiding there.

Ping.

Ping.

Ping, ping, ping.

Pingpingpingpingping.

He rushed to the bathroom, flinging the door open to find his laptop lying open on the floor. The screen was cracked, but the messages that covered the screen all gave the same notifications.

ADMIN: Corrupted files detected. To repair, first allow system to access:

Show hidden files, folders, and drives.

He slid down onto the bathroom floor, pulling the damaged computer into his lap as he hesitantly clicked Show.

His desktop background had once been a family photo but now was nothing more than a black screen, a void of his own making.

The empty background was suddenly covered in files and folders.

"What we've hidden ..." he muttered to himself, clicking the first folder that was titled Rose - Medical File.

He clicked the first file, taking a deep breath. He didn't remember hiding these files; he didn't even remember having them on this computer ... except he knew that they contained the counseling sessions and evaluation Rose had been given when they realized she was suffering from some kind of mental illness.

When the video started, though, Ryan felt like he had fallen through the floor.

A doctor spoke to Rose in front of a window, voice quiet and barely audible. "It's an acute psychosis. I'm afraid I don't know more than that right now. I do think the medication will help."

"Is he ... dangerous?"

"I really don't believe so. I think he's just confused."

The video cut to Ryan, sitting at a table, muttering, "That isn't him. He's not ours. He's been replaced."

Rose leaned over, trying to comfort him as the doctor wrote on a chart.

"Stop gaslighting me, both of you. How do you not understand? That is *not our baby!*"

The screen jumped again to Rose, tearful, holding their baby just out of reach, tilting him toward Ryan as he sat restrained and screaming. The baby's facial deformity wasn't as bad as it had been before he died. The progression had been rapid.

Everything became very quiet. The point of view was now looking down at Ryan's own arms as he cradled the baby, rocking him and then shaking him. The screen blurred with colors of flesh and black.

And then—

Screams.

"Ryan! You're sick, honey, please. You need help. Our baby is real, this is real."

"*Ryan! What have you done?*"

The sounds of her sobs were like a twisting knife in his gut.

He closed out of the file and searched the other hidden files, buried logs he had hidden from himself. A security video feed showed him standing outside the hallway door like he always did in the dream. He dropped the computer when it ended. Couldn't pick it up again. Couldn't touch it.

He had been the one who had snapped, the one who believed something had replaced his child, who believed Rose was part of it. He had killed the baby, and then Rose had burned herself alive while he had stood outside and watched.

And built the lie around her, piece by piece, until even he believed it.

Another video played without prompting. Ryan was sitting at a desk, looking right at the screen.

"I'm sorry... This is our fault. Traveling to uncharted planets was bound to eventually have a cost. The same parasite that is eating my brain is the same one that I infected my son with. My loving kisses transferred it to him somehow. It destroyed the cartilage of his face, little by little, then the bone.

"I have these periods of lucidity, like now. It's my last chance to record this message to myself. We knew the risks, but we wanted the money. We loved the travel, the adventure. Rose knew better too. She knew better than to get on this damned ship. After all she had witnessed, after all the doctors told her. She still thought she could fix it." The version of him on the screen looked down and then back up, tears welling in his eyes. "I think she's still here somehow, in the walls. I hear her.

Sometimes I see her. I don't know what's real and what's a hallucination anymore. My brain's cored out like a bad apple. There's not much left but those indigestible seeds. Her, him, us. That's all that ever mattered."

The screen went black.

Ryan thought that he could lay there and die. He could just sit there until he forgot again and start all over until he was incapable of thought at all anymore.

"Ryan?"

The distant sound of his name had him crawling to his feet, following it to the door that led to the hallway. He heard it again, opening the door and peering through the crack into the empty hallway.

"Where are you?" he called, clamping his eyes shut at first.

"We're outside. We're inside."

He saw a bloody trail on the hall's white flooring, crudely drawn arrows down, down, down ... all the way to the debarkation bay.

The airlock hissed, depressurizing with a slow, mechanical sigh like the ship itself was weary of the burden it carried. Ryan stood at the threshold of the door, bathed in the sickly blue glow of warning lights. The cold hum of the ship faded beneath something deeper now—a silence so vast it felt alive with intent.

Beyond this door lay the expanse of nothingness that had appeared around him. It was a perfect void: no stars, no light, no sound. Just a gaping wound in the universe. The dark heart of existence.

He saw a faint trace of Rose cradling their son, spinning him as she hummed in her throat. Her gossamer skirt spun around her like a twirled flower. The baby cooed. He was perfect, whole. His face was intact and present. He was not deformed or suffering. He was *happy*.

Ryan touched the glass, breath fogging the pane.

"I remember now," he whispered. His voice cracked, hollow with horror but not surprise. "It was me." The words didn't echo. The void beyond didn't care.

No one else knew. Everyone who knew was dead, and deep down, wasn't he too? He could return to Earth with the burden of the truth on his shoulders, the pain of guilt wrapped around his throat like barbed wire. But here in space, in this void between existence and nonexistence, there was another path presented to him.

Rose paused, turning to look at him. Her face was a ghosting of light, and he could barely make out her features. But he knew she was smiling.

"Hey, you," she said quietly.

Ryan jerked the handle downward, pressing in the four-digit code to override the remaining protocols.

The door slid open.

A wall of black greeted him, thick and endless. He stepped forward, weightless, and drifted from the safety of the ship and into the cosmic ink. Rose put out one arm toward him. Their son giggled.

Ryan reached out for them.

Their fingers touched, then they began to unravel together. Their atoms spread and everything unwound. Flesh, memory, grief, and regret all fell apart and succumbed to the void's insatiable thirst. Just unmaking, devouring, *rearranging*.

Nothing remained other than the faintest glimmer of light before it was consumed by the negative.

There was a crackle on the ship's speaker, then a whisper that sounded like a contented sigh.

TRANSMISSION LOST
VESSEL: SOLIVAGANT
STATUS: DERELICT
CURRENT LOCATION: UNKNOWN
UNRECOVERABLE

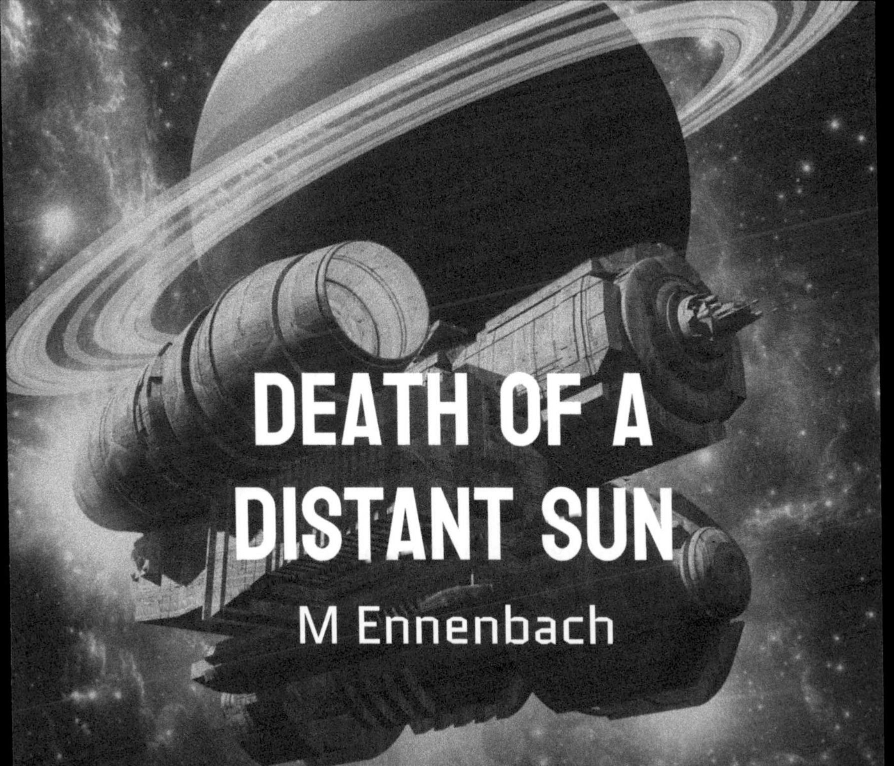

DEATH OF A DISTANT SUN

M Ennenbach

The bridge was dark except for the flashing lights on the myriad of consoles. Deb leaned back in her pod and kicked her bare feet onto the console in front of her as she tapped out a nic stick from her pack. The sudden flare from her torch temporarily blinded her, but she quickly adjusted to the darkness again, the orange ember adding new shadows to the cockpit. She didn't have to see him to know L was glaring at her from his console.

"All these years dreaming of space, and the only twinkling lights I see tell me Paddy is pulling his pud for the fourth time this cycle," Deb said with a cloud of smoke.

"You know you're always welcome to come down and give me a hand. With this monster, I could certainly use the help," Paddy responded through the comm.

"Brad, did you hear that? Paddy needs the tweezers down in engineering," Deb answered with a laugh.

"He has to wait his turn like the rest of us," Brad replied, his booming laugh reverberating from the comm.

"For fuck's sake, sounds like Brad is already into his secret stash. Need to ease up; we've got a long way to go before we hit the next station," Paddy said sternly.

"Too fucking long," L lamented as he swiped a nic stick.

Deb sighed. Paddy and L were right. They had been in the middle of fuck all for the past six months chasing salvage claims with a half empty hull to show for it all. They should have been on their way back home by now, not headed deeper into dark space searching for enough credits to call the entire excursion worth it.

"My horoscope says there is great fortune in my future," Brad said.

Deb felt as if she was going to sprain her eyeballs with how hard they rolled back at this. She held up five fingers and counted them down quickly.

As the last folded, Mick got on the comms. "More of this jorinshit? You're going to fucking tell me that constellations, ones not even visible in the quadrant in which you were born, mind you, can somehow still influence your life? By the Silence, you're either insane or mentally deficient if you believe any of that idiocy!"

"Such a Scorpio!" the entire crew said as one.

"Ooooh! Guys! I think I figured it out!" Brad shouted. "Leroy!"

"I don't know why we have to go over this every cycle," L muttered around a cloud of smoke. "It doesn't stand for anything. It's a letter. That's all."

Deb arched an eyebrow at him. "Just go ahead and tell us so he'll find something new to hyperfixate on. Leroy."

"I sorta like Leroy," Paddy said.

"If you degenerates put half as much effort into finding scrap as you put into solving the mystery of what the fucking L stands for, we'd all be on beach somewhere," Mick muttered.

"Yeah, Leroy!" Brad added helpfully.

L glared at Deb as she laughed, then steepled his fingers. "Silence, I beg you. Distract these imbeciles before I go insane. Please."

Suddenly, the bridge erupted in red lights, and the proximity alarms sounded throughout the ship.

"What in the fuck did you do, Leroy?" Mick shouted as they dropped out of hyperspace.

"I didn't so shi—" L began, but went silent as the display lit up. An old star-class cruiser hung in the vast nothingness of space. It was ancient, at least in terms of space exploration, but it appeared fully intact. And it was gigantic, dwarfing their trawler by at least three times.

"Take a pass around her, Deb. Nice and slow. I want full scans, L. Brad, wake the night crew. We need all hands," Mick said. "Get yourself topside, Paddy. We need to plan."

"Downloading specs now. Gimme five," Paddy said.

"She isn't going anywhere," Deb said, transfixed by the image, chills making the hair on her arms stand up.

"You know what that is?" L asked, a rare smile breaking his stoic demeanor.

Deb shook her head; whatever it was, she had a bad feeling about it.

"That's our fucking ticket home," he answered happily. "That is a museum-quality relic right there, and worth even more broken down."

"Uh huh," Deb replied, unconvinced.

"It's the kind of haul scrappers dream of!" Mick said as he entered the deck. "Would you look at that bastard? Damned thing looks near pristine."

He wasn't wrong. As they slowly circled the silent ship, the confusing issue became trying to figure out why it was listless in the void when everything seemed in working order.

"Scans indicate some systems remain online within the vessel. Basic filtration systems seem active. I'm not seeing any indications of life, though," L said, studying the console.

Deb pointed at the display suddenly. "What's that?"

She clicked on the image and zoomed in. Stenciled on the hull of the ship were the words *Distant Sun.*

"Expedition class freighter, early Earth III pioneer vessel," Paddy said, perpetual cigar clenched between his teeth as he exited the lift. "Seems they only built ten of these suckers back in the day. Seven were destroyed. Two were retired 300 some-odd years ago."

"Fuckballs. Are you guys telling me you've never heard of the *Distant Sun*?" Brad asked through the comms. "Ship is a legend in every port across the mapped regions."

"Why is it a legend?" Deb asked despite herself.

"You haven't heard of the *Distant Sun*?" Eric asked around a wide yawn as he stepped onto the bridge with one of the other two night crew members, Jamie. They stared at the monitor at the image of the quiet freighter as they circled.

"Where's Moose?" Mick asked, breaking the silence.

"And what's the story about this ship?" L added.

"Moose is getting ready, and she is not happy. Now about the *Distant Sun*—" Brad began.

"Wait until everyone is gathered. I don't want to have to listen to this idiocy twice." Paddy scowled.

"I'm listening. Not a one of you wants to see me before coffee and make-up! Ha!" Moose laughed over the comms. "If the bearded bastard is going to disturb my beauty sleep, he may as well tell me a story while I evac the old bowels! Ha!"

"Now, mind you, this is second-hand information from a second, second-hand source," Brad began, a curious bubbling sound rumbling over the comms.

"So this is coming from, like, a sixteenth-hand source?" Paddy grumbled.

Brad let out a long cough, ignored Paddy, and continued. "The *Distant Sun* was the pride of the fleet on Earth III, meant to usher mankind into the future of space exploration. The best of the best headed out on a one-way trip to the edge of the universe, marking habitable planets with beacons as it went.

"From all accounts, things went bad nearly immediately. Engine issues. Crew squabbles. But they continued on. Reports returned sporadically. The relays were few and far between back then, so a message could take months to return. Then years.

"Then nothing. Decades passed. The ship was believed lost."

The bubbling noises returned, and Mick slammed his fist on the wall. "By the Silence! Finish the fucking story or your rations are getting put in my safe for three months!"

Brad sputtered and coughed for a second. "Sorry? What was that? Quasar fluctuations scrambled comms for a second.

"Anyway, decades go by. And then a new message arrives from the *Distant Sun*. They found something. Signs of life—"

"Oh, fuck me, it's one of *those* stories," Moose moaned, and you could hear her eyes rolling in the tone.

The crew began grumbling, but Deb spoke up. "Let him finish. It might be bullshit, but he knows more than the rest of us."

"Every now and then a pile of shit hides a raknut," Mick said begrudgingly.

"Right. After that message, there wasn't anymore from the *Distant Sun*.

"The way it was told to me, though, about 200 years back, a trawler spotted a derelict ship and tried to hail it. They didn't receive a response so flew closer to get a better look. They were running low of everything, so they marked the ship's location with a tracker beacon and returned to port to restock and plunder their newfound treasure.

"Except the beacon went dead, or so they thought. They became laughingstocks at every port, talking about a ghost ship. About fifteen years later, they get a ping. It's from the *Distant Sun*. This is their chance at redemption. They're gonna hook the *Sun* and bring it back like a trophy.

"Their last transmission was a fuzzy image of what was allegedly the *Distant Sun*. After that, every couple of years, sometimes decades, a new ship would report seeing it. Each ship which saw her was never heard from again," Brad finished.

"I heard a story about a ship called *The Gullible Dumbfucks*. Anyone who saw it had to tell ten people or they were swallowed whole as they slept," Moose said into the quiet.

"Why in the hell would you tell us that when there aren't enough people around to tell?" Brad asked in a near panic.

Everyone laughed, a little nervously at first, but once Brad added his own booming laugh, the tension was eased a little on *The Kabouter*, even as they stared warily at the image on the display.

"Well, it was a nice ghost story. I vote we tractor lick the haunted son of a bitch and return to civilized space, where we then all retire into obscurity," Mick announced.

"Easier to just scrap out what we can now, come back with a bigger ship to grab the rest. Databanks alone would entitle us to palatial estates on the nicest planets in The Belt," Paddy rebutted, ever the pragmatist.

"Enter the death ship of doom and come back later? Did you not hear my story?" Brad asked incredulously.

Paddy scowled even harder. "A bunch of hoodoo and idiocy. There isn't shit out in space except salvage and mineral rights. No ghosts. No gods. No aliens except us. Just a series of fucking coincidences."

"Right. Nearly a millennia of space exploration with zero contact with any species smarter than a dog, yet the one ship which reportedly did, centuries before, just happens to be floating in *our* flight path isn't awfully Silence be damned *coinci-fucking-dental*!" Deb snapped, uncomfortable with the entire ordeal.

Paddy shrugged. "Is what it is. And what it is, is the chance of a lifetime."

"We have something those other morons didn't," Moose announced as she entered the bridge. "Superior tractor beams and me! Ha! Why scrap it piecemeal when we can take the entire thing back?"

The crew settled into arguing logistics of pulling the beast of a ship across an alarmingly large section of known space.

"We don't have the resources to head all the way back to base without at least one stop. May as well send out invites to pirates!" Paddy argued.

"So you'd rather enter the ghost ship? For fuck's sake, do you hear yourself?" L retorted.

"Leroy makes a valid point," Brad added.

"Who in the fuck is Leroy?" Eric asked.

It went on for most of the morning.

Paddy nearly broke the cigar as he clenched his jaw in a scowl that was perhaps his finest ever, absolutely dripping with incomprehensible exasperation as he glared at Deb. "What do you mean the tractor beam can't find a lock on the *Sun*?"

Deb managed to fire back a suitable counter-scowl, which only seemed to deepen Paddy's in a reciprocal, rancorous instance of indignation, and spat, "The. Tractor. Beam. Can't. Find. A. Lock."

"It's like watching two dagger fish about to hate fuck one another from existence," L whispered.

"I got fifteen on Deb. Paddy's all scowl," Mick said, sliding his credit chit onto the console.

"No bet," Brad replied.

Paddy and Deb turned their scowls on Mick, who flipped them both off and said, "Not on my ship, princesses. Deb, what's going on with the tractor beam?'

Deb sighed. "As far as I can tell, they're functioning properly. It's the *ship*—it's not responding. I would say they have a jammer on, but jammers came out around fifty years after the invention of tractor-beam tech, and that came out roughly a hundred years *after* the *Distant Sun* vanished."

"I have a theory," Eric said, staring at the monitor.

"It's a literal ghost ship?" L asked.

Eric shrugged. "I have two theories. One, these old ships still ran on hydrogen-fusion engines. Judging by the various windows being ice free, we can hazard a guess some systems remain active."

"The *Sun* has one of the last full-hydrogen systems. Is this little science lesson going somewhere?" Paddy said, his scowl needing a target.

Eric smiled. "Well, class, what is a byproduct of hydrogen fusion? Something not discovered until years after?"

"Oooh! Oooh! Stockton particles!" Brad answered excitedly.

Eric reached into one of his pockets and tossed Brad a candy, which he greedily snatched out of the air, before continuing, "Correct. And what does a tractor-beam jammer use to jam tractor beams?"

"So you think the centuries of accumulated Stockton particles have imbued the *Distant Sun* with a permanent anti-tractor field?" Deb asked.

Eric nodded and steepled his fingers. "It's a theory."

"And your other theory?" Mick asked.

Eric shrugged. "It *is* a ghost ship, and we're *all* going to die."

The silence was heavy for a moment as the crew considered the theories, until Deb snapped her head up and glared at Eric before demanding, "Where in the fuck is my candy?"

"Only good boys get candy," Brad said with a grin.

"I say if we're going to die because of a ghost ship with a magical aura, we all deserve candy," Moose said with a hint of malicious intent.

L whistled and pointed at the display. "The entire vessel is saturated with Stockton particles."

"That explains why it was never brought back to known space. This new wrinkle makes me lean toward boarding the ship, restoring power, and piloting it back ourselves," Mick grumbled.

"Are we really going to get back into why boarding the mysterious death ship of death is a terrible idea?" Jamie announced as the grumbling began to ramp up again.

Everyone turned to glare at Jamie, except Deb and Moose, who were eyeing Eric and waiting for candy.

"And what is your big plan, Mister Jamie? Except for being too chickenshit to board the *alleged* death ship of *alleged* death?" Paddy asked, one eye completely closed as his scowl intensified and the cigar bowed dangerously.

Jamie spread his arms. "Tack weld big fucking metal mounts to the bow, hook her up with some plastisteel chains, and tow the harbinger of death back to a fat payday. Yes, it's a giant Kick Me sign for any pirates or raiders, but in that unlikely event, we're only out the metal mounts and maybe the chains." He looked at Paddy. "Or you board the *Sun* and let the death ship eat you. Whatever."

Metal mounts it was.

Paddy floated in front of the *Distant Sun's* bow, his breathing the only sound as he gazed upon the hull of the vessel. It didn't have the sharp lines calculated for optimal sub-light traversal, nor the common propulsion vent ports. Paddy turned and looked at Eric, who was using controlled bursts from his suit to wrangle the now-weightless metal mounts from *The Kabouter*, and asked, "You ever see any holovids from Earth I? The ones where they still used petroleum-based fuels?"

"Never really got into primitive sciences beyond the basics. My dad loved all that old stuff. Always said ships these days lacked the danger of the original explorers. Why?" Eric answered.

"I saw a vid in college, back on Larson XII, where they showed the different iterations throughout the decades before the planet became unsustainable. The *Distant Sun* reminds me of my favorite. I can't remember the name of the model, Crocodile or Clickity Clack, something strange like that. Where the other automobiles seemed designed for speed, these were atrocious land beasts made for pure comfort. Shiny metal with long lines, this retro, futuristic approach that caught the eye from every angle. The *Sun* is like that. It was designed to be larger than life," Paddy replied.

"With your cut of the haul, you could digi-print yourself a Crocodile. Maybe without the pollution factory," Eric said as he maneuvered the first metal mount into position on the red dot projected by *The Kabouter*. "You ready? Plasma tack these twelve, and it's a slow ride back to retirement."

Paddy raised the plasma torch and precisely welded the metal mount to the hull. Neither spoke as they floated through the void, stopping where the red laser marked the perfect position. It was slow but steady, and both men moved diligently up and across the hull.

The final row was to be placed just beneath the massive transparent helm of the bridge. Paddy floated up and shined his suit's lights into the quiet vessel. Eric took up position at the opposite end, and together, they illuminated a good portion of the bridge.

"*Kabouter*, you seeing this?" Eric asked as he swept the light across the bridge.

The skeletal remains of the *Distant Sun's* crew were strewn across the bridge. Partial remains lay across the consoles or were held in a sitting position by raggedy clothing. It was a grisly sight, but not necessarily an unexpected one: it simply stood to reason the crew would still be aboard the ship and long deceased at this point, but death was always shocking when it chose to showcase itself to those ever drifting closer themselves.

"Paddy, can you zoom back in on the left center of the room, behind the captain's chair?" Deb said into the hushed silence which had fallen over the crew.

"Sure," Paddy said, immediately following with, "now what in the fuck is that?"

It was difficult to tell, but it appeared there was a black triangle floating in the air near the center of the bridge.

"I call first dibs on the death pyramid!" Brad shouted.

"Fuck!" L cursed with a glare toward Brad.

"You snooze, you lose, Leroy," Moose cackled.

"You think that's what they found? The alien artifact?" Jamie asked.

"The *alleged* alien artifact," Mick corrected him. "Not our concern for now, though. Paddy, Eric, get those last metal mounts attached ASAP. Oxygen's wasting, boys!"

"On it, boss," Paddy said.

Eric held the metal mounts in place as Paddy welded them, then they slid down and knocked the next one out.

"Last one. First round is on Moose," Eric said as he pressed the metal mount to the hull.

A sudden black flash erupted, blinding Paddy momentarily and sending the live feed into a burst of static. Paddy regained his senses and found the metal mount spinning off into space. He blinked away the black spots and looked for Eric, but he was nowhere to be seen.

"*Kabouter* to Paddy and Eric! Come in. Silence be damned!" Mick suddenly shouted into the now-working comms.

"I'm here," Paddy said, grimacing as a migraine level headache gripped his entire skull. "But I can't find Eric!"

"What in the hell happened?" Mick demanded.

Paddy opened his mouth to answer, but the pressure in his skull made it hard to think.

"Come to us," a strange voice seemed to whisper into his helmet, and then Paddy only knew darkness.

"Tell us again, Paddy. A person cannot simply vanish," Mick prodded.

Paddy's scowl seemed to be a permanent addition to his face. "You saw exactly what I did! A black flash and he was fucking gone!"

"We didn't see any flash. One moment you were about to weld the final mount, then nothing but static for eighteen seconds. Moose was ready and on her way out of the hold as soon as you went dark," Mick said, a helluva lot calmer than he felt.

"The second I stepped out, I only saw you floating. By the time I got to you, you were passed out and Eric was gone," Moose added.

"Eric's signal just went dead. We should have at least a range of two light years of reception, and a lone man in a suit has zero chance of making it sixty kilometers before the rocket needs to cool down," Deb stated.

"Captain!" L called out through the comms from the bridge. "I think I found Eric! The signal is super weak."

"Where is he?" Mick demanded.

"It shows him to be 700 or so meters in front of us, sir," L answered.

"That doesn't make any sense. The fucking *Distant Sun* is 500 meters away," Paddy muttered, and his eyes grew wide as he looked at Mick. "That isn't possible."

"None of this bullshit seems possible. Convoluted and growing more fucked by the minute, yes. But possible? We left that in our ion wake light years ago," Mick muttered.

"We can send in Elmer. He can get in, snatch Eric, then we tow this cursed relic back and pawn it off on some uber-rich dick monkey. We'll all be laughing about this in our mansions," Brad offered.

"Fire it up," Mick said, shoulders slumped. "Let's pull back from the *Sun*, though. Put a buffer between us and whatever the flash was. Maybe it's a weapon of some sort."

Brad nodded. "Smart, smart. A little space between us and the ghost ship. I like it."

E.L.M.E.R. (Electro-Liminal Mechanical Engineering and Recon) was Brad and Deb's pride and joy. They spent countless hours of downtime tweaking and modifying it into, what they considered, *the beefiest bitch in the entire universe*. It was indisputable in its ridiculousness, so it was allowed.

The entire crew stood on the bridge watching the display as Elmer powered up in the bay and ran through diagnostics, except for Paddy, who could barely sit up due to the headache. Scans had shown nothing wrong with him, so Moose added a tranquilizer shot to help him sleep after the incident outside.

"Mornin' y'all," Elmer said as the final check was passed.

"What the fuck did he just say?" Deb asked, glaring at Brad, who sat with his mouth hanging open, clearly in shock.

Moose cackled loudly, and they both glared at her. She quickly raised her hands. "It wasn't me. But Eric was chuckling the other night as he returned from the bay. You know that asshole. Bet ten credits he did it to mess with you guys."

Everyone smiled, but the tenseness around their eyes remained as they thought of how Eric was somehow on the ghost ship. Alone.

"Hey, buddy. Just sent you a super important mission," Brad finally said.

"Duh ding dang dippity doo! Roger that one, good buddy! Reckon I should be off if'n that rascal Eric needs my assistance!" Elmer replied slowly, if not happily, as he flew out of the charging and diagnostic pod.

"What did he do to my baby?" Deb asked, devastated, as the display showed the *Distant Sun* growing closer.

Elmer flew to the aft docking door, and a probe extended from his middle and snaked into the control pad. "This dang ol' security is easy peasy. Be in in a jiffy."

"Engage silent mode, Elmer. We don't know what's on the ship," Deb ordered.

"Roger that. Best be quiet, critters are skitterin'," Elmer replied before muting himself.

"Whatever hell Eric is experiencing on the *Sun* is only the beginning of his torment," Deb muttered as they waited for the hull door to open.

After what felt like an eternity, the hull slid open and Elmer boarded the *Distant Sun*. The feed showed an opulent interior in rustic decay as the door slid silently. Dust motes hung in the air as Elmer floated around the corridor, streaming. Elmer's main camera focused and zoomed in on a disturbance in the thick dust that covered everything.

"That has to be Eric's boot print!" Brad exclaimed.

"If it isn't his, then he's definitely not alone on the *Sun*," L added in a macabre tone.

"Find him and get him back, Elmer," Deb said.

Yes ma'am appeared on the display.

"What the hell? Look at his footprints. They just suddenly start there," Jamie muttered.

"Almost as if he just popped up there," Moose added uneasily.

Elmer cast his lights across the floor, and the boot prints did seem to just appear. The silence of the *Sun* seemed to infect *The Kabouter* as the crew watched the sepulcher-like interior of the ship pass by. Despite the amount of bodies that littered the bridge, the corridor of the vessel seemed abandoned in the last days of the *Distant Sun*. Elmer hovered through the corridors, following the brazen trail through the dust until he came to doorway covered in strange writing which appeared black in the LED glow.

"Analysis confirms the writing is in human blood," L intoned flatly as the strange writing filled the screen.

"What in the fuck happened there?" Mick asked softly.

"Whatever it was, I say we grab Eric, tag the *Distant Sun* and get as far away from here as possible," Deb answered, a quiver of fear in her voice.

Elmer interacted with the door and it slid open. The lights illuminated the room, and the writing covered almost every inch of the walls, ceiling, and floor. Standing in the center of the room, with his back to Elmer, was Eric.

"Howdy there, Eric," Elmer announced as he hovered into the room. The dust was heavy in the air, and it seemed each and every mote had been disturbed and was moving, the tiny particulates fragmenting the light.

Yet Eric didn't turn or even shift to acknowledge his visitor. He just stood stone still, staring at the wall in front of him.

"Eric, hey buddy, snap out of it! Let Elmer bring you back to *The Kabouter*. We can get you all fixed up and back to port ASAP," Mick said through Elmer's comm.

Eric remained motionless.

"C'mon, man! Wake the fuck up!" Deb shouted.

Elmer moved forward into the room, and as he did, the signal began to break up. Brad and Deb quickly tapped on their consoles, and the image grew clear once again as Elmer circled in front of Eric. The crew gasped in horror as the light shone into Eric's helmet, exposing his face to the harsh glare. Both of his eyes seemed to have been burned from their sockets, and black oil seemed to run down his cheeks as he stood mouthing words inaudibly. Then a flicker of motion from the corridor brought Elmer's attention to the hallway. Flying full speed with his rocket pack, a gigantic wake of dust behind him, came Paddy, racing toward them.

An insane grin tore his face in two as he propelled through the *Distant Sun* to stop right in front of Elmer, the malevolence enhanced by black dripping from his melted eyes as he spat, "See you soon."

Then the stream went dead. Silence filled *The Kabouter* for a few moments as they stared at the black screen. Before any of them could form words, multiple alarms rang out through the ship, along with various explosions.

"The motherfucker sabotaged the ship! Everyone get your suits on! Now!" Mick screamed into the cacophony.

Before he could move, the console in front of L exploded, and he didn't even get a scream out before his face was shredded. A large chunk of plastisteel jutted from his throat. His arterial spray caught Deb mid scream, and she began choking on the sudden mouthful of blood. Brad and Jamie managed to grab her as they rushed toward the door. Fires began to flare from the destroyed equipment.

As they pushed from the bridge, the artificial gravity failed, and the confusion turned to one on all planes as they suddenly found themselves floating among sparking devices as the ship rocked around them.

"Suits! Now!" Mick ordered.

"Then what?" Moose demanded as she awkwardly spun while pulling on the suit.

Deb sealed her suit then began frantically tapping on her wrist interface. "*The Kabouter* is fucked. The drive is nearing implosion. We have maybe twenty minutes before we're sucked into a mini singularity. We need to get to the escape pods."

"Why in the fuck did Paddy blow *The Kabouter*?" Mick seethed.

"It has to have something to do with that black flash. Whatever grabbed Eric must have infected Paddy as well," Jamie said as his helmet was almost snapped into place.

Four explosions went off one after another, which caused *The Kabouter* to tilt.

"That was the escape pods!" Deb yelled.

"Fuck!" Mick screamed.

"The *Sun* is the only option," Moose said, way calmer than she felt.

"The derelict ghost ship with the creepy fucking triangle thingy? What about the implosion?" Jamie asked.

Deb tapped faster. "It looks like it should be far enough."

"I might have an idea," Brad said quietly, his words nearly swallowed by the chaos.

"What the fuck is it?" Mick demanded.

"I was going over the plans of the *Sun* that Paddy found and comparing them to the actual ship. I think the *Sun's* escape pods are still intact. They should still be functional," Brad answered. "Maybe."

Mick nodded. "Head to the bay. We grab as much essentials as we can and head to the *Sun*. Once on board, we find the escape pods and eject."

"And Paddy and Eric? What about them?" Moose asked.

Mick looked away and shrugged. "I don't think Paddy and Eric are there anymore."

"We can't just give up on them!" Deb shouted.

Mick looked at her with sad eyes. "We don't have any choice. Our chances here are less than 10 percent as is. Paddy left us to die. Or to feed us to whatever monster is inside of him and Eric. You saw their eyes, Deb. They're already gone. Now get a move on, or we'll be next."

The five of them used controlled bursts to propel from the bay of *The Kabouter* to the still-open hull entrance on the *Sun*. They paused and watched the silent convulsions of their ship as it was slowly pulled into itself in a captured storm of whirling blue sparks, tongues of flame, and rolling clouds of black smoke which compacted itself tighter and tighter until it expanded once more in a jittering ball of pure energy. It dissipated in a wave of concussive force that was still felt over the great distance. The only sound was their choked sobs in the emptiness, an orchestral hollowness in which the stars wept.

With overwhelming hesitance, they enter the open door of the *Distant Sun*.

Mick gestured to them and tapped a message onto his wrist. *Drop comm channel to 101.9*. Once they did, he spoke. "Cannot trust they aren't listening, or whatever is inside of them isn't, at any rate."

Brad projected the plans of the ship into the air between them. "Near as I can tell, the escape pods are located roughly starboard middle. They're marked blue."

"There has to be some stores or rations. Silence only knows how long we could be floating out there waiting for rescue," Jamie muttered as he studied the plans.

"There are only two of them. We could just incapacitate them, repower the engines, and take the *Sun* back to port. Be a lot more comfortable," Moose offered.

"And what about the evil black triangle which melts eyeballs?" Deb asked flatly.

"It's on the bridge, right?" Brad asked. "Everyone knows the bridge is not the only helm for the vessel."

"Paddy and Eric don't seem to be in the mood to work with us, and it took a crew of eight to keep *The Kabouter* going. There are five of us, and the *Sun* is triple the size," Mick countered.

"L would have had a plan. He always had a plan working," Brad said sadly, his head hanging.

"L would have us in an escape pod. There's no way he would want to spend more than a minute on this ship," Deb said, on the verge of tears.

"He wouldn't want us to stand here arguing. Fine. Let's move toward the escape pods. Do you guys remember what Paddy said before *The Kabouter* went down?" Mick asked.

"See you soon," Moose whispered. "They wanted us aboard the *Sun*. Are we supposed to be their crew?"

Deb shrugged. "Whatever has possessed them likely does. We need to avoid them AND the bridge."

As they crept down the corridor, Moose said, "Low level systems are still functioning. All the doors should be operational, at least. Oxygen levels are low but breathable."

"I don't think whatever it is Paddy and Eric has is infectious. We were in contact with Paddy directly, and near as I can tell, no one has had their eyes melt into black goo," Deb said.

"Still, keep your suits fully sealed. We don't know what caused them to change. The black flash seems most likely, which implies it must have been the triangle," Mick added.

Moose shook her head. "They were both infected outside of the ship. It had to be the flash. Nothing else could have survived outside of the ship. And if it did, we all flew through it a few minutes ago."

"Umm, guys?" Brad said.

They turned to see he had opened one of the doors and came over to see what was inside. Four desiccated bodies were kneeling around a crudely drawn circle on the floor. The walls were covered in the same stage writing.

Jamie scanned the bodies. "Less than one hundred years dead."

"I think we found out what happened to one of the other crews who stumbled upon the *Sun*," Moose said.

"Is that what the ship does? Floats in space seeking a crew? Or are we all just sacrifices to whatever the triangle is?" Brad asked.

"Why not both?" Eric asked from the corridor, causing them to lurch in fright. "We all do our part to fulfill our Master's orders."

The *Distant Sun* suddenly hummed back to life around them. Dust swirled as the full air circulation kicked on, filling the air around them with a thick, gray cloud. When it abated, Eric and Moose were gone. The others scrambled down the hall, checking each room for any sign of them, but there was nothing at all.

"Now Eric has magic powers? Fuck this shit. We need to get the fuck out of here fifteen minutes ago," Brad said, near panicked.

Deb nodded. "They can come pick us off one at a time. Fuck supplies. We need to go."

Jamie frowned. "Might be more difficult now that the *Sun* is powering up."

"How so?" Deb demanded.

"Weapons systems will be live, for one thing," Mick said.

No one said anything for a few moments as the weight of the statement settled on them.

"And?" Deb asked. "You said for one thing."

Mick sighed. "We need to destroy this ship. This will all happen again if we don't. Or worse. We don't know what they're planning, but this isn't the first attempt."

"We could try and disable the engines, maybe cut power totally," Brad suggested.

Mick shook his head. "Not now that they have Moose. She is, was, the best engineer on *The Kabouter*. If they turn her, she can get the system going no matter what we do. It has to be destroyed."

"So, what? We go to the engine bay and rig it to meltdown? Then race the countdown to the pods? We'll all die," Deb said.

Mick nodded. "You three head to the pods. I can take care of the engines."

"Then meet us at the escape pods for a wicked cool launch to watch this ghost ship go BOOM!" Brad said with a nod and grin.

Mick shook his head. "Not this time. I should have gone down with *The Kabouter*. A captain shouldn't abandon his post. This is my chance at redemption."

Deb and Brad opened their mouths to argue, when Jamie held up his hand. "That may be the dumbest thing I have ever heard. I'm going with you. Don't argue. You're right. This ship needs to be reduced to debris. Whatever the fuck the black triangle is, I know for sure it isn't benevolent and kind."

Mick squeezed Jamie's shoulder, then looked at Deb and Brad. "Be silent. I don't know what the black goo does to them, but Moose knew our entire plan."

Jamie smiled. "We could do something to grab their attention."

Brad's eyes grew wide. "Gimme a second! I got an idea!"

They watched him run back down the hall and go back to the room with the kneeling corpses. Soon enough, he was running back with something clenched in his fist, above his head. He handed the object to Mick then put his hands on his knees and tried to catch his breath.

Mick glared at the strap Brad handed him. He ran his hands over the six egg-like nodules hanging off of the belt. "What in the fuck are these?"

Brad smiled. "I've only seen them in vids. Those are six highly illegal plasma grenades. Guess the last crew wasn't exactly on the up and up."

Deb whistled and looked at the grenade belt. "Can we set them on a timer?"

Brad nodded. "Yes ma'am."

Mick smiled. "Deb, you and Brad prep the pods. Jamie and I will distract Paddy and Eric, plant these, and meet you guys."

Deb frowned. "And if you don't?"

"The two of you get the fuck out of here either way," Jamie answered as Mick just stared at the floor.

"We don't have the time to waste arguing. It's an old ship, but I can't imagine it takes too long to get all the systems up and running again. I can't imagine what the end game is, but melting eyeballs and killing off entire crews cannot be a solid first step," Mick said bluntly.

Deb shook her head. "Set the grenades to explode now. We can all go to the escape pods *together.*"

Mick shook his head. "Silence be damned, Deb. What if they don't go off? Or the damage isn't enough to take the ship down? There are too many factors at play to hope."

"He's correct, Deb," Paddy said, suddenly appearing at the end of the corridor. "There can be no playing at hope. Now we work toward a higher power. There is no point in fighting the inevitable. Join us."

"Is the eye make-up optional? I don't see myself wanting to apply that each morning, Paddy. How about we all just take a moment, stop acting all fucking creepy, and maybe talk about this?" Jamie suggested.

Patrick smiled. "I have gazed upon infinity, and it spoke to me, whispered the secrets of the universe as it shattered who I once was. Moose saw it. Eric saw it. We were chosen to complete a divine mission which began eons ago. Let it speak to you."

"No," Mick said simply, then raised his sidearm. Without warning, Mick fired once. A searing blast of lavender burst from the weapon and punched through Paddy's helmet then out the back with a shower of brain and skull fragments.

But Paddy's head stopped mid explosion. Tendrils of black shot out from his head and caught every fragment, and for a second, time seemed to slow before the pieces snapped back into place. Paddy looked at Mick and smiled before he blew out a smoke ring. Then he launched himself at the group, the smile infused with madness and rage. The four stood their ground and unleashed a barrage of flashing bolts into Paddy, yet still he continued forward. The black tendrils did their best to mitigate the extreme damage Paddy's body endured, but eventually it was overwhelmed. He fell to the floor in a wet slop as his body shuddered and dissolved into chunks that spread across the floor in a pool of red and black.

"Fuck," Brad said, stunned.

"That was for L," Deb growled.

"Idiots," Moose's voice came over the ship's intercom. "You would abandon divinity for what? To continue your pathetically miniscule existence a few more years?"

"We need to move! Now!" Mick shouted.

"There is no escape from this sacred duty. Soon you will understand the glory of serving," Moose said flatly.

"She's going to purge the escape pods!" Deb said as they ran. "It's what I would do!"

Mick pointed left at an intersection. "Two of them, four of us. Get to the pods and stop her. We'll take care of the engine."

"Comm channel 120.111 once you're ready. I'll contact you on there once we have the grenades set," Mick said, not slowing.

"Then meet us at the pods," Brad reiterated.

"Good luck," Jamie said as he and Mick turned right.

"Do you think we can do this?" Jamie asked as they sped down corridors toward the engine bay.

"They can die. Whatever the goo is, it doesn't make them immortal," Mick said, sidestepping the question.

"It took four of us firing full bore to take down Paddy alone," Jamie replied.

"That's a later problem. The present issue is if these grenades will do enough damage to meltdown the engines," Mick said gruffly as they slowed down.

The doors to the engine bay were directly ahead, and both men were sure they weren't going to be alone. Mick popped three of the grenades off the belt and handed them to Jamie. The two didn't speak as they checked their gear and caught their breath. They eventually looked at one another and simply nodded, then Mick opened the doors to the engine bay.

Eric turned and smiled at them. "At last." Black tentacles burst from his back, and he rose into the air to look down upon them. "*We* have need of the two of you."

"Deb, I gotta be honest with you; I am not in the best shape," Brad wheezed.

Deb looked at Brad. The skintight suit strained at his heavy breathing around his prodigious belly. "Still look six foot three and 230 to me, cutie."

Brad, who was more like five ten and pushing 280, blushed and nodded. "I think they must have messed with my suit. Been a while since I put it on."

Deb nodded absently as she scanned the doorways around them. Then she cried out and rushed forward.

Brad gulped nervously and started moving again to see what the commotion was, fearing the worst. When he entered the room, his eyes grew large as he saw Deb cradling Elmer. The bot was badly damaged, the main plating around the center was deformed, and the LEDs on his display winked randomly. Brad fell to his knees, tears streaming into his voluminous beard as he touched Elmer.

Deb touched his hand and smiled. "Now we have a project to kill time on the long wait for rescue."

Brad nodded at her through tears. "We can fix him right up!"

"Sorry, kids, but you're going to be far too busy to put your robot back together again," Moose taunted from the hallway.

Brad looked at Deb. "Get Elmer to the pods."

Deb shook her head. "We stay together, dammit."

Brad smiled. "Just do it. I'll be right behind you. Promise. Wait for my signal, then run. Okay?"

Deb shook her head. "I, *we*, need you. I can't fix him alone."

Brad nodded. "Duh. You're helpless without me."

Brad hugged Deb, patted Elmer, and tugged at his spacesuit with a sigh. "Must have been Eric. He must have switched suits with a smaller one. Asshole."

Then he stepped into the corridor and smiled at Moose. Without a word, he shot her twice in the head then looked at Deb and nodded. Before she could speak, Brad was already barreling toward Moose.

Jamie cried out as Eric slammed him down onto the console. Blood sprayed from Jamie's mouth as he bellowed and fired three times, point blank, into Eric's chest.

"You cannot win. This has all been foretold, long ago. Submit. Serve," Eric said, his voice coming out gurgled as his chest reformed and the ragged wound sucked in air.

"You need to snap out of this!" Mick screamed as he swung a wrench from off the table into the side of Eric's face with enough force to turn his head 270 degrees with a wet snap. Eric collapsed to the floor, and Mick hurried over to help Jamie up. "We need to place the grenades before he recovers!"

Jamie stumbled across the room, Mick pulling him along, and the two began to place the egg-shaped devices across the room.

"Get the last one in place and go as fast as possible to Deb and Brad!" Mick shouted. "I can set the timer!"

Jamie opened his mouth to agree when he felt something odd. Before he could recognize what the sensation was, he found himself flying across the room to face Eric once more. He looked down to see a tendril of black had torn through his chest. He gasped as his body grew cold, and he stared into the blackened holes where Eric's eyes had once been.

"You could have joined us, been part of something which will change the entire universe. And instead, you choose to die without meaning, doing absolutely nothing to change fate," Eric said coldly. "Pathetic."

Jamie looked at Mitch and tried to speak. "Suh-sorry, buh-buh-boss."

Mick stared at him, seeing the plasma grenade light up a virulent green as Jamie slammed his hand against Eric's chest. Mick felt waves of pain and heat as the explosion knocked him across the room. His head hit the wall, and he crumpled to the floor in a smoking heap.

Deb grabbed Elmer and peered into the corridor to see Brad bashing at Moose and trying to knock her into another room. She took a deep breath and fired her rockets full throttle down the corridor.

"No you don't!" Moose yelled out, and Deb cried in pain as a black tendril pierced her calf. Elmer flew from her hands through the doorway to the escape pod bay with a clatter as she tumbled across the floor, snapping her right wrist in the process.

Deb felt her suit compensate, the arm growing tighter to keep the broken wrist straight. Black circles flickered at the edge of her vision as she pushed herself to her feet. A beeping caught her attention, and she staggered into the console.

Escape pod purge engaged read across the screens. As Deb tried to figure out what was happening, the first two pods ejected. She quickly typed on the console, ignoring the nausea and the sounds of Brad screaming from the corridor. The third escape pod began to fire its engines when the alert went off, something in the mad pressing of buttons and prompts having cancelled the purge. Deb slumped forward, the black circles growing thicker, and shook her head. She opened the hatch to the fourth pod and slid Elmer in. Then she staggered back into the bay and searched for anything she could use. Her eyes lit up as she saw something she had only seen on old holovids, leaning in the corner.

With a burst of adrenaline, she grabbed the relic and went back to the corridor. It didn't look good, to say the least. Brad was on the floor, Moose hovering in front of him, two spiked tendrils driven through his wrists and into the floor beneath. Deb didn't say a word. She thumbed on the power button on the shaft of the electric spear, one once used by early explorers to capture and kill new, exotic species from the edges of space. She angled it upward, piercing Moose through her clenched anus with 50,000 volts flaring along the sharpened tip, all the way up and through her, finally erupting through her soft palate and nose in a shower of gore. Moose collapsed, the electrified rod still discharging as it ran through her like a spit.

Deb helped Brad up, neither capable of speech, and they staggered back to the pod, where they collapsed into the seats.

Deb changed comm frequency to 120.111 and moaned, "Mick, Jamie, what's your status?"

"... status? Stop fucking around and answer. Brad and I made it to the pods. We aren't great, but we made it. Where are you?" Deb's voice sang into the darkness.

Mick opened his eyes and immediately wished he hadn't been forced from unconsciousness. His whole body was in agony. His entire torso was charred and bubbling from the plasma explosion. He tried to stand, but his legs didn't seem to be connected any longer. He could see them, twisted at an odd angle, but they may as well have belonged to someone else.

He looked around the room and saw the remains of Jamie baked into a fifteen-meter radius in the center of the room.

"Silence damn you! Mick, Jamie, fucking answer me!"

Mick smiled, and the movement tore the flesh off his face. "Mick here. Good job, crew. One last thing to do. Go ahead and take off. Jamie's dead. Got Eric, though."

"We can come to you! Don't be stupid!" Deb cried.

Mick sighed. "Ain't enough of me left to gather. Leave. That's my final order as captain of *The Kabouter*. It's been an honor."

Deb responded, but the words didn't make sense any longer. Mick had only one goal. He pulled himself down the wall, leaving a trail of stuff he was sure was meant to be inside behind him. He reached up and shakily set the timer for the grenades then leaned against the wall and smiled. Soon enough, it would all be done.

Deb pressed the launch button through a curtain of tears. Brad lay passed out in the seat beside her as she let the sorrow take full control of her, sobbing so hard it was indistinguishable from the racket of launch. Before the black circles overwhelmed her completely, she set the distress beacon. Finally, she let the dark take her.

Neither Brad nor Deb saw the explosion of sheer white light behind them as the *Distant Sun* erupted, nor felt the shockwaves that rattled the pod and rattled Elmer from his seat to hit the floor with a jarring crash. The crash dislodged the deformed front plate off Elmer, though, and a black light flashed in the escape pod as an ebony pyramid slid from Elmer's chest cavity and slowly hovered above the sleeping crew.

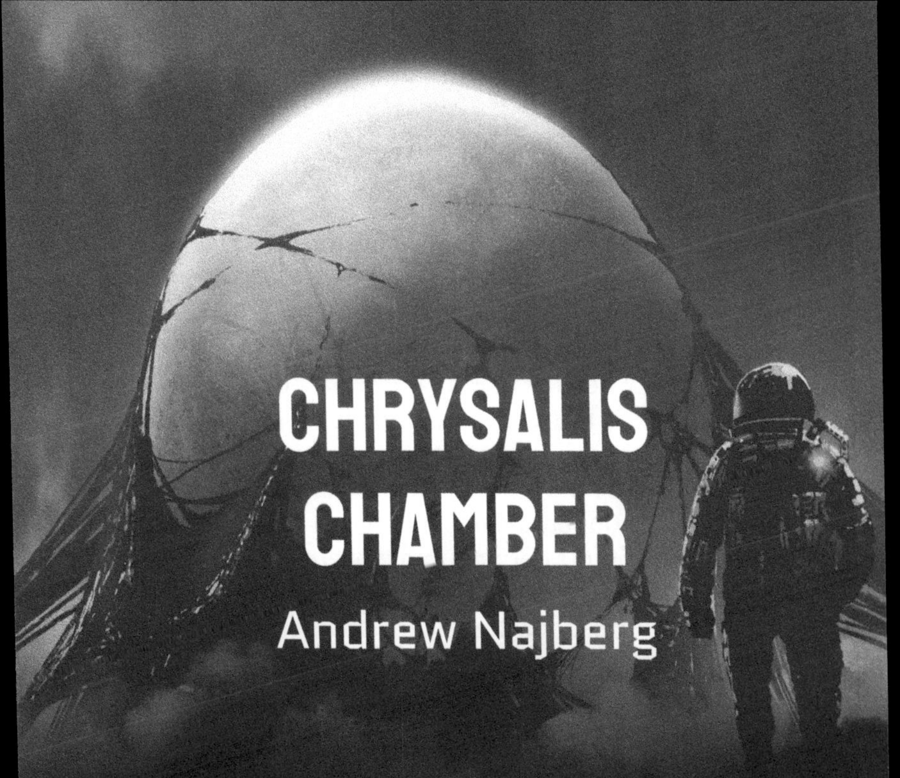

CHRYSALIS CHAMBER

Andrew Najberg

Belts of something chitinous affix me to the wall of a subterranean chamber that serves as a burrow and hatchery. At least, I assume that's what it is due to the pervasive presence of fibrous bundles in which our captors render themselves inert for periods that feel like hours and the ovoid objects reminiscent of ostrich eggs that ... unravel to yield writhing offspring. Though the surface temperature is -273 degrees Celsius, in here, below this moon's surface, it's a perfect 22 degrees Celsius, or it was according to my vital data readout before it failed.

Otherwise, I would have died really quickly when their larvae burrowed through my suit.

Unfortunately, the perfect temperature is the only comfort this place offers. I am immobilized for all intents and purposes, though I can move my arms below the elbows and my legs below the knees. All that serves to do, however, is underscore how much my joints ache from hanging like this and just how badly I want to change the bend in my back. Honestly, the agony comes in waves in my spine so severely that I feel like my vertebrae are being crushed, and I have doubts that were I free I would be able to walk again.

It's been three months since we crashed, and three days since basecamp was overrun. Everyone in the habitats died when they broke the seals. I only survived because I was on the team in rotation for a shift salvaging a new load of supplies from the wreckage of the colony transport. Before the reactor shut down and all systems went dark, the onboard databanks led us to believe that the caverns of the Alternian Range were devoid of life and would be a safe refuge until the rescue ship arrived. That it was the belief of Command, that the whole moon should have been barren.

Even now, I wonder who messed up the telemetries. Was it Silvano? Hortex? Could it have been a coding error in the navigation processor? The people back home will want to know who they're supposed to sue.

But I digress.

For lack of a better word, I'm currently a captive of a species of indigenous fauna, and I suspect I am being used as some sort of livestock to support their young. When the first egg hatched by my feet and I felt that long, undulating thing burrow its way through my boot and into dense meat at the base of my heel, the sinking feeling that fell from my heart to my gut was like jumping from a plane without a chute. Since then, I've been infested by at least nine larvae that I'm aware of, though who's to say how many burrow into me when I pass out from pain and exhaustion? I feel them all my waking hours, crowding my organs as they find things inside me to latch onto. It's hard to explain what it feels like except maybe that painful knot you get when you swallow too much water at once—but all over the place.

Their level of sentience is uncertain, but I suspect it is likely comparable to our own. I believe this because despite the fact that they have not tried to communicate with me, it seems pretty clear that they dislike looking at me. It might be guilt or it might be superiority—either way, their attitude is one that indicates higher-level processing. The chittering sounds they make to each other are probably a sophisticated language, though I honestly can't differentiate them from the sounds of your average Earth insect or rodent.

They go about their business with the anatomical structure I assume to be their head oriented away from me. Their bodies are rather insectile or perhaps crustacean externally—they seem to have segmented, semi-translucent carapaces through which I see fluids churning and what might be muscles or tendons flexing. Their bodies are divided into roughly five sections, and they ambulate on four to six legs—I have begun to wonder if the difference in limbs may be connected to gender dimorphism. They also have two hands that seem to be their primary dexterous appendages, as well as a pair of vestigial arms that hang limply from what is most easily understood as their armpits.

Even now, I look at them and I can't help trying to analyze. Categorize. Understand. There's a Nobel prize or a Kelgiziak Grant in this for someone for sure, but I also know that someone isn't me. Every second I watch them, I'm aware how far out of my depth I am now. I was a low-level researcher in the ship's biological crew, but I was meant to look for microbes. A research director should be giving me daily objectives, procedural steps, protocols. I thought I would be loading ice and soil samples into centrifuges and taking notes and readings from the microscopes.

Something spasms in my back. I feel the bulge there atop my liver, the strange pull of the thing that burrowed into my back just below my ribs three days ago. A trickle of some warm fluid runs down my back. It could be blood. It could be pus. It could be something else. But

I'll never know because I can't see the place where the trickle absorbs into the padding of what's left of my suit.

"Hnnnnnnnnnnngggh," I say, clenching my jaw and closing my eyes. The tendons in my neck stand out, and my back tries to arch.

Unfortunately, the suit is restrictively bound to the wall, and I fight the confine more than I channel my pain into the tension.

Thompson whimpers, and when I open my eyelids our gazes meet. She's pouring sweat from her forehead. The bulges hanging off her torso are far larger than mine—her suit is distended in several places, and spines have extended through the suit fabric like she was trying to conceal massive sea urchins in there and failed.

Would my parasites grow spines? Would they go out through the suit or upward into my organs and flesh?

I would ask Thompson how hers progressed, but one of the parasitic larvae hangs from her mouth, having affixed itself to her tongue. I can't help but wonder if they're drawing the same thing from her tongue that they are from my liver.

I look over to Rodriguez. The one hanging from her neck pulsates, and some of the plating of its carapace seems to be peeling off. Is it beginning some sort of molt?

When I wiggle in my suit, I can feel something that feels empty and dead jabbing against my lumbar region, and I believe it could be a discarded shell.

I hate Rodriguez more than anything. If she hadn't recruited us to her salvage team that day, we would have been in the shelter with the rest of the crew when the seals broke. We would have died with all the rest.

The larvae that seems to be sucking the meat out of my left inner thigh spasms and emits something hot and wet. I've seen the visible masses on Thompson and Rodriguez do what I believe to be the same thing enough to suspect the parasite has just defecated. If my assumption is correct, the viscous slime running down the side of my knee like some boiling snot must be a bright, shimmering green.

Yay.

"Fuck you, Rodriguez," I mutter. My words can hurt her, so it's something I feel like I have some measure of control over.

Our captors have thus far ignored every one of my pleas and screams. I suspect they regard it more like the bleating of sheep or lowing of cattle.

Rodriquez looks up slowly at me. Her face is a death mask, utterly pale, her eyes as vacant as plastic beads. Nonetheless, her forehead knits and her crow's feet deepen as she fights to process my words. Then, as if remembering where we are all at once all over again, her whole visage twists in anguish.

"I didn't know," she weeps. "How could I have known?"

"I'd be dead now if it weren't for you."

It's like all the muscles from her neck vanish, her chin drops to her neck so fast. Her shoulders tremor in their encasement as her lungs convulse with her sobs. Her torso is twisted so that one shoulder is higher and forward, while the other is unnaturally far back. Good. I don't like that I seethe with such venom at her because it wasn't intended, but damn it, it feels better to be angry than to just straight up suffer and loathe what's happening to me.

My bowels churn painfully, and the thing that is burrowed among them churns against their grain. There's nowhere to use the bathroom but where I am, so I purge myself yet again in my confinement. The stench is awful, and the feculence teems with acidity. I hiss at the horrid burn, and my head lolls back. When it does, a juvenile version of the creatures that cling to the wall above me takes my cheeks in its front arms, leans its upper mass forward, and vomits a thick, grainy fluid into my upturned mouth. I try to retch it back up immediately, but razor-sharp talons in its fingertips dig into my upper and lower mandibles when I do.

I reflexively swallow to draw breath to cry out, and I sputter uselessly as a second torrent splashes right into my gullet.

The worst part is that on the biological level, my body immediately feels better at this. My stomach knows it's receiving nutrients. A feeling of contentment wells out from it. Against my will, I almost feel grateful that I've been fed like a hatchling in the nest of some horrid mama bird. How could this species exist? How could something have evolved like this?

I would ask Thompson, she was my supervisor in the biological studies department, but again, she has a thing for a tongue now.

I study what's left of the articulations of my suit. The major joints were reinforced with neuro-linked, servo-driven bars. The servos burned out when I woke the first day and spent hours attempting to thrash against my restraints. The chitin was fresh then and hard as stone. It's more brittle now, but so much of my strength is gone that it's hard to put any real force into my muscles. Every time I'm fed, my resolve wanes further, and it occurs to me that perhaps there is some sort of psychotropic compound in that regurgitation.

Nonetheless, the metal reinforcements that provide the strength for the suit articulations appear to be escaping from their housing. The sharp edge glints where it broke. I doubt it would cut through their exoskeletons, but the soft flesh of my wrist or throat ... All I need is to have one free arm. I stare at my fingers as I wiggle them in the dim light. Where the light is coming from I don't know. The walls are strangely corrugated, almost like the folded surface of a brain, and the light seems to escape from somewhere inside the folds. However, if I peer into the ones I see most directly, their bottoms seem dark, like deep, deep trenches. Maybe the light sources only glow when I can't see them.

But that metal shard—I see that metal shard. I love that metal shard and hate it because it is so close to me.

I hate Rodriquez because she is so close to me and because she did this. There has to be someone to blame.

One of the things inside me burrows up between my lungs and my rib cage. My vision tunnels, and my head lolls back. The juvenile creature grabs my face and vomits down my throat. I can hardly breathe because my lungs can't expand with that thing between my lungs and my rib cage. I feel like I'm drowning, like I'm sinking deep into an ocean trench covered in weights like the diving tests they gave us during flight training.

Thompson whines. Her face is pinched and spasming. She thrashes her head side by side, repeatedly trying to pull the thing that has attached itself to her tongue into her mouth. It must hurt so bad to keep her mouth open so long. It's been like that for days.

I think Thompson is nodding as if she read my thoughts, but then I realize she is building momentum. She snaps her head back and drives her chin down to her chest.

With a squish and a clack, she bites her tongue off. The thing falls from her face to the floor and squiggles among the weird writhing tendrils that cover everything.

"Gwah," she says as a glut of blood pours out of her mouth.

I dream that I'm back on the *Demeter* and that we're on a wake cycle in transit. I'm lying on the dinner table, holding a coffee flask, those weird curved things that look like a glass-blowing accident, and someone is using a carving knife to open me diagonally across the gut. Rodriguez is there to the side, rising up and gazing with curiosity while Commander Sullivan, the head of Tyco Deep Space Launch Station, holds a set of barbeque tongues and clacks them together.

"Mmm," the commander says. "I really outdid myself."

I look down at myself, and there are roaches crawling in and out of the coils of my intestines. I wonder if they're wanting to eat me or if they're "my" bugs. Memories of seeing through the eyes of the bugs as they burrowed their way among and through my organs strobe through my vision. The thought of someone else eating them revolts me.

"But those are my bugs," I say.

And that's the bridge between sleeping and waking, the words tumbling from my mouth in a dry rasp that makes me think of cracker crumbs. My eyes roll open as I retch, and some hot, brackish fluid trickles down the corners of my mouth and drips off my chin.

"I trust the merchandise had the correct genetic markers?" a voice says.

A voice I know.

Commander Sullivan's voice.

I haven't heard him for months, not since the *Demeter* set forth on that long and lonely transit and he bade us Earth's best wishes and the unending thanks of mankind. But that gruff rasp is unmistakable.

A human in a heavy-military atmospheric suit enters, followed by someone in the green, lighter tactical-command model. The one in green is flanked on either side by two of the adult creatures. Unlike the ones I've seen, these creatures have ripples in their carapaces, almost like wet skin. They glisten and seep a teal fluid from between their plates, and they seem to be attentive to the one in the green suit. One of them chatters away in its language and gestures at the room.

Even without hearing his voice again, I am certain: the green suit holds Commander Sullivan.

My heart leaps. I look to the sharp piece of metal on the joint frame of my suit, and I'm embarrassed that I had considered taking my own life.

He stops just inside the entrance and appears to survey the room with a slow pivot of his hips. His suit's faceplate is reflectively opaque, but I imagine the horror with which he surveys the scene before him. Do his eyes widen in surprise? Or narrow in anger? What if he throws up in his suit?

The fact that the creatures aren't actively killing the commander means that he's managed to engage them in diplomacy. Somehow the creatures with him—they understand. No doubt he's negotiating our release.

I can only imagine that one of the gunships hovers in orbit. Maybe *The Brigadier*. Her phalanx missiles must be trained on whatever space we're hidden in, ready to break the moon in two on Sullivan's command. It would, of course, be strange for the commander to come down if that was the plan, though. Feels kind of special that he would put himself in the line of fire for us.

His steps are careful as he enters our hatchery, avoiding the ovoid eggs that litter the ground. The strange tendrils that writhe and knot all over the floor seem to draw away from his suit as he moves.

"Thank god you're here," I say. "I'd given up."

Commander Sullivan stops in front of me. My face reflects in his visor. The whole bottom half of my face is streaked black, no doubt the accumulated stain and splatter of the creature feeding me. Two nodules under my skin—one where my jaw meets my ear and one in my forehead over my left eye—jut out nearly half an inch. Strange that I don't feel them like the ones burrowing inside me, but even as I think that, I register a gentle scraping against my skull from the one in my forehead.

Perhaps the thing that shocks me most is that all my hair has fallen out except a few scraggly whisps. How had I not noticed? How had I not felt it slipping away? When I left Tyco, I had a crew cut, of course, but it had since grown to a floppy ear-length in transit. Right before we made our disastrous approach to the moon, I had been admiring it in the mirror after hygiene protocols.

I close my hanging jaw, try to lift my chin to look dignified. This man is here to rescue me. I need to look worth rescuing.

"You son of a bitch. You swore," Rodriguez snarls at the commander. Her gaze flicks up to me and Thompson. "You swore it would just be them."

The tactical suit, despite being lighter than the heavy combat suit of his escort, is still fairly rigid, so the commander's shrug is almost lost to its bulk.

"Unfortunately, they really can't tell us apart above the genetic level unless you're wearing their transponders," Commander Sullivan says. He reaches forward and scrapes the chitin from over her nameplate. "And you just happened to be compatible with their brood too, Rodriguez. Rodriguez. Your sacrifice is noted, Rodriguez. I'll read your file tonight, commit it to memory."

Rodriguez's whole body strains, but she's more immobilized than I am, and the contorted position her body is stuck in can't possibly give her much leverage.

I look back and forth between the two of them.

That same drop from heart to gut.

On some level, I probably recognized it from the moment I heard the commander's voice, but now I know that when Rodriguez asked how she could have known, she was lamenting her own capture. I wasn't chosen for the salvage expedition by chance, and neither was Thompson. We were sold.

"Why, sir?" I gasp.

The commander turns to face me again. He reaches up to his helmet, and I think for a moment he's about to take it off or open his visor. Instead, he pushes a button beside where his ear might be, and a suitcam feed appears on the visor's outside. His eyes are devoid of any form of emotion. No regret. No anger. They're moving, but that's the only thing alive about them.

"The alloys of this moon are worth more to the space program than you could ever imagine, and this exchange grants us access. We *need* those materials the way this species *needs* you to fill a gap in their life cycle. If it's any consolation, we hadn't meant the ship to crash, and we didn't know you'd be among the selected candidates until afterward. Your patriotism will be—"

With a grunt, I twist my hips and pivot my shoulder as hard as I can simultaneously. Anger sends adrenaline unrestricted through my system, and I feel ready to move a mountain. The chitin swathes that fix me still shatter, and my hand flies to the broken frame of my suit. Blood sprays from my hand as I scrape my palm on the sharp edge before I jerk the piece free. I swipe my shiv at the commander, but he steps back easily. The escort in the heavy suit is between us before I can blink, and the mechanized hand of his suit takes mine at the wrist.

A squeeze shatters all the round bones of my wrist, and the piece of metal frame falls from my hand as I cry out.

"I understand your reluctance to commit to your part in the expansion of our species," Commander Sullivan says from behind his escort. "It's not the part I would choose for myself, for sure."

"Go fuck yourself," I say.

I slump forward. The restraints that held me keep me from a complete face-plant, but I sag like a sack. One leg is fully free, and I brace myself as I clutch my forearm just below my crushed bones. The flesh is already red and throbbing, and my pulse grinds through the pulverized joint.

The commander turns to the creature with whom he had been interacting when they entered.

"I trust the shipment is ready for extraction?"

My eyes fall to his suit, to the black box on his suit. There's a little red light on it.

I don't let myself think. I throw my upper body back to the wall and kick out. My heel connects with the box on his hip, and the plastic housing collapses under the impact. The commander stumbles sideways, swinging his arms like a drunk, until he falls down on all fours with a bellow.

The little light on the black box is no longer lit.

The two adult creatures swivel and lunge at him.

The escort joins the fray and grapples with the creature closest to him. The creature shrieks and spasms at his touch, and I see that he has his own transponder on his belt.

The other creature closes tighter up Sullivan's back. Its vestigial arms elongate and narrow, and they dig at the underarms of Sullivan's suit. I hear plastic crunch and canvas tear as they rip their way into his arm pits, and suddenly the commander is screaming. The creature drives at his body with those arms in a swooping, wavelike motion, and each time, they seem to drive deeper.

The screams taper into a thick, gurgling whine.

The escort takes in the convulsing form of his officer, lets go of the creature, and runs out of the chamber.

Silence descends.

My breathing is the only sound for a precious moment before there's a long squelching sound as the creature pulls its arms out of the commander's torso. They keep coming and coming, retracting into the alien's body, dripping with the commander's blood and chunks of flesh and sinew. The creature the escort grappled twitches and looks about as if bewildered and dazed.

The shiv shines at my feet like Excalibur.

I pick it up, look at Rodriguez.

"You piece of shit."

"I'm sorry," she says. "I'm sorry."

I regard the shiv in my hand, picture myself driving it into her face over and over. Extracting my revenge for what she's done to me.

I swing the blade and drive it right into Thompson's ear. She squeaks in shock and falls instantly silent as the blade crunches straight into her auditory canal. I then look Rodriguez straight in the eyes.

"I hope you live forever," I say, right before I jam the blade into my own jugular.

RARIFIED-AIR

Sean McDonough

The visitor notification *pinged* urgently at the corner of his Ex-visor, but Lonnie was not urged.

These people, they were used to being granted their every whim at the drop of a hat. They treated him like he was just one of the trained monkeys running around on the solar deck with a tray of synthetic oysters, as opposed to a one-man team responsible for every heating coil, power supply, and exhaust chamber on the ship.

They would replace him with an AI if they could, but there was no algorithm that could account for every quirk and idiocentric hiccup in a three-mile-long star cruiser. For that, you needed a glorified monkey, like Lonnie Grennon.

And if you needed Lonnie Grennon, you could wait until he finished his afternoon jerk.

When the deed was done, Lonnie wiped his hands and crossed the invisible line that separated his living quarters (cot, radon microwave, sonic sanitizer) from the maintenance deck (tools, spare parts, radiation shields). He was back on the clock.

His Ex-visor pinged at him again as he was within steps of the door, and Lonnie deliberately slowed his gait as he climbed the oil-stained, metal steps leading to the airlock.

Before opening the steel bulkhead doors, Lonnie activated the video monitor. The visor had already identified his visitor, but Lonnie hoped against hope that there was a glitch somewhere and it was actually Miss Jupiter on the other side of the door instead of some dumpy admin with a soil monitor jammed up her ass.

"Ah, shit," he muttered as the display revealed not Miss Jupiter but, indeed, a dumpy admin with a soil monitor jammed all the way up her ass.

"Mister Grennon, I have an urgent assignment for you. Are you there?" Admin Gower called. The woman was such a shrimp that her severe blonde bob and black-rimmed visor barely made the bottom of the display, but he knew from experience that she walked around the cruiser like she was twenty feet tall.

And she would never personally come down to Zeta deck unless there was a fucking disaster happening.

Ding. His Ex-visor fired off another notification in glaring red, agreeing with his assessment.

"Mister Grennon, I see my notifications are being read. Please open the door."

Better get it over with, he thought. But he waited another half a minute before actually pushing the button to slide open the airlock. The metal panels slid apart with the dull grind of gears that he never got around to oiling properly.

"Grennon," she began without so much as a how do. "We have a protocol 27-G incident on Zeta deck."

Lonnie responded with a look of deliberate ignorance.

Fresh annoyance flared behind the crystal panel of Gower's ex-visor. It almost made her look human. "Grennon, you're supposed to recertify on your terminology SOP every six earth cycles. It's in your employment agreement."

"Septic system must have failed that day," Lonnie said agreeably. "Shit backing up all the way to the tennis court. I've requisitioned for an assistant everytime we dock, but it never seems to be—"

"A 27-G means a murder on board, Grennon."

There was nothing deliberate about Lonnie's expression now.

"It happened in a living quarters," Gower continued, gratified to see Lonnie's smirk disappear. "The dwelling needs to be preserved. That's procedure. Get over there. Now."

Lonnie was certainly not a smart man, never better than 70th percentile in school evals. But he was blessed with a certain animal cunning, and that beast raised its head and sniffed hungrily at the air. News of the killing may have briefly wiped the smirk off his face, but that sly devil was back in full force. "Procedure also says that the ship's Security Director has sole authority in the event of criminal activity on board, Administrator Gower."

He was pleased to see her mouth pucker up. "You need to fulfill your responsibilities in compliance with Protocol 27-G," she said. "The person directing you to do so is irrelevant."

"Space-Ex is very particular about procedure, Miss Gower. You said so yourself. I don't even have a properly signed work order for this task."

He busied himself by stroking his gray stubble while she stewed at his doorstep, clearly wishing there was another maintenance manager anywhere on this side of the Asteroid Belt.

Finally, there was a small chime as she did the only thing she could do. An infusion of Ex-credits appeared at the corner of his visor.

"I'll begin preservation protocols right away, ma'am. What quarters did you say it was?"

"I didn't. Zeta Unit 34. Get it done."

She spun on her heels, the synthetic material barely a whisper against the oily steel deck, and disappeared down the corridor, back to the luxurious confines of her Alpha–deck suite.

Leaving Lonnie to wonder why Zeta 34 sounded so familiar to him.

The circuit didn't complete until he was actually standing nose to steel with unit Z-34 and saw the nameplate next to the unit number. Somebody had traced the letters in red semi-gloss paint in a misguided attempt to add a little cheer to the sterile hallway.

Torrence.

The name on the door is the same as the name on the wrinkled work order twisted in the girl's clutching hands.

Lonnie takes it from her. A paper order is suspect to begin with, used only in case of some kind of network snafu, and Lonnie has to peer even more closely just to try to decipher the writing. The sheet is badly crumpled and damp with sweat.

The same unit number. Zeta 34.

"I can't go by this," he says.

"It's the 1272 form," she insists. She means to insist, anyway, but it comes out like more of a plea. "It's the right form."

Lonnie shakes his head in annoyance. He's missing his break because this little pain in the ass grabbed him in the hallway. "Yeah, but it's not signed. Not to mention that a legitimately approved service call would already be on my itinerary for the day." He taps near his temple, and the Ex-visor helpfully brings up the panel of assigned tasks. "And it ain't."

The girl's work order is a scam. He knows it, and so does she. Maybe he would be tempted to look the other way for a brunette with baby blues who knew how to use them, but for not this sweaty sack of laundry with a pumpkin-shaped head and acne scars peppering her face like constellations in the space outside the ship.

"Get back to wherever you're supposed to be before I make a report to the FSO." He doesn't bother trying to weasel some credits out of her, not if she's quartered on Zeta. He tries to slide past her, but her hand clutches his wrist with the desperate strength of somebody trying not to get sucked out of an airlock.

"I need my unit's access code changed!" she screeches. Her desperation echoes off of the steel walls.

Lonnie yanks his hand back. "So get a work order."

He keeps walking.

And there he was after all.

And he still didn't have a proper work order.

It was quiet. Zeta deck was the quarters for the bottom slush of ship staff, the longest hours for the least Ex-credits. There were a dozen identical bulkheads on either side of Unit 34, each of them just as silent. For all Lonnie knew, there was a dead body lurking behind every one of them.

Dead as the woman who wanted you to change her locks.

Lonnie's dry heart did not bleed. Whatever happened to this girl, it started long before she came to him with a phony piece of paper. It was called a *personal* passcode for a reason. If you give it out to the first person who called you pretty, that was what happened. That wasn't Lonnie's problem. His problem was getting this done and getting back to dinner and his date with an AI blonde.

With a grunt, he slipped the vacuum pump off of his shoulder. These rare Mars minerals were supposed to be lighter than Earth metals, but they weren't getting lighter fast enough to keep up with the wear and tear on Lonnie's old bones.

The Elon was a standard issue Cyberliner. The dimensions on each one were identical from stem to stern. The number of tennis courts on the Solar deck was the same. The output on the collider drive was the same.

And the atmosphere purge port was hidden in the same discreet panel at the base of every bulkhead door.

That was the protocol if a murder occurred on a ship in between planetary jurisdictions. Seal off the area and vacuum-purge the atmosphere. Keep the crime scene perfectly preserved until the proper authorities could gather evidence.

Or bundle everything neatly away once you reached port and nobody was around to see you take it to the incinerator.

Lonnie refused to dwell on that. He focused on getting a good seal on the connection between the vacuum pump and the port with his clumsy, grease-stained fingers that were made clever by years of repetition. He sat down on the floor once the pump was turned on and working, preferring the chill of hard steel against his back to the pressure on his knees while he waited.

There was a small blob on the floor near his hand, an angry red planet of a rusty smear.

Blood? Maybe she had died right there in the doorway, opened up and gotten a knife in the throat before she even knew what was happening.

If the killer had her access code, he wouldn't need to use the bell.

"Bullshit," he muttered.

Still, he wished the vacuum would work a little faster.

Procedure said that the SSO would come to claim the tank of purged air from Unit Z-34. These days, even air was evidence. Once the ship reached Jupiter, Planetary Police would take custody and the air would be examined for particulate matter that might reveal the killer's identity.

With whatever weird shit was going on around this, Lonnie didn't see anyone coming anytime soon.

Still, just to cover his ass, the first thing Lonnie did after slumping into his workshop was to make sure the tank was properly stored and labeled in a corner. If somebody did come for it, he knew where to find it.

Until then, the radon oven and a couple hours with the algo-reel beckoned.

Lonnie had meant to spend an hour working on a disassembled algae filtration tank, but a mixing bowl of mac and cheese and a steady stream of AI-generated dick kicks and bikini car washes worked him over better than a sedative and a long weekend at Las Venus Spaceport.

It wasn't until three hours that Lonnie jerked back to wakefulness with an ugly snort. The small of his back throbbed from sleeping in his chair. His crooked neck felt like it was full of strained steel cables.

And somebody was screaming in his ear.

He realized that was what had awoken him. Somebody was in his workshop, and their high-pitched scream was working at his eardrums like a diamond-tipped drill bit.

Impulsively, he lifted a pipe wrench off his combination workbench/dining room table and hefted it to shoulder height. The ugly pounding of blood in his temples urged him to crack a skull if need be, and god help the Hargan's feeb kid if he got out again and wandered into the wrong unit.

There was nobody else in sight. His dimly lit workshop was as empty as always except for Lonnie and his quivering shoulders and darting eyes. He was alone.

But the screams. The screams carried on.

The adrenaline kept his body in a miserable state of tension, but Lonnie's lifetime as a mechanical technician gradually took over. There was noise—trace it to its source and fix the problem. It was no different than chasing a creaky fan belt.

He eventually followed the screaming sound to a corner of the shop, a section of the work room where he kept obsolete parts, uncalibrated equipment, and mismatched screws and caps.

It was also where he stashed the air tanks from Z-34.

A leak, he thought in a wash of relief that he refused to acknowledge was relief. *Just a leak.*

A leak that sounded for all the world like the last, desperate howls of a woman about to be stabbed to death. But that didn't matter now that he found the source. The tank he used to vacuum-purge Z-34 was defective. There was a pinhole leak somewhere, and it was pitched just so to make the fillings in his teeth ache. He knew how to fix a pinhole leak, no problem at all.

Except when Lonnie examined the tank, he found nothing. Not a hiss. Not so much as a breeze. The fittings were snug and secure. There were no perforations in the body. The tank itself was complctely intact.

It was also unquestionably the source of the terrified howling that was causing his eyes to water and his knees to twitch in sympathetic response. It was no reel scream, no machine-algorithm approximation of terror. It was the genuine article, human howl of death, triggering a fight-or-flight response that made his sedentary heart race in a way he struggled to constrain.

Lonnie sat on the oily steel floor and rubbed the back of his neck. "What the fuck," he muttered. "What the fuck?"

There was something he was missing. There had to be. He pressed his ear against the cold, chrome convex of the air tank.

There was no sensation, no telltale caress of leaking air. There was only the bottled-up screaming stabbing at his eardrum. No pause to take a breath. Just a constant, endless scream.

Sudden movement flashed in the corner of his eye, and all of the bottled tension in Lonnie's body went off like a collapsing star. He leaped up with a speed that made his brittle knees boil in protest and flung himself back against a wall of parts, sending capacitors and coils to the floor in a rattle of metal rain. He screamed, but not as loudly as the voice roaring in his ear.

"Grennon! Where the hell are you!?"

A call. You just got a call.

He couldn't respond yet though. Lonnie's scream had been brief, only the merest exhale, but it seemed to take him forever to get his breath back. HIs throat was as tight as a bolted-down lug nut. He felt cold sweat pouring down his face.

If the silver-haired, bristling face at the corner of his Ex-visor noticed Lonnie's obvious distress, it didn't seem to matter nearly as much as his own anger.

"Grennon, we scheduled our sonic whiteners for calibration an hour ago!" the man yelled. Get over here right now!"

Declan, his mind supplied, finally working again. *The dickweed who manages the spa.* Lonnie found his voice and fought to hold it steady. "Your whiteners aren't due for calibration until Tuesday."

"It *IS* Tuesday, shit for brains. Your ass better be up here in the next five seconds!"

The video cut off before Lonnie could retort that that wasn't possible. He just had dinner. He was looking for an air leak. He had ...

He had spent all night listening to the screams coming from the tank.

Lonnie grabbed his tool bag and fled the workshop.

The visit to the spa on Solar deck was exactly what Lonnie needed. Even the staffers there were upper deck, finely chiseled men with windswept hair and LED iris implants for that subtle sheen. The women were all custom models, genetically modified in utero to grow into perfect tens. No surgery required.

The dirty looks he got for showing up late were of no consequence. Lonnie was just happy to be there. It was bright. It was clean. The music was low and pleasant.

You couldn't even imagine anybody screaming there.

He didn't hear the screaming when he got back to the workshop.

That wasn't to say that it had stopped. The high, keening wail continued to leak from the tank of dead air. Lonnie simply decided that he didn't hear it anymore. There was no sound. There was just his combination shop/living quarters. Same as always. If he had a headache so powerful it made his eyes water, so what? *The Elon* had been in space for the better part of three weeks. That kind of thing happened.

The pharmaceuticals wing was closely monitored. Prescription sedatives were supposed to be carefully controlled and never distributed without authorization.

But when a person had backdoor access to climate controls for the medical head's private quarters, "exceptions" could be made in exchange for prompt services. Lonnie dry swallowed two green pills he couldn't identify, and the effect was an instantaneous rush of sweet, warm liquid filling his eyelids. He barely made it to his cot before he plunged into a deep, unshakable slumber

There were no dreams. But there was fear.

When he awoke, Admin Gower wasn't just at his door, she had used her executive override to enter the room and was looming over the bed, shaking him so vigorously that Lonnie briefly thought he was aboard an old Earth ocean liner instead of a star yacht.

"Lonnie! *Lonnie Grennon!*"

He opened his eyes, and she was directly on top of him, her bulging eyes practically pupil to pupil with his own. Her nails were dug into his shoulders like a dozen 12-gauge bolts.

"Unit 47!" she screeched.

"Wha?" Lonnie slurred, still soup-brained from whatever he had taken.

She hauled him up into a sitting position and rattled him back and forth until his teeth clicked together. "Unit Z-47! Vacuum it now! Hurry!"

He'd fallen asleep with his Ex-visor still on, and now numbers were flashing across his eyeballs. Credits. Far more credits than the last time Gower had asked him to vac a room.

"Do your job!"

Lonnie didn't have the bandwidth to question what was happening. His muscle memory took over while his slurring brain was still in a pharmaceutical haze. He was out the door with the vacuum pump and an empty air tank before he thought to ask Gower if she heard the screams too.

Two tanks couldn't leak.

One? Ok, sure. One tank happens. But even with Space-Ex and its low-bidder bullshit, you didn't get two leaky tanks in a row.

So how could it be that Lonnie now had two different voices screaming at him inside his workshop?

He sat on his stool drinking the sludge coffee they served on Zeta deck and fighting the urge to check himself into the med bay.

You should just vent them. If planet-side police were going to collect these tanks, security would have already come to confiscate them. Empty the tanks. Hell, put them to an exhaust port and let them scream into the fucking void. Problem solved.

No. Problem not solved. Problem swept under the rug.

Lonnie had been in Spaceliner maintenance for thirty years, since a trip to the moon was the height of luxury. In all his time on-ship, there had only been one other occasion where a murder happened on board, and that had been a fucking circus. There were curfews and security patrols for the remainder of the voyage. No precaution was considered too much.

On *The Elon*, there had been two murders in less than a terra-week, and there had been no response except to call maintenance.

Because this time it's just dead Zeta deckers.

Boo hoo. Everyone had problems. Suck it up, buttercup. The world wasn't fair.

It sure wasn't. If you wanted proof, come down to Maintenance on *The Elon*. Listen to the women screaming in their pressurized gas canisters.

Damnit, they're not actually in there.

"So what the fuck is?" he muttered.

Lonnie slurped more sludge. Christ, the sound just didn't *stop.*

His visor flashed green, a notification that the Bell Engines were due to be greased.

It joined the faulty gas sensor on Beta deck and the menu monitor at La Bon Giorno where the AI kept insisting on making everything Japanese. The issues on the ship kept piling up.

But Lonnie couldn't stop listening to the trapped screams.

They still terrified him. The reaction to the deafening horror was still a deep, primal fear. But he also found himself spending more and more time just...listening to it.

Music worked that way too, didn't it? Lonnie hated all that synth crap they played at the clubs at night, hated the way it always managed to vibrate down through the pipes right into his fuckin' ears. But goddamn if he didn't sometimes find himself repeating that little boppy shit all day to himself while he replaced ion cores and adjusted HVAC controls.

Why couldn't the screams of the dead work the same way? Why couldn't terror get its hooks in you until you liked it that way?

Lonnie closed his eyes and drifted.

It was another day before he opened them again, maybe two. Lonnie couldn't say with any certainty. All he knew was that his stomach hurt and there was a stain at the crotch of his pants that had dried into a consistency like cardboard.

If Gower noticed this, she didn't care. She didn't seem to care about much of anything.

"There's another one," she announced tonelessly. "Z-23. Seal it."

"What's her name?" Lonnie asked.

Gower had to stop and turn around. She was already halfway back to the door.

"What's whose name?"

"Z-23," Lonnie said. "It's a 'she,' isn't it?"

Gower sighed. "What difference does it make?"

"None, I suppose. Just curious."

Gower sighed. It was a sound like the color seeping out of a sheet. "We reach dock tomorrow. It's someone else's problem then."

"Sure it is," Lonnie said.

Gower shook her head. "It won't be yours anymore. Isn't that good enough?"

Three was better.

Three tanks. Three screams.

He understood that now.

Together, the three screams brought clarity. They had a voice. Lonnie understood now.

He knew what he had to do.

The Elon's atmosphere circulation system was stowed in a chamber off the maintenance workshop. The oxygen genny and the 100K HP compressor worked in tandem twenty-four hours a day to keep breathable air pumping through the entire ship. For obvious reasons, it was the single most important system on *The Elon*, and Lonnie spent a great many hours of his week changing the filters, greasing the bearers, and testing the emergency batteries.

Moisture was a constant concern. Humidity built up in the system over time, creating the risk of mold formations in the air lines and exposing the entire ship to a host of airborne diseases. It was necessary for the maintenance manager to periodically introduce purified nitrogen into the system to dry out the lines and prevent any kind of fungal growth.

It was procedure.

In a happy accident, the nitrogen tanks used for this chore were the exact same size and configuration as the tanks used for sealing a living quarters.

"I'm working on it," Lonnie told the screams as he pushed the tanks toward the junction where the main duct connected to the air generator. There was only one connection valve, but Lonnie had a multi-tap valve he could use to connect all three tanks at the same time.

He could still hear the screams as he opened the tanks, but they gradually grew softer and farther away, borne by the air pressure and carried out into the ship.

Lonnie found that he missed it.

That night, he slept quite peacefully.

And awoke feeling better than he had in twenty years.

He didn't even wait for his alarm to go off. Lonnie simply awoke and arose and made his way to the small galley kitchen that was his privilege as manager of a one-man department. He fixed a cup of tar coffee and dug a tray package of frost-coated pork sausages from the back of the freezer. The genuine raw article as opposed to the pre-cooked, radon-oven meat bullets he usually scarfed down.

The sausages were just starting to sizzle when his visor informed him there was a caller at his door.

Trusting that the sausages would be alright for a moment, Lonnie went to the bulkhead.

"Mr. Grennon?" a timid, youthful voice asked.

Lonnie looked down at a fidgeting, acne-faced assistant who looked like he was ready to wet himself. *Malcolm Warden*, Lonnie's Ex-visor helpfully informed. He nodded briefly at his visitor, enjoying the youth's discomfort.

"Mr. Grennon," the kid pressed on with a gulp, "I've got a 27-G situation that needs to be addressed." He lowered his voice. That means a-—"

"I know what it means," Lonnie cut him off. "What room?"

"A-4, sir."

Lonnie tilted his head. "Alpha deck?

Malcolm winced even hearing it. "Obviously we'll need you to be as discreet as possible. It wouldn't do to distress the other Trump Card holders."

"What happened? Who is it?"

"I'd really rather not say." Malcolm hemmed and hawed.

Except he would rather. Lonnie could tell. Some tales just demanded to be said.

"I'm just asking in case there's anything I need to know," Lonnie clarified. "For procedure."

"Well," Malcolm began, "A-4 is Mister Bayzo's suite. His masseuse showed up for his morning deep tissue and found ..." He shook his head. "It seems Mr. Bayzos had some kind of breakdown during the night. He stuffed both of his ears with toilet paper. And then he took a stylus and punctured both eardrums. On the second try, it seems that he shoved one in so deep that he stabbed into his own brain."

"Jesus," Lonnie said.

"Nobody knows why he did it. He had such a rich, invigorating voyage."

"I'll bet he did," Lonnie muttered.

"I know there should be an official work order," Malcolm pressed on. "But as I said, we're trying to keep this discreet. Do you think—"

"Don't worry, discretion is the order of the day," Lonnie assured him. Then a thought occurred to him. "Not that it matters, but usually Admin Gower makes these kinds of requests. Where's she this morning?"

Malcolm winced. "About that ... We're going to need you to go to suite A-7 as well."

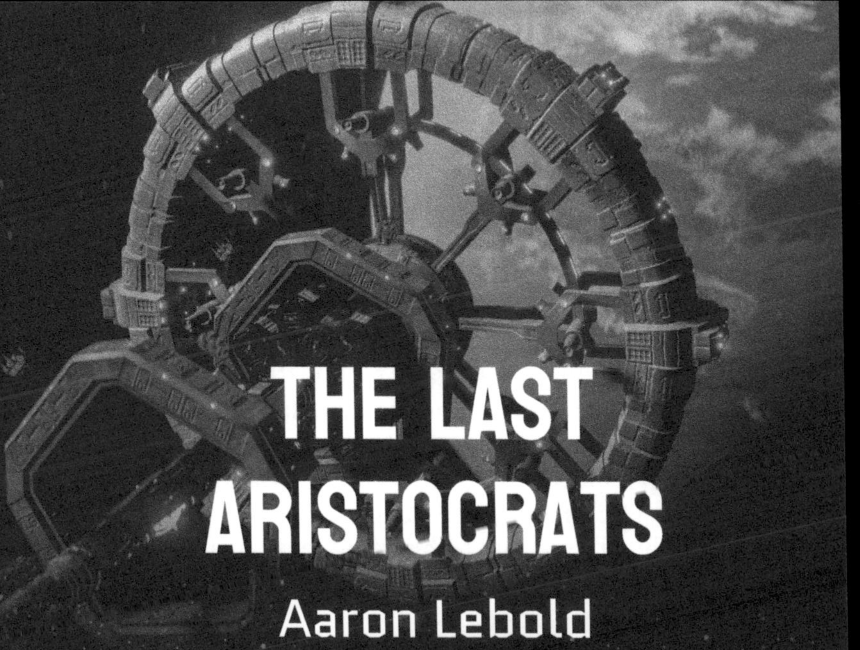

THE LAST ARISTOCRATS

Aaron Lebold

I sat with melancholy as I stared out the small porthole. As a child, it had been a dream of mine to see outer space, but somehow the novelty had already worn off. I would catch myself daydreaming.

When I was younger, I heard a story that there was a dead Russian astronaut floating aimlessly in space. After some basic research, I ended up learning that the story wasn't true, but I still liked to think of it sometimes. The thought of constant peace, the magnificence of the universe being revealed bit by bit with each passing day, the solitude, the lack of need for basic human necessity, being lifeless and drifting around sounded a bit like Heaven to me.

I watched as they all took turns drawing numbers. It was the only fair way. Carla wasn't used to fair; none of them were. Fair was never a concern when you had money. Circumstances, however, had changed dramatically since the destruction of Earth. There were twenty-seven of us on the large vessel, down from thirty-five. They had all paid to be on the ship, and paid handsomely. I was surrounded by the richest of the rich, the painfully accurate definition of an aristocrat.

My presence caused a bit of animosity for some. I earned my money with my words. Apparently my words meant enough to enough people that I was voted onto the ship. I didn't even want to join the elite, but I was pressured. People who found solace in my work advocated for me to go, to help the new world with a baseline perspective that they all felt would help with survival. The fact that I had some basic training in engines didn't hurt, and by agreeing to do maintenance on the ship, I was granted passage. So there I was.

I drew number sixteen.

It was understood that humanity had found another habitable planet that was already flourishing. The issue was the craft only had one small escape pod. It took the pod seven days to take the chosen one to the new world and then to return to the shuttle to pick up the next.

I always had a baseline of distrust for people in general, and the fact that I knew almost every inch of the ship and had never seen the pod myself caused a bit more than skepticism.

Carla and her daughter sat near me. I watched her look up at the large timer that now read zero. She looked at the number in her hand. She had seven. She glanced down at the young Ophelia. "It'll be our turn this time, princess."

The young girl looked up with an impatient sneer. "You said that last time, Mother." Her voice matched her words—spoiled and entitled.

I watched Carla look her daughter up and down with judging eyes. "Be sure you aren't overdoing it at the feast tonight."

"I know, Mother."

Though the escape pod only held one person, there was an exception. Children under nine or children who weighed less than eighty pounds could accompany their parents if they were the chosen one. Though her daughter was nearly thirteen, she had remained quite petite. Carla had her on the scale daily to ensure the two could travel together when their day finally came.

The room fell silent as the number was about to reveal itself. I watched Carla as she looked down at her card and back up to the screen. She was praying for a seven. She held her breath. For a brief moment, she became flushed with excitement, but it faded into disappointment when she realized she was looking at a nine.

Jonathan jumped from his seat with his number in the air. "It's me! I'm nine!" There was a unanimous sigh in the room as the entitled hopes of many became crushed. Jonathan didn't maintain much modesty as he danced toward the back door, the door that only opened every seven days. The door that was off limits and kept guarded around the clock.

There was an airflow vent that ran above it, but I was the only one who knew about it. There had been more than one occasion where I had debated skipping the draw and seeing what happened on the other side, but I always figured that fate would decide. I would get called just like everyone else at one point or another.

The light above turned from red to green, and the guard opened it to allow Jonathan to pass. He turned around to face his fellow passengers. "See you guys on the other side."

The door closed behind him, and the guard resumed his post. All the passengers went back to their regular routines, muttering to one another.

About five minutes later, the clock reset to 168 hours. It would be another week before another was chosen.

Carla ran her hands down her designer dress and straightened her diamond rings that she had attempted to use as a bribe in the early days, before it was made clear money couldn't get you anywhere when everyone was rich and like-minded. She moved to the table next to me with William and Betty.

I always preferred to sit alone, and nobody seemed overly interested in getting to know me, anyway.

I watched Ophelia run off to play games with the other children.

During the seven-day wait, everyone did their best to pretend everything was normal. They were the social elite, and treating each other as such kept them all feeling significant.

The safe passage to the shuttle had certainly not been cheap. It was unclear how many people managed to get off Earth before its implosion, or how many were already recolonizing on the new planet. There were a lot of holes in the story as far as I was concerned.

William straightened his tie and adjusted his top hat. "So, what do you guys think the new planet will be like?"

Betty finished applying her lipstick and gave a quick pucker before responding. "It will clearly be inhabited only by the wealthy and successful. Surely they wouldn't allow any commoners to tag along."

Carla nodded in agreement. She glanced briefly at me. I could feel her judgment. "Well, they will need people to do the dirty jobs. Possibly the most skilled of the lower population will be there to keep things going for us."

They all agreed and took turns glancing in my direction, not as subtly as they may have thought. Maybe they didn't care.

William pulled out a deck of cards. "A little bridge until the feast?"

Carla and Betty both agreed, and they played. Time could move slowly in the shuttle, and cards had become a regular way of passing the time.

Soon enough, the bell rang to summon everyone to the dining area. The table was set with elegance, as it usually was. All the proper silverware and serviettes were placed as they should be. Water was the only beverage on board, and vegetables were few and far between.

Betty placed her cards on the table. "Finally."

Ophelia was already in her place when Carla returned to her previous table.

I knew that the main reason Carla was feeling so impatient about being chosen was that she had noticed the food selection continued to dwindle as time went on. She wasn't afraid to vocalize it, as if we hadn't all noticed the same thing.

The thing with these people was that they didn't have many problem-solving skills. Like most things in life, they all seemed to figure that being rich was the only solution that was ever needed. Maybe at one time they had rational thought, but it seemed like that day was long gone.

The waiter emerged from the back door with a cart stacked with plates. The guard held the door for him as he passed and resumed his post as soon as it closed again. Each table was served as though it was being catered.

Ophelia got her plate and reached for her food, and Carla slapped her hand. "Manners, girl. We wait until everyone is served. You know this." She then took a small portion of her daughter's food and placed it on her own plate. "We need to keep you at the right weight."

Once everyone had their food, we all dug in. The meat, always the star of the show, always perfectly seasoned, was tenderized beautifully and tasted like heaven compared to the previous day's meal. I savored every bite before swallowing. Everyone else at the table was doing the same. For most, it was best to savor the day of the feast because everyone knew it would be a steady decline as far as rations were concerned over the next week.

The meals were always fancy, but the quantities would decrease each day. On the day of the feast, there was always something extra. Today it was a baked potato. By the last day, they usually served a stew that consisted mostly of leftovers all mixed together with seasoning, presumably in some sort of large cauldron or pot.

Once it was over, they all used their napkins to dab the edges of their lips and placed them on their empty plates.

I wiped my face with my sleeve.

The waiter came by and collected them all before taking them back through the forbidden door.

I heard Ophelia pleading with her mother. "I'm still hungry."

Carla scoffed. "You just need some time to digest."

Once the dishes were all cleared, everyone went back to killing time. Books, cards, art. People did just about anything to keep their minds occupied. I had always been lucky in the fact that my imagination could keep me busy for hours. Once a story started in my head, it could completely take over.

The routine was something that most people had become accustomed to, but every now and again someone would complain. Any time this would happen, the unhappy guest would be given the option of leaving the ship. Only once did anyone take the offer. Once it was discovered they would be leaving without a shuttle, it was never again considered.

The last man who took the option was taken into the back room and literally kicked out into space. No protective gear or oxygen. The rest of the passengers watched him drift by the large windows, gasping for air that wasn't there. He was unconscious after about twenty seconds. It was interesting to see his bodily fluids boil then freeze due to lack of air pressure. Then he began to expand, like a dead raccoon on the side of the highway.

His body nearly doubled in size before it exploded in front of us. The speed in which it happened made me think of what a frozen watermelon would look like hitting the ground from a thirty-story building, vaporizing into shattered specs of its previous being. I made the decision on that day that I would come up with my own plan if I was going to jump ship.

With complaining eliminated as an option, all of us onboard did what we could to make it through another week. Each day felt progressively longer than the last.

Inevitably, we went full circle, and it was once again the day we all anticipated—the day to draw numbers. When the timer showed only two hours remaining, everyone began to keep a close eye on it. Card games stopped, reading stopped, everything stopped. The mundane routine turned back into the exciting feeling of watching a horse race. Who was going to win?

When there were ten minutes left, we chose our numbers. I chose twelve. There were only enough numbers as there were people, so if I didn't take one, my absence would be noticed.

I slipped away from the crowd, which was easy since everyone's eyes were glued to the screen. It felt impulsive, but at the same time, it felt right. I slipped up into the air vent and watched the crowd below me to see if I could tell who was selected.

Through the vent, I saw Carla clutching Ophelia and staring at their number. Her voice was muffled. "This time. This time for sure." The guests rarely spoke among themselves during this time and never shared their numbers. I typically knew what others had because I went so easily unnoticed.

Carla waited in anticipation for everyone to be ready and the clock to expire. She held her breath as it turned to zero and the number was about to reveal itself. She could feel her nails digging into her palms as he clenched her fists. There it was. It was a four.

From above, I saw her jump up, nearly knocking her daughter over. "That's us, baby. We're four!"

The usual energy of jealousy and resentment filled the room like a thick cloud. I couldn't see her face, but I knew Carla well enough to know that she paid it no mind. It was inevitable. Jealousy was always a major part of the seventh day, and it was one of the biggest reasons most of the passengers never really let themselves get close to anyone.

Still holding her daughter's hand, she made her way toward the back door.

I crept through the vents until I was in the next room. I heard the mag locks on the doors and knew the guard was letting her through.

From above, I could tell that the room was bright and clean. Nothing seemed to fill the space but another door. I slid deeper into the vents until I crossed over to the next room, keeping pace with Carla and Ophelia.

I heard the young girl address her mother. "Is this where the escape pod is? Are we really going to the new planet?"

Carla had a huge grin on her face as she looked at her daughter. "Yes, dear. I told you we just needed to be patient."

As they crossed the threshold of the second door, the atmosphere changed. Hand in hand, I watched Carla and Ophelia try to take in their surroundings. I was doing the same. The room was not like the rest. There was machinery all over the place, and the floor had dark stains all over it. Looking at how unkempt it was, I started to see the bigger picture. Carla did not. She looked down at Ophelia. "Makes sense that the elite are not allowed back here. It wasn't because we aren't good enough but because we are *too* good for something so vile."

I wanted to shout out. I wanted to warn her. At the same time, I really didn't. I almost wanted to break out in laughter.

A man approached the mother and daughter. He was wearing common clothes, a T-shirt and jeans, covered in stains. Dark-red stains. His right hand was behind his back.

"Hi, we are this week's chosen. Can you direct me to the escape pod? My daughter is surely under eighty pounds. You can weigh her if you wish."

I could see pretty well through the vents. I watched Ophelia develop a look of horror and confusion as the strange man brought a small sledgehammer down onto her mother's forehead. It happened so fast that Ophelia didn't even think to let go of her mother's hand.

Two men came from behind a curtain and lifted Carla's body. She was still alive, and Ophelia refused to let go. She was dragged along behind the curtain.

I pushed forward in the vents, being cautious not to make any sounds. My movements were surely a whisper when covered by the screams of the young child.

A meat hook hung from the ceiling, and after seeing the extra person, one of the men began to affix another. The other two hoisted Carla and speared one foot with the hook, then the other.

Ophelia stood frozen. I could only assume she had never seen the true horrors of our species. Some of the things that people were doing to each other as the planet began to slowly crumble. The things that people did to each other in everyday life, for no reason other than the fact that people were fucked up. I assumed Ophelia was never exposed to any of that. Now she was getting an intense crash course.

They kept Carla alive so her heart would continue to beat and they could bleed her out like a deer. One of the men pulled out a blade and ran it down the veins in Carla's arms. Her blood came out in spurts in rhythm with her heart.

The man looked to the other. "Get the kid on the other one."

They didn't bother to subdue her. The two men just grabbed the flailing child and dropped her onto the second hook. Bleeding her wouldn't be as important due to her small stature. The hook went through her back and popped out from her chest. Blood spilled to the floor, mixing with her mother's. A grate was underneath, swallowing the serum as it fell.

The man in the T-shirt looked up at her. "Sorry, little girl. There is no other planet." He slashed her throat, and the blood splashed across his wicked grin as it evacuated her small body. He then looked to Carla, who had been mostly drained. He proceeded to slash her throat as well, before taking a step back.

I wanted to get out of there, but I could feel myself shaking. I ended up staying in place for the entire skinning and deboning process. They were preparing for the feast. A room full of impatient, self-righteous pricks were all salivating in anticipation of Carla and Ophelia's tender flesh.

It was all making sense, and I wished I felt more surprised than I did. I had probably used the phrase "eat the rich" myself a few times. And thinking about it was a bit satisfying, but I could never join them. My place was outside. Outside of social status and hierarchy. Away from the masses.

I kept going forward through the vents, knowing they would lead me to a maintenance room at some point. I picked up the pace, though I doubted anyone would notice my absence. Soon enough, I found myself in the location I was looking for.

The spacesuit was in the locker. I had only used it once, to patch a hole on the outside of the ship, but I knew enough of how it worked. I was going to choose my own fate. I wasn't going to let the social elite consume me like game. I was certain that back in the lobby the clock had already been reset to 186 hours. It would be a week before another was chosen.

I suited up and found the hatch to the outside. It was time to live the life of the Russian astronaut that I had made up in my teenage imagination. I didn't know how long the oxygen would last, but at least I knew that my last days in the world we knew would be peaceful and silent. Nobody would even notice I was gone unless something broke on the ship or they noticed at the next draw that there was one more number than there were people.

It didn't matter. Nothing mattered. I slipped out the hatch and enjoyed the spectacle. It was beautiful. Drifting in space until I died, and then some.

ELDRIDGE

C S Jones

The landing craft defied the frenzied throes of the gods and hastily threw itself through the planet's atmosphere. Its rickety hull courted death as it plummeted, carrying its two nervy passengers and their terror-stricken pilot to the silent research station somewhere below.

Hafgan IV was a barren desert planet, prone to prolonged bouts of intense electrical storms and tempestuous cyclones. It also served as a base of operations for the Eldridge research facility, a sole tubular structure that carried out studies no civilized society would dare comprehend. It was a discovery that salvage coordinator Xander Langley was dismayed to learn when his ex-wife, Harriet, sent out a rogue transmission pleading for him to collect her.

"It's not here!" said Zhou, the pilot, his voice almost drowned out by the turmoil around them.

"What's not here?" called back Xander, breaking from his reverie and following his friend's gaze to the flight computer. "The landing pad?"

The ship swayed then righted itself.

"No, the facility. The *entire* facility. These are the coordinates, I'm even getting a return signal, but the whole thing's gone."

"What?" Puzzled, Xander leaned into the cockpit and peered through the window. Through distorting elements and blankets of swirling dirt, he could make out nothing but an empty crater. "Maybe the craft needs calibrating?"

"Not a chance. I performed a navigation sync before we set out. That there is exactly where it ought to be, and this here computer, it's getting a signal from down there, telling me the same. Only, well, look for yourself."

Xander checked the coordinates stored on his wrist unit against the shuttle's display, dismayed to see they matched. "That shouldn't be possible," he said, and took a seat to run through the transmissions on his wrist unit, specifically the last one from Harriet, sent only one cycle ago, pleading for him to bring her home. As if sensing his confusion, from somewhere below, the words of another transmission appeared and lit up the screen.

Harriet: Not alone. Please hurry.

It was similar to the first one he received almost a week ago, encrypted to hide its true purpose from anyone who might be monitoring. Harriet served as the facility's comms expert, one of only a select few capable of sending out such a distress call, and at the drop of a hat, Xander called in a few favors from his fellow crewmates. Before he knew it, he was on his way with Zhou and Callahan, his pilot and salvage partner, to rescue her.

As they ventured nearer, he remained in constant contact, and while trickles of what the Eldridge facility had been up to startled him, he and his wife had reconnected. For Xander, there was a chance to salvage everything he had lost.

But as the week had progressed, he had to confess he had become increasingly uncomfortable. The more he communicated with Harriet, the more she hadn't seemed like herself. An abruptness grew with her messages, an uncharacteristic coldness that soured his tender approach. It was so unlike her. Admittedly, they hadn't been on good terms when she initially took the position, Xander having dragged his feet when signing the divorce papers, but this past week, after showing such promise, had begun to feel like he was talking to a complete stranger. Still, he knew he had a responsibility to get her out of there, and no matter his reservations, he would move heaven and earth to make it happen.

"Xander, I don't know how it's possible, but we might have to seriously consider heading back," said Zhou through pursed lips. "I'm sorry, but without anywhere to land, we—"

"Over there! Anyone see that?" Callahan shouted from her seat at the back, pointing at something through her porthole.

Xander hunched beside her and followed her pointing finger. Something hid within the storm, its dull, steel outline growing vaguely visible through intermittent breaks in the hellish atmosphere.

"Wait, that's the facility," said Zhou, and brought the shuttle around. "It shouldn't be ... It's moved half a mile west."

"Can we land?" asked Xander.

There was a tense moment as he waited while Zhou studied his monitor.

"Zhou?"

"Seems the LZ is intact. As for the building around it, I dunno, parts of it look decimated."

"Decimated? Look, can we land?"

"Maybe it's the storm, but the entire facility looks warped. Plus, it seems to be wrapped in something, like metal piping's all around it. You ever seen that before? I guess we can land, but for the record, I don't like it. What we're seeing, this shouldn't be possible. It's as though someone's picked it up and thrown it somewhere else. Besides, you see any landing lights down there? It's dead."

"Please, Zhou, Harriet's been talking to me. She's down there somewhere. I need to bring her home."

Xander still sensed Zhou's hesitation when Callahan spoke up. "Take us down. You can wait with the ship while we take a look. You owe it to Harriet, Zhou. You'd never have met Alex if it wasn't for her."

Zhou's reluctance was palpable, but after a lingering moment, the sensation of the drop ship descending sent queasy ripples through Xander's stomach. He was going to bring her home.

The ship touched down at the center of the facility, its donut shape helping shield the LZ from gales that threatened to punish anyone brazen enough to face them head on. Clad in their EVA salvage suits, Xander and Callahan ventured out onto the deserted landing pad in search of a way in.

Together, the two shuffled their way in slow motion, their movement impaired by forceful gusts that continuously threatened to blow them off their feet.

"I can't see shit," said Callahan through muffled comms, her head lamp barely brightening a path filled with nothing but the glisten of dust and debris.

"Just a little further," said Xander, his voice an echo around his helmet as he followed the tiny blip on his wrist unit. "Fifteen feet to the airlock."

The device had been a birthday gift from Harriet after her last posting, a state-of-the-art trinket that proved to be a piece of kit he hadn't known he needed. At the time, he joked she must have felt guilty about something to spend so much, but she brushed it off and asked if he liked it. They divorced not long after, something that hit Xander harder than expected. Still, despite all the pain and, yes, even at times, hate, he wore that unit. Healthy or not, he couldn't imagine life without this connection. "Watch yourself, it should be right—"

A metallic thump rang out, followed by a tirade of cursing.

"Cal, you alright?"

"Fuck! What the hell is ... Yeah, I'm OK. I walked into it."

"Into what?"

"It's some kind of diagonal coiling. I think it's copper. Huh, weird, it's hot. Hang on there a sec, I think I see more." Callahan wandered off along the structure.

Left to wait on his partner, Xander peered back to where the shuttle should be, wondering just how long Zhou was prepared to wait. He was a good friend in normal circumstances, but he could be skittish, and Xander sensed his distress at having to land.

He was about to call Callahan for an update when a break in the weather revealed a vaguely humanoid shape in the distance. Hunched, it shuddered and collapsed, then vanished among the elements. He couldn't say why, but Xander had the distinct sensation it had been watching him.

He was about to take a step toward it when Callahan reappeared. "Yup, there's more of those diagonal coils. They disappear into the ground; must be a single piece wrapped around the complex."

Xander nodded and looked back, but the figure was lost to the elements. "What the hell?"

"I know, right?" Callahan went on. "Didn't Harriet mention anything about the structure being wrapped in copper?"

Xander shook his head. "No, I meant ... Never mind. No, nothing. Whatever, fuck it. The airlock should be right up ahead."

"I think I see the access panel. Give me a sec and I'll bypass it."

Callahan took a lumbering step and was about to reach for the panel when something caused her to recoil. Her scream was bloodcurdling. In slow-motion, she backtracked, her lethargic movement doing little to match the terror in her voice.

Through static screams that bounced around his helmet, Xander grabbed Callahan and pulled her in.

She writhed, desperate to get away. Still she screamed, until her voice settled into the words she so hurriedly wanted to yell. "Fingers! Fucking fingers!"

"What? Cal, rein it in. You'll burn through your air supply. Breathe. Slow and deep. Breathe." It took a moment, but when she was steady enough on her own feet, Xander approached the panel.

Through glassy torchlight, he found the rectangular panel then the familiar square buttons within. Only there were other shapes as well, foreign and impossible. Four gnarled fingers, weathered by the atmosphere, poked from the panel as though pushing out from within the wall itself. Xander gasped but found he couldn't look away. He was transfixed by the sheer absurdity of such a ghastly sight.

Without warning, the fingers flexed, tearing him from his mesmerised stupor.

"They're moving," mewled Callahan, her voice an octave higher. "Oh god, we have to leave, Xander. They're fucking moving. *Moving*. Tell me you see it as well."

Xander stumbled over his words. He had never felt so exposed. Then he remembered the figure in the distance and was instantly terrified by what was out there. Tendrils of poisonous doubt wormed their way up his spine and nestled within his brain as he fought the urge to turn and run.

"Zhou, come in," Callahan spoke into her comms, but there was no answer. "Zhou," she tried again. She was about to try a third time when Xander's wrist unit sprang to life.

Harriet: Hurry Xander.

"You might want to ask her what the hell's going—" Callahan's words were cut off by a series of rusty, wet squeals somewhere behind them.

Through swirling pillars of dense fog, that same humanoid figure took shape again. It was difficult to gauge its distance, but Xander knew it had gotten closer. The strange mass shimmered and flexed, its body contorting. As it continued its choked babbling, it edged ever closer, but still the fog masked its features.

Somewhere behind it, the shuttle roared to life.

"No, Zhou, can you hear me? Don't you dare! Don't you—" cried Callahan, but all she received was static before the sound of thrusters blanketed the air. There was a rumble as the ship zipped by overhead, kicking up swirls of dirt and fog, and they were left with the awful wails of whatever was out there.

Xander hurriedly typed into his wrist unit.

Harri. Can't get in. Open the landing bay airlock.

"We need to move. Whatever it is, it's heading right for us," said Callahan, all thoughts of the panel far from her mind.

As the figure grew closer, strange, wispy tendrils took shape all over its body, loose and trailing in the wind. Faint, wet slaps struck the floor with each labored step as its body pulsed menacingly.

Xander checked his wrist unit—nothing.

"Xander, come on." Callahan pulled at his arm, urging him to move, fully aware that any attempt to flee would be far slower than either would like.

Another figure formed behind the first one, then another. Before they knew it, there was an entire group of these strange things, all sluggishly converging on them.

Xander and Callahan were about to flee when the airlock door slid open with a hiss.

Xander spun. "Harri?"

Someone in an EVA suit, not dissimilar to theirs, stood in the entryway. "Inside, quick," came an old, worn voice.

Xander and Callahan didn't argue; they practically threw themselves in.

The old man glared out at the figures that slowly shuffled their way forward then, with a sigh, closed the door.

"What were they?" asked Xander, scrambling to his feet. Beside him, Callahan lay frozen like a statue.

"Those things? They're not of our reality," said the old man.

"Xander ..." whimpered Callahan.

Xander ignored her. "Not of this reality? What's that supposed to mean?"

"Xander ..." Callahan said again.

The old man sighed and removed his helmet. He had to be in his sixties, wispy, gray hair hanging limply, framing a haggard face, worry lines and age combining to show someone who must have been through hell. "Temporal displacement. Outlying mitigations in matter transition caused them to come back with us, and—"

"*Xander!*" screamed Callahan.

He spun to see her gaze fixed on the body of a person, or what was left of them. Their lower back, along with a trailing leg, was all that was visible, the rest disappearing into the wall. It was as though they had tried to run right through only to get stuck halfway. No doubt it was that same person whose fingers they had seen outside.

Xander reeled on the old man and grabbed the scruff of his suit. "What the hell happened here?"

Unmoved, perhaps expecting this, the old man remained limp and stared at the airlock door.

"*Answer me!*"

The old man's focus shifted. "The Eldridge phased."

"Phased?"

It's what we're studying here, a way to phase through reality, negating the need for extensive bouts of space travel. We've been trying it for years, going back as far as the Philadelphia Experiment and Operation Causeway. We thought we'd cracked it, but the Eldridge's structure became unstable and, well ..." He motioned to the trapped person. "My name's Doctor Stein. You want answers? Come with me. It'll be easier to explain once we're safely back in my refuge. I promise you all the answers you want."

"They're still fucking moving," mewled Callahan, eyes still set on the person. "Tell me how they're moving?"

Calmly, the old man knelt beside her. "My dear, poor Doctor Datsun there, he's melded with the structure. There was a series of aftershocks, and we shifted as he fled one of those creatures. When the Eldridge finally set, the unfortunate fellow happened to be exactly where this wall was. Tragic, really. Now, here's the thing—it hasn't cut him in two. He is in one piece, but now he's melded. He's inside there, his body and this structure as one. There's quite a few with this issue, some somehow still with us, others mercifully not, though I will say those that still are certainly aren't conscious like you or I."

"Is there any way to get him out?" asked Xander, forcing a lump in his throat back down. Instinctively, he checked his wrist unit to still see it blank.

"Not without great risk to ourselves, I'm afraid. It was a minor miracle we made it back at all. I dare not tempt fate a second time. Besides ..."

"Besides what?"

"Well, I believe scrambled would be the most accurate description for what he would be afterwards. I hardly recommend it."

"Where's Harriet? She's my wife—"

"Ex-wife," said Callahan, somewhat calmer.

"Whatever, she's in here somewhere. We've been communicating. I need to get to her."

A clunking noise like the patter of heavy rain slapped across the airlock, followed by a series of faint, wet groans.

"I don't recommend we stay here. I'm afraid there may still be one or two of these creatures within the facility, but if we keep quiet, we should be all right. I shall warn you, though, if we do come across one, I implore you to avoid it like the plague. They're radioactive beyond anything of our world. Even the slightest contact would unravel your DNA and render you nothing more than mush within seconds. Doctor Keegan was the last to encounter one, and well, let's just say we needed a mop to dispose of him afterwards. Now, please, if you will, my refuge?"

"Harriet, she was in charge of communications here. I'm really keen to check in and make sure she's OK," said Xander.

"You have my word, if you come with me, I promise I will lead you back to her."

The trip to the refuge was a grim pilgrimage, but at least they didn't encounter any more creatures. However, Xander and Callahan did bear witness to the devastating aftermath of a whole host of frightful ends. While many were due to being melded into the structure—walls and floors displaying hellish, writhing murals, their various limbs and body parts now part of the Eldridge—others were no more than unrecognisable, sloppy messes.

A number of times Xander had to stop, his stomach churning with each awful sight. It was a feeling compounded by the growing concern he held for Harriet's safety.

Please be OK, Harri. Please be OK, was all he could think, this repeated thought a mantra, chugging along inside his head.

She had hinted at some of these atrocities in her covert messages, but to see them up close and in such vibrancy chilled him to his very core. Never in his wildest dreams had he expected things to be this bad.

Again, he checked his wrist unit, apprehension building at the lack of response. "Doctor Stein, what about my wife?"

The doctor seemed distracted as he studied a darkened corridor.

"Doctor?"

With a huff, he said, "Do you seek annihilation? Or will you let me inspect the route before we end up charging head first into one of those things? Look, I assure you, Mr. Langley, she's fine. Now, my refuge is just down the next corridor. Things escalated rather quickly here once the creatures appeared. Many of us became separated. But fortunately for us, I've managed to construct quite the stronghold."

"How many of you are there?" asked Callahan.

"Ah, now, along with yourself and Mr. Langley, I count our number to be four. Well, three and a half."

Their faces dropped.

"Yes, unfortunately only myself remains of our little faction. Rogers won't be much help to anyone. Originally, we were made up of a number of scientists and engineers, you know, pragmatists. Everyone had their own idea on what to do. So, naturally, that led to a whole host of failed attempts to correct our dour situation, until, eventually, only myself remained."

"But you said you were taking me to Harriet. You said she was with you," said Xander, his features tensing.

"No, no, I said I can point you in the right direction. I never said she was with me. Now, if you please, it's imperative we get inside. These creatures, they like to roam, and I fear we've already announced our presence."

Xander wasn't listening. He was ready to throttle Stein, until Callahan cut in front of him. "Thank you, professor," she said in the hope of leading Xander away from doing something he would regret.

"Doctor. I'm a doctor."

She gritted her teeth. "All right, *doctor*. But what happens once we're inside? We'd be essentially trapping ourselves, wouldn't we? It's not like we've got anywhere to go?"

"Your shuttle won't have gotten far. I'm assuming your pilot is trying to leave without you, am I correct? Not very selfless of them, I must say. Well, they should still be within signal range. If you'd be so kind as to give me the shuttle's system code, I can patch in via our retrieval system—"

"Retrieval system?"

"Yes, a function installed in case anyone got cold feet. It's a way we can bring them back in."

"Wait, cold feet? What the hell is this place?" asked Callahan.

Stein ignored the last part. "It'll mean we can remotely recall the shuttle. At least that way we can all get out of here."

A wet wheeze echoed down the corridor.

"Ah," said Stein. "That's our cue to move."

Once inside, they removed their helmets and took in the room, while Stein resealed the entrance. It was the communications center, with a console and hologram display of the facility in the middle. Along the walls were more consoles, some familiar, some practically alien in nature.

But nothing could prepare them for what was next. Beside them stood a tall man. His features were gaunt, as though he had not eaten in days. His eyes were glazed, his mouth opening and closing, giving the expression of a goldfish at feeding time. It took them a moment to understand, but the back half of his head and shoulders were inside the wall.

"Ah, take no notice of Mr. Rogers, here," said Stein, and tilted a bottle of water into his mouth. "He's no trouble. Though, I will concede he's more of a pet these days."

Callahan tugged at Xander's arm. "This is all kinds of fucked. What do you make of this guy?" she whispered as Stein's back was turned.

Xander glanced at his wrist unit. "I can't weigh up if it's some kind of deception or he's just flat-out bat shit."

"Agreed, and I don't know which is worse. This place is nightmare fuel. Do you think he really knows where Harri is?"

Xander's jaw tensed. "He'd better."

"Well, something's been bugging me, and I think I've just worked it out. He used your last name, Xander."

"So? He probably got it from Harri."

"Sorry, Xander, but you're divorced. There's no way she's using Langley."

Xander was about to call to Stein when his wrist unit lit up.

Harriet: Stay there, I'll be with you soon.

Doctor Stein turned back and smiled. "Now, the code? I know I said I'd provide answers, but this is surely more pressing, wouldn't you agree?"

Xander and Callahan side-eyed one another, their thoughts on the same wavelength. After a tense moment, Xander said, "Alpha, six, eight, six, zero, delta."

"I thank you." Stein typed the code into the center console. "There, that seems to have done the trick. I'm afraid it's merely a waiting game now, so why not pass the time."

"OK," Xander said. "So, about Har—"

"Reinsert principle."

"Reinsert principle?"

“Yes, that’s why things are as they are. We didn’t take it into account. We phased as planned. Our aim, a distant, uninhabited place on the far side of Jupiter. Only once the coils were charged—those copper things you encountered, to generate the power needed—there were a series of malfunctions, and before we could switch it off, we found ourselves phasing, not only through time and space but through dimensions, as well.

“We tried to stop it—while your wife did her best to warn the top brass—but by the time we managed to shut down the coils and dispel the excess power, we were somewhere we really shouldn’t have been.”

“Where did you end up?” asked Callahan.

“We’d traveled the entire length of the cosmos, and then some. We were at the end ... Or the beginning. It really was difficult to tell. But there was this, well, a colossus is the simplest way to describe it. An all-seeing eye, a harbinger of all things chaotic and malevolent. Not to be hyperbolic, but, simply put, this being was madness personified. Anyone who gazed up at it we instantly lost to its influence. It tore through the facility, scything and decimating at will. The destruction you no doubt saw upon entry was the result of this god-like colossus. It was truly a force like no other. Those creatures you’ve seen, they were of this thing. Now they roam the facility only for mayhem’s sake. Life seems to be an affront to them.

“Needless to say, panic set in. I mean, wouldn’t you panic? There were nearly two hundred personnel stationed here, and we lost almost half right away to that behemoth, more to those creatures, and the rest due to the phasing. In our haste to get away, though risky, I sought to return us to our initial phase point. But I negated the planet’s orbit when implementing the reinsert principle.” Stein brought up a hologram of the facility on the main console. While the two levels above ground were mostly a standard shade of grey, the section that had been destroyed, along with three sublevels, were marked red.

"The planet moved, and we wound up some distance from our origin point." He paused a moment to let the implication fill the room. "My miscalculation killed everyone in the lower levels. When we emerged, there was solid rock beneath us. No one down there stood a chance." He stood and trickled more water into Rogers's mouth.

Neither Xander nor Callahan could speak. They looked to Rogers, who only gawped as water dribbled down his chin.

Eventually, Xander spoke. "Doctor, this is all awful, and I hate to sound like a broken record." He took a stifled breath and gritted his teeth. "But Harriet, the only person I'm here for, the only person I give a damn about, where is she? She's meant to be on her way here. I've let you go on, let you lead us into your web, hell, even let you feed your pet goldfish, all while waiting patiently. Now please, for the love of fucking Christ, will you tell me where my wife is?"

"He's *not* a goldfish."

"Doctor Stein, *please.*"

Stein looked Xander up and down. "Fine. I was hoping to do this painlessly, but if you're going to insult Mr. Rogers, then—"

The comms station blared to life. Zhou's voice crackled through. "What the hell is this? Let me go."

Callahan flicked the comms switch. "Zhou, you prick, you were gonna leave us."

"Cal? Shit. I didn't want to, but something was trying to get in the shuttle. I panicked."

"Save it. We're bringing you in. Wait for us this time."

"But Cal, something's—"

"Save it," Callahan said, and severed the comms.

"So, where were we?" said Xander, still staring down Stein.

Stein side-eyed Cal, who now faced him too. With a sigh, he said, "Long story short, she's dead."

Callahan expected Xander to buckle, but still he stared at Stein.

"Impossible. I've been communicating with her," he said, and tapped his wrist unit. "She's on her way to us right now."

Stein pursed his lips. "Well, that's not strictly true, I'm afraid. I assumed you'd already worked it out, but it seems love truly is blind." He lifted his sleeve to reveal Harriet's wrist unit. "Yes, duplicitous, I know, but I had to maintain your interest."

Xander stood frozen. The entire room was closing in.

Stein carried on. "She ventured out around a week ago, while we were still suffering the aftershocks. I don't believe she trusted in my practices and chose to spend her final days in her own quarters. Comfort, I believe it stifles even the most acute of minds. Anyway, once I discovered her passing, I retrieved the unit and contacted you. It was the only way to communicate without alerting the overseers; they certainly wouldn't want any of what's gone on here to get out, so a stealth extraction was my only option. Just know I truly am—"

Xander threw himself forward and swung his fist against Stein's temple. The doctor's head snapped sideways, and he stumbled back. Before Stein could regain himself, Xander struck him again, his fist smashing into Stein's jaw. Stein fell to the ground and immediately curled up as a barrage of frenzied punches rained down.

"Xander!" screamed Callahan, and tried to pull him away.

Xander shook her off and carried on his assault. "You just left her there?" he roared as tears began to well.

"She'll still be there. Please, I can show you. Please. Stop," Stein tried to say as he weathered another flurry.

Xander paused, a fist still raised. “Show me. You agree to show me where she is and I'll let you get up.”

Cowering, Stein said, “Her quarters, they’re on the other side of the facility.”

“Xander,” tried Callahan, again, softer this time. “Listen, we’re not even meant to be here. If she’s, you know, maybe we should just—”

“I have to see her,” said Xander, and slumped beside Stein. “I have to know. We didn’t end on good terms. Cal, I need to see her one last time, even if it’s just to say I’m sorry.”

Callahan shook her head. Her unease was palpable. “Xander, the shuttle will be here any minute. I’m sorry, but it’s a detour we can’t afford to make.”

Xander rose to his feet and looked to the hologram floor plan. “Then if I’m not back by the time you’re set, go without me.”

“But, Xan—”

“It’s non-negotiable. I’ll meet you at the drop ship. If I don’t make it, give Zhou a good slap from me.”

Stein shakily sat up and wiped blood from his mouth. “Perhaps this will save the trip,” he said, and crawled over to the center console. He pressed a few buttons, and a camera feed displaying Harriet’s quarters appeared in the holographic interface.

Xander’s chest hitched.

“Yes, abhorrent, isn’t it? I believe they thought the worst of the aftershocks were over when they decided to slip away, human nature and all that. If only they’d stayed; it’s only really this room that’s any sort of Faraday cage. Well, minus the outside walls, of course,” Stein said, glancing at Rogers. “I did try to warn them, but, well ...”

Xander didn’t hear; his focus was on the interface. In a bed lay Harriet and another man, their bodies entwined and distorted to create a single, grotesque being. Their faces were conjoined at the cheek, their features meshed as one. A host of limbs, impossible to assign, reached out, spread wide.

"Xander," said Callahan, her shock causing her own voice to quiver.

Xander didn't answer. He could only stare at the image. It was as though he was a skipping record, trapped in his own awful stasis.

"Yes, they'd been seeing a lot of each other leading up to the experiment," said Stein. "Like a couple of teenagers, it really was quite sickening."

"Not helping, doctor," said Callahan.

An alert flashed on the console: SHUTTLE DOCK SUCCESSFUL

"Xander," Callahan said again, more assuredly, and squeezed his elbow.

The world fell back into view, and Xander turned to Callahan. "I, erm, I think we should leave."

It was then they realized Doctor Stein had already slipped away.

Xander and Callahan charged their way down darkened corridors, ignoring the weak grasps of hanging arms that reached from the walls and ceiling. With their helmets on at the ready, a wet gurgle came from around the corner.

One of the creatures shuffled into view, and Xander almost didn't stop. Callahan was quick to yank him away, using his momentum to swing him back around.

The creature was so much worse up close, a walking, living disease that reeked of death and ruin. Yet there was an uncanniness to its movements despite the dozens of wispy tendrils dancing all along its body. Though slowly shuffling, as though walking wounded, it had what could be considered the usual human extremities, joints and all. The shape of a face was even vaguely visible, though it was a detestable mess. As it lumbered on, lumps of discolored flesh oozed away, sliding off its soggy body, leaving a gruesome trail in its wake.

"Shit, the airlock's on the other side," said Xander. "We need to get to Zhou before Stein tells him to take off." He still carried the look of someone lost, but more and more he was understanding the need for survival.

"Zhou, come in," Callahan pleaded into her comms, only to be greeted with the hiss of vacant static. "Shit. Wait, what about the ruins?"

"Ruins?"

"Where the facility had been destroyed, remember, we saw it while we were landing? It'll lead right outside. It should only be a few hundred yards. Maybe there'll be somewhere we can climb through?" she said as they backed away.

"Good a place as any, I guess. Come on," said Xander, doubling back. "For what it's worth, Cal, I'm sorry I dragged you both into this."

"You didn't hold a gun to our heads, Xander. Just, maybe learn to let go next time, yeah? No more keeping your head buried in the sand."

They were panting, the exertion of running in their EVA suits taking its toll.

They were almost to the ruins when another flash of static deafened their comms.

"*Oh shit, oh shit!*" came the grainy voice of Zhou.

Callahan paused. "Zhou? What? What's—"

An awful cry pierced their ears, but before they could react, it abruptly cut off.

The entire facility shook, causing both to stumble to their hands and knees. The sound of moans and crunching rubble echoed all around.

"I'm sorry," Xander tried to shout, but Callahan could only cry out as the ground beneath her shook.

Doctor Stein surged past, almost tripping over Xander. He didn't stop, made no attempt to lessen his haste. "It's here! It's followed us! Oh Christ, it's followed us!" he cried over his shoulder. "We have to get away from it before it can—" His voice trailed off as he disappeared out of sight.

"He's headed back to his lab," said Callahan. "He's going to phase us."

They clamored to their feet just as the entire roof ripped away, raining down rubble and gory pulp. Atmosphere rushed into the open space, causing the corridor to transform into the eye of a storm.

Xander dove for cover, doing his best to ignore the painful thumps of debris striking his body. He turned to see Callahan stood, gazing out the cavernous hole above them. At whatever was staring back.

Her eyes were wild, disconnected. Words wouldn't form, and when Xander reached for her, she snarled and pulled back. A darkness had overtaken her, and with her mind lost, she cackled, resisting Xander's grip. She outstretched her arms as one of the creatures emerged from the corridor beside them.

"Cal, please, come on, Cal," Xander pleaded, tears forming.

But she wouldn't move; she only cackled and babbled.

"Don't you know? Don't you know?" she repeated between flurries of indecipherable chants.

A huge rumble rattled the glass of Xander's helmet as whatever towered above unleashed a bassy growl. He resisted the urge to look up, as tempting as it was. Its aura was all-encompassing, oppressing, oozing pure malevolence.

He pleaded one last time to Callahan, but it was hopeless. She was lost. The smaller creature in the hallway shuffled closer still. Mere feet away now.

With no other choice, Xander turned. He didn't want to see what came next. But when he went to step away, he found he couldn't move.

He peered down to see his leading foot had sunk into the floor. Doctor Stein had started the machine, and there was nowhere to run. Xander fought to free himself, but it was like fighting against quicksand. Again and again he tried to pull away, resisting the urge to push with his hands.

Beside him, Callahan screamed. Her screams still sang with that god-awful cackle even as they descended into gargles, putting an abrupt end to her madness.

Xander did his best to ignore his partner's death throes. Like a mouse in a trap, he mustered one final lunge, but it was useless. From his own momentum, he lost balance. The floor rushed to meet him, and all that was left to wonder was how it would feel. Would it hurt? Would it be quick? Who would be waiting for him when the end finally came?

No grand slideshow of his life flashed before his eyes when his face sank into the floor, only a few final seconds of nothing that seemed to last a lifetime. There was no lingering thought of Harriet, nor Callahan or Zhou. There was nothing but the long, labored sting of trepidation.

Then it was over.

SKIN

Blaine Daigle

An ocean of stars twinkled and shimmered across a black canvas outside the viewing platform, while a metronomic *beep* was birthed and lost in the vast, metallic space of the ship. Cold air filled the space in steady breaths from the ventilation systems, the smooth, metal surfaces dull and lifeless in the artificial light. The space was bare, and what few items did exist outside of the stationary chairs and monitors were held in place only by the gravity systems built into the ship's electrical systems.

For Roy Arastey, the room just felt cold and dead, the only sign of life beside his own being the subtle feeling of descent as the ship, the *IDE Clover*, slowly dropped from the thin atmosphere of the mining planet below. The rock surface of Ethera-2722 awaited his landing platforms as he took long breaths of cold, sterile air and stared upward to the stars above.

He was at the farthest extent of humanity's long understanding, a spot in space known as The Reach. This area, seemingly between galaxies at the edge of the Andromeda, was quiet, unadorned with inhabited planetary colonies. Rather, it was just dead rocks floating lifelessly through the void like jellyfish in a black ocean. Ethera-2722 was the only planet humanity had attempted to settle this far out, and that was only ten years ago. It was a mining colony, meant not so much to pull minerals but to simply see if that area of space was even worth the costly investment.

Roy reached to his ears and activated the voice recorder on his headset, hearing the soft *beep* kick the device on and signify what he was saying was being recorded and broadcast to his superiors monitoring the mission.

Not that it really mattered. The results of the mission were already concluded. Ethera couldn't sustain life, even with the atmospherics installed in the colonies. When the radio went silent and transmissions stopped coming six weeks back, a thermal reading from a surveillance drone showed no signs of life within the colony. The conclusion was already understood; they just needed someone to certify them. Someone already out in space. Someone with a small ship that didn't need a crew. Someone who didn't care about potentially not returning home because there was nothing for them to return to.

Someone like Roy.

Roy moved down the halls of the ship, passing by empty dorms that hadn't slept a soul in years. He hadn't had a crew since the accident, since the simple mistake of a missed reading had caused the living quarters to flood with carbon dioxide while Roy slept peacefully in the captain's chair, oblivious to the death befalling those he was in charge of.

He shook his head, trying to dissolve the memory. It didn't matter now anyway. Nobody would ever die under his watch again because there would be nobody under his watch again. Now, he existed as little more than a cheap hire—someone who would go on jobs others wouldn't, the deal sweetened by no risk of a lost crew.

Only one man.

"This is Captain Roy Arastey of the *IDE Clover* reporting in. The date is March 13th, 2329, and I am in active descent toward the surface of Ethera-2722. Primary mission objective remains to locate any survivors of Ethera Mining Colony Alpha and provide escort back to Andromeda Checkpoint 3288. Secondary objective remains to collect samples of rock and mineral ore as well as atmospheric residue to determine environmental causes for colony failure. Current distance from surface at seventeen meters, closing at 1.4 meters per second. Requesting final confirmation to land."

The radio crackled with static, and for a while, Roy actually began to doubt whether he would actually get the clearance. For all he knew, nobody had received his message. All the technological advancements of a civilization, and there they were, still reliant on obsolete tech from three centuries ago.

That was if anyone was listening in the first place.

"Repeat, this is Roy Arastey of the *IDE Clover* requesting final clearance to land on Ethera-2722. Currently at eleven meters and closing."

The radio crackled, and a dull, lifeless voice filtered through the speakers.

"Clearance confirmed for landing on Ethera-2722."

Roy smirked. Of course, an artificial voice. Nobody was listening to him. Nobody cared. There was no living soul watching over him, only the cold and lifeless AI that worked the jobs they couldn't find actual people to do. It was only marginally better than the silent apathy he expected to receive, but it was a level of apathy nonetheless.

Yet even the confirmation of his expectation did not stop the chill from working its way down his back at just how alone he really was as the landing platforms touched down on the rocky surface of the planet. He held on as the vibrations of landing shook through the craft and listened as the computer ran through its diagnostic checks before another solitary beep confirmed all systems were good to go.

He reached the exterior hatch and dressed himself. The gravity on Ethera was nearly twice that of Earth, so a specialized suit designed to reduce and disperse the pressure was required for travel. The helmet was light as well, hooked to an automatic rebreather system that took the traces of oxygen in Ethera's atmosphere and converted it into breathable air.

"All checks completed," said the robotic voice of Mission Command. "Is there anything else you need, captain?"

Roy chuckled. How nice. "Run diagnostic check for heat signatures," he said, tightening the latch that connected his helmet to the rest of his suit.

"Diagnostic check has already been run," the machine responded. "No life forms detected."

"Run them again. I don't like surprises."

He finished securing the rest of the latches along the suit as the distinct hum of the ship's machinery filled the silence around him.

"Diagnostic complete. Confirmed. No life forms."

Roy nodded. "So be it."

He pressed the button on the wall, and a hiss of pressurized air filled the room as the door loosed and slid open to reveal the hard surface of the planet. Jagged, black rocks that shone like crystals jutted from the cracked stone surface. Across the rocky expanse, the colony sat a ghost in the distance. Roy could hear the machinery running, could see the lights engaged at the entrances to the mines, but knew there was nobody there.

He stepped off the platform and onto the planet, feeling the immediate change in gravity as he did. The suit clicked to life, adjusting for the new change. He paused and let it work, the pressure slowly lifting as it was dispersed around him. Within a minute, he felt as though we was on Earth again—a foreign feeling given he hadn't been home in almost fifteen years.

He moved across the dark planet toward the colony. EMC-Alpha was a standard colony comprised of four single-story buildings lined with thick, tinted glass. It was laid out in the middle of what was assumed to be a crater as it was cheaper than trying to crack the hard mineral stones of Ethera's crust. *Typical of humanity*, thought Roy. *Why do the work yourself when you can let a meteor do it for you?*

But the real colony was below the surface. With the hard crust already destroyed by the meteor, the softer underlayer was exposed, and cracking through that was easier. The colony went down five floors: the top two dedicated to scientific and technical wings designed to keep the operations going, the middle two reserved for living quarters, and the bottom operating the electronics and the oxygen levels of the colony. Preliminary scans when the colony had stopped communicating indicated that each of those levels was devoid of life. Cold and hollow. Subsequent scans showed the same.

Even as Roy approached, he turned on the infrared scanner in his helmet and saw nothing but cool blue across all four structures. As he walked closer, he felt an uneasiness rake its nails across his skin.

"Command?" he asked.

"Yes, captain?" replied the artificial voice.

"Run electrical and oxygen diagnostic."

"Specific parameters?"

"Look for elevated levels of carbon dioxide or nitrogen in the air. Maybe ..." His voice trailed off. The memory returned, stopping him in his tracks.

"Captain?"

"Maybe there was a malfunction in the machinery and it flooded the colony with toxic gases. If I can get those readings, it would confirm what happened."

"Official protocol is to record evidence."

"I know, but I don't want to walk in there and see bodies all over the fucking place if I don't have to."

The sharpness in his voice surprised him. For a moment, he forgot he was talking to a machine, an artificial mind that didn't care about what had happened to him before. For a moment, he forgot he was alone on this desolate rock.

Command was silent for a while but then returned. "Oxygen levels normal. CO2 levels normal. Nitrogen levels normal."

Roy exhaled. It didn't provide many answers outside of what *didn't* happen, but it was an answer he was happy to receive.

"Understood," he said. "Continuing approach."

When he arrived at the colony, he immediately looked for any debris, anything that might signify an explosion or extreme malfunction. But there was nothing scattered around, nothing aside from the fine, black mineral dust that sat atop the cold rock. He glanced over to one of the many mines dug into the side of the crater then flipped on the infrared again and again saw nothing but blue.

But maybe.

"Command? How far into the crust can the life sensors reach?"

"Probes from outer atmosphere can push through 80 percent of mineral structure. Inner atmosphere can push through 100 percent of mineral structure."

"So they aren't in the mines."

"Not according to preliminary and follow scans."

"Ok. Preparing to enter colony structure."

Roy moved to the door and activated the opening mechanism. It opened slowly, revealing little by little the empty room within. Metallic structures—tables, chairs, walls lined with digital boards still operating—all lined the confined space. Roy walked the room but saw nothing. Nothing out of place. Nothing sprayed messily across the floor. It was just an empty control room, a blank space effectively dead yet still operating under the guise of life. He continued his search and found nothing.

"Control area secure ... Wait."

Something caught his eye, something on the far wall next to a digital readout. From his vantage point it looked like ... rust? But that was impossible; the entirety of the structure's interior was composed of stainless material.

But the closer he got, he saw it wasn't rust.

It was blood.

"Control, I have verification of blood."

He leaned in, trying to make out the shape of what was on the wall. It was smeared, clearly dragged across the walls by what looked like a hand. But the spread was inconstant as if whoever had done it had struggled to keep the pressure as they did so. For a few moments, he traced over the design, trying to connect dots and pieces until the message finally became clear.

SKIN

"Command, run atmospheric diagnostic. Look for anything airborne outside of natural parameters."

"Oxygen levels normal..."

"No, not that. I think there might be something that causes problems when exposed to skin."

"Please stand by."

Roy turned his head toward the elevator. A new coldness overtook him, and he was grateful he had the suit. His skin still crawled at the sight of the blood spread across the walls, the cryptic message clearly written long ago yet seemingly so fresh.

He pressed the call button, and the mechanical whir of the elevator filled the quiet as the car came up from the lower levels, which meant that the last time the elevator had been used was someone leaving this area and going down. Was it the person who wrote the message on the wall? Someone else? As far as Roy knew, he was the only person who had been sent to investigate the vanishing communications of the colony. But how much did he really know?

"Command, diagnostic update."

"No airborne anomalies detected."

The elevator arrived, and Roy got in. He went to press a button to go down and froze. A bloody fingerprint was plastered over the 3rd level button. Whoever wrote the message had gone down to the third level.

Roy followed suit.

The elevator descended deeper into the compound, and the wide-open windows became featureless walls bathed in artificial light. The car stopped at level 3, and Roy stepped out into the living quarters. A long hallway lined with doors opened up before him, the harsh light above still humming and shining, throwing a sterile glow down upon the space. Roy switched from internal communication to external and called out.

"Hello?"

There was no answer aside from the mechanical hum of the compound's systems. For a moment, he considered taking off the helmet. The atmospherics were normal, and he was starting to get claustrophobic inside the suit. But he remembered the message.

SKIN

"Command, diagnostic update."

"No airborne anomalies detected."

"Run it again."

"Please stand by."

"Fuck," he said, and with careful steps, he moved down the hallway. He stopped at the first door to his right and pressed the opening mechanism. The door slid open sideways.

There was so much blood inside the room.

Roy staggered at the sight. At the center of what was a living space for the small quarters, a body lay on the floor. For a moment, Roy struggled to make out the twisted mass of bone and tissue, but then he realized that whomever this was had their skin removed completely. Roy was looking at a skinless corpse. Muscle hung loosely and sagged with time from bones that were starting to change color from shock white to dull gray. The floors were covered in blood, and the corpse's eyes stared wide and lifeless from the exposed skull.

Roy fought the urge to vomit, reminding himself he couldn't afford to take off his helmet, especially when thinking about both the message and the condition of the corpse.

"Command! Diagnostic status!" he said, his heavy breathing fogging up his visor.

"Please stand by."

Roy stumbled out of the room. Against his better judgement, he moved down the hall, checking the rooms as he went. Inside each of them, a similar scene awaited him. Some individuals, some couples. Occasional families with both large and small bodies. He thought about having found his own crew, poisoned by the very air they had breathed while he had slept unaware. They had been so still, so peaceful. The only indicators they were dead were the lack of breathing and eyelids that were destined to forever remain asleep.

But this ... this was different. Worse.

What the fuck had done this?

"Command! Diagnostic status!"

"Please stand ..."

"Don't fucking tell me to stand by!"

"Please stand by."

He needed to get out of there. Something horrible had happened, and for all he knew was *still* happening. He had his answers, well enough of them to satisfy a report. Command could send a full team to evaluate what he found. This was beyond whatever expertise he possessed. Whoever had come down here from the top level was probably in pieces all over the place.

He began heading back to the elevator when something hit him from behind, knocking him over. He hit the ground and rolled onto his back, turning to see what hit him.

It was a man.

Wide-eyed and panicked, blood drenched his work uniform. Deep, heavy breathing interrupted any attempted communication. His mouth contorted as though trying to figure out how to speak, how to make words exist outside his mind. Roy stared back.

Finally, the man spoke. "Please! We have to get out of here!"

Roy stumbled to his feet and pushed away from the man. Involuntarily, he found himself scanning the exposed skin—face, hands, wrists—looking for any signs of what he had seen inside the rooms. But there was nothing. Sure, the man was covered in blood, but there didn't seem to be a source.

"Please!" he cried again.

Something moved from farther within the quarters—a rattling sound, moving furniture sliding across metallic floors. Roy froze as the man's breathing grew even faster. The sound was moving all around them. In the walls. The ceiling.

They were not alone.

"Please," said the man. "We have to get out of here, now!"

A crash in the distance.

"Command," said Roy, "diagnostic update."

"Please stand by."

There was another crash, followed by the telltale sounds of scurrying, something moving quickly across the floor. The walls around him started to shake in small tremors. The ceiling above slightly buckled in spots. Whatever was in there with them was on the move.

"Let's go," said Roy. He helped the man to his feet, and together, they ran to the elevator.

The sounds intensified. It was moving quicker.

Roy pressed the button to open the elevator, pulled the man through the doors as they opened, and almost punched the button to return to the top floor.

At the end of the long hall, something crashed into view just as the elevator ascended upward, something that resembled a mass of organic material, red and fleshy and rolling over itself as it fell into view. But it was gone as soon as it appeared, relegated to the floor below as the elevator moved upward. But Roy had seen enough of it to freeze his blood.

They arrived at the control room on the top floor. Roy helped the survivor out and hurried to the hatch that led outside. But as he went to press the button to disengage the hatch, he realized the man didn't have a helmet and wouldn't be able to breathe, not to mention that his lack of suit meant the walk back to the *Clover* would be impossible. If he didn't freeze, he would suffocate as the gravity would slow him down far beyond breath-holding capabilities.

They were stuck. Roy paced across the room, trying to figure out the next step. There were more than likely some variation of the suits in the mines, but that walk was just as treacherous as the walk to the ship. There was another suit back in the *Clover*. He could run back to the ship, grab it, and bring it back to the man. He would have to make the trek on foot as there wasn't nearly enough flat ground in the immediate area of the compound for Roy to land.

It was his best play.

"Listen, I have to leave now ..."

"What? No! No, don't leave me!"

"I don't have a choice. You won't make it without a suit, and I'm not going back down to get one here. The best option is my ship."

"You can't leave me here!"

"I'm not going to leave you. I promise, OK? I'm not going to leave you."

The man looked up at him with heavy eyes, eyes that seemed almost alien with how wide they stretched. The color dull, pupils dilated and deep black. Something wasn't quite right with them. Roy remembered he still hadn't gotten clarification on any airborne pathogens that might attack someone's skin.

But he had seen something down there, something that resembled a rolling mass of tissue. Something that *had* to be responsible for what had happened at the colony.

"What's your name?" Roy asked.

For a moment, the man didn't answer. His mouth hung slightly open like a curious dog.

"I'm Captain Roy Arastey," Roy said. "What's your name?"

The man's mouth shook as though he was trying to speak but something was holding him back.

"I need you to listen," Roy said. "I'm going to go back to my ship and grab you a suit. I promise I will be right back. I won't leave you."

The man stared at him with those wide eyes a moment longer, and then solemnly nodded his head.

Roy returned the nod and stood back up, turning to face the hatch.

Then Command beeped to life.

"Diagnostic complete. Unknown organic anomaly detected."

Roy froze, the new update lingering in his ears even seconds after he heard it.

Organic.

He had been so focused on the concept of something airborne that he hadn't even considered the possibility of an *organic* threat.

Something living.

Something from the mines, maybe.

He thought of the thing that had crashed into view in the living quarters. It had been organic. Biological. It was moving.

Command was reading it now. Had it crawled up? Would he return to find the survivor yet another victim of whatever it was?

"Location?"

"Two meters."

Roy's arms and legs went numb, and he turned slowly back to the survivor, the unnamed man he had carried all the way up to the exit.

The man's skin was retreating from his face, revealing a bloodied skull beneath. The skin from his arms bubbled and rolled as it seemingly came to life and slid down his body to the floor below. Roy felt a sharp rise of panic at the realization of what was happening. The absent eyes, the almost unworking mouth–whatever this was, it had been imitating human skin, wearing the corpse like a suit and animating it to get Roy to bring it up.

And now the disguise was up.

Roy retreated until his back hit the door. The skin crawled across the floor toward him, and he blindly felt around for the release button for the hatch. His heart racing, his hand slammed violently against anything and everything that might have been the button, but the signal never sounded. The only sound was of his slamming fists on metal.

The skin reached him, and he felt it swarm around his foot. A ripping sound joined his cacophony of screams as it tore open his suit at the ankle and slunk inside. It wrapped around his leg, and an instant searing pain shot through his nerves like lightning. Roy screamed, but there was nobody listening.

"Status update?" asked Command.

Roy howled in pain as the skin slowly worked its way up his body. He could feel it dissolving his skin and taking its place over his throbbing muscles and screaming nerves.

"No! No! Don't!"

"Confirm status?"

The skin reached his face and molded over him like a glove. The pain was intense, more than at any other point in his body. He felt himself melting under the slick and slimy embrace of the being. He felt it slip into his mouth and fill his throat. His whole body convulsed momentarily, violent shakes as what was left of him tried in a final, doomed effort to fight off the skin.

He went still. Slowly, Roy's vision grew black at the edges. His arms moved but not by his own volition. He was a puppet. He could feel his mind slipping away, but for now, he was still aware, still conscious, filled with enough life left to hear his own voice speak, words he had no intention of saying coming from a mouth he hadn't told to open.

"Status report. Multiple survivors in compound. Requesting immediate rescue. Returning to ship now."

No! No, goddammit, no!

Command responded..

"Report confirmed. Relaying information to mission superiors. Thank you for your service, Captain Arastey. Safe travels."

The last thing Roy Arastey felt was his legs move as the hatch opened before him. Across the black, rocky surface he was led, guided by the puppeteer which now pulled his strings. His vision blackened more and more as he watched his ship come into view. What remained of his mind found solace only in the realization that it would hopefully be over soon.

SCREAMS FROM OUTER SPACE

Heather Ann Larson

Hurtling through space, the salvage spaceship *Xenom* was locked in on its final destination. The crew had left the last outpost fifty-six days prior, and they were ready to get the hell off the ship, even if it was only for a day or two. Not only did they need to restock their supplies, but they needed a break from each other. They normally would have been in stasis, but the thermal control broke at their last stop, and there were no parts to be found to fix it. They had finally found something duct tape couldn't fix.

Alerting central command, Charles said, "Base, this is *Xenom*. We are approximately 32,000 meters from our final approach and closing in fast. Do you copy?" The *Xenom's* comm operator, he had been with the ship since its maiden voyage; he knew the ship like the back of his hand.

"*Xenom*, this is base. We copy; 32,000 meters from dock."

The captain, John Houston, stood behind the pilot, watching the screen as they began their approach. "Looks like we're right on target?" he asked.

"Yes, sir, should be a smooth entry," Smith answered. He couldn't stand Houston hovering over his shoulder. He had been on board as long as Charles and had been flying longer than that little piss-ant captain had been alive. He didn't appreciate the man micromanaging his job.

Initiating communication with the outpost, Charles said, "Outpost Zeta, this is *Xenom*. Do you copy? We are on our final approach and will be landing in three minutes." When he received no response, he repeated the message.

A sharp squelch across the radio drew everyone's attention. All six of the members currently on the bridge whipped their heads toward Charles, who was staring in horror at his screen. "Houston, we have a big fuckin' problem here," he said as he backed away from his monitor. "I don't know what that thing is, but I believe it best we hit full reverse thrusters and get the fuck out of Dodge right now."

Houston stomped his way across the bridge, his heavy footsteps vibrating the flooring. "Charles, we just spent the last fifty-six days getting here. Why in the fuck would we ..." He lost his words as the monitor came into view. The screen showed a dust storm on the planet's surface, a swirling of blues and teals set against the black void of space, that concealed the midnight- and pink-colored rock protrusions. But there was something else there as well. That something looked a lot like giant tentacles. Each one had to be five klicks long and well within reach of the outpost. And they were nearing them.

Smith came up behind the men and watched what was happening for a moment before he said, "Son of a bitch. I thought the stories were just that. We best do what Charles says and back the hell out of here. If we get within reach of those things, we're done for."

Turning as if in slow motion, Houston's head took time to catch up to his body, which was rotating toward Smith, as his eyes were glued to the screen. When he finally looked at Smith, understanding lit his eyes. "You guys are fucking with me. That's a good one—mess with the new captain, get him to shit his pants. I'll admit, you had me for a minute or two there. How did you get that video to override the comm monitor?" He shook his head; he couldn't believe they tricked him. He didn't believe himself to be that gullible.

The crew was stunned. The captain could see on the monitor there was something otherworldly out there, and he didn't believe them. He thought it was all one big joke.

Smith decided to take matters into his own hands. Striding back to his controls, he slammed reverse thrusters on full. The ship lurched, its descent stopping abruptly and throwing the crew off their feet. "C'mon, c'mon, c'mon," he muttered repeatedly under his breath. They weren't moving fast enough for his comfort; having already well entered the atmosphere, they had a bit of gravity working against them. The air on that planet wasn't breathable, and nobody was suited. With the outpost not responding, he assumed they were all dead. There would be nobody there to let them in. If they got any closer or didn't back up any faster, those things whipping around on the station were going to grab the ship, and they would be well and truly fucked.

Jumping off the floor and barreling toward Smith, Houston started yelling. "What the actual fuck do you think you're doing, pilot? This is my ship, and I did NOT give you the order to back off. You get this thing back on course or you're done for. I'll make sure you never fly another ship for the rest of your pathetic existence." His face was as red as Mars, and if the situation was a cartoon from the ancient days, he would have steam coming out of his ears.

Spinning around with his fists up, Smith was ready to brawl. He had taken on guys twice his own size and walked away; Houston was three inches shorter, and it was clear the man had never picked up anything heavier than a freeze-dried food packet in his life. Taking in a breath for a retort, Smith stopped short when the ship again lurched, only that time in the wrong direction.

Everybody became frantic. There was a tentacle as thick as a man's torso wrapped around the outer hull. There would be no getting away.

Houston pulled his head out of his ass and realized the gravity of the situation. He ordered everybody to suit up in the event the hull was breached or if they had to evacuate into space. There was a protocol for the situation, and Houston had book smarts. He knew exactly what to do in a simulation. But the simulation was real; he had to pull through or every life lost would be a mark on his record. Being the selfish, smarmy prick he was, he didn't want to look bad. However, he was more worried about his own skin than theirs.

As the last of the personnel was donning suits, which took exactly two minutes and five seconds for everybody to comply, there was a deafening screech as the ship cracked from the pressure the tentacle was exerting. The ship was certain to implode from the trauma.

Houston knew he had to order everybody to launch at that point, and there weren't enough capsules for everybody on board. Having cheap-ass company owners meant cutting costs and paying under the table to pass inspections. He loaded first, picking one of the two fully operational pods, and ordered everybody behind him to find a vehicle to exit in.

Not knowing there wouldn't be enough, all crew members rushed the launch pods, creating a bottleneck in the corridor outside the pod launch dock. During the commotion, somebody was pushed into the control panel, and the door to the inner part of the ship closed. Three people were crushed in the process—one from the door and two from being trampled in the stampede and chaos.

Whipping tentacles lashed out at pods as they attempted escape. Two were snatched from the air, and another five were knocked to the surface by the thrashing appendages. Those were the lucky ones, crushed or slammed into the ground, death immediate and a blessing. One was knocked out of the atmosphere to float through the vacuum of space.

Others weren't so fortunate. Their pods failed to launch or they launched without direction and no way to navigate (more cost-cutting measures ensured that). The suction cups on the tentacles ripped through other pods and suits, explosive decompression and its subsequent consequences taking far longer than the human body should have to endure.

Smith managed to get his pod launched. His controls had steering, but only half his thrusters worked, denying him the ability to evac as fast as he wanted. He did what he could to maneuver around the lashing stalks of the alien arms that continued to grasp for anything they could get hold of. His years of experience gave him an edge the others didn't have, and he dodged swipe after swipe, the small pod rocking crazily.

He felt like he was ten years old again, playing *Asteroids* in his uncle's basement. That arcade game, at least that was what he was told it had been called, had been in his family for over 150 years. His Uncle Hank had taken very good care of it, cleaning out the guts and getting a converter kit so it could be plugged in. Blasting aliens out of space had been his favorite pastime when they went to Uncle Hank's house.

Unfortunately, the pod wasn't equipped with guns, and his steering was getting erratic due to all the lashing limbs. He had launched off the back of the ship, but the *Xenom* having entered the atmosphere, he was on a slow downward trajectory when he came out. With limited boosters, he continued falling. After a collegiate effort to avoid the creature, a tentacle came in contact with his vehicle, and his gradual descent became a rapid one.

His vision was limited as the hit shattered the windshield, the spiderwebs making his view a kaleidoscope of imagery. Blues and teals of the dust thrown up by the creature blended with the dark greens, grays, and deep purples of the monster's thrashing tentacles. Smith got lost in the miasma of colors, entranced with the beauty of his impending end.

The collision detection was still functioning, and he was ripped from his reverie by alarms blaring. With no real way to prepare for a fatal impact, he closed his eyes, hung his head, took a deep breath, and wished for his mother. He had a few seconds to ponder whether or not he would feel anything before he was slammed into the surface.

But his descent suddenly slowed. Opening his eyes one at a time, he felt his pod go from what felt like supersonic speed to near zero in moments.

There was no sound. The alarms had stopped blaring and he could hear nothing of the outside world. While the alarms had been overstimulating, the silence was deafening. Looking out the destroyed windshield didn't help as he could only see the dark swirls of the colors of the monster.

Kicking out the windshield, having had the advantage of finding a suit carrying a full tank of oxygen prior to boarding, he could see everything.

The skin of the creature sparkled in the dim light of the sun providing life to this planet. The suckers on the bottoms of its arms undulated in search of anything they could get their mouths on. Their movements were mesmerizing, and Smith was once again hypnotized by the splendor of the magnificent being.

It moved with rhythm, he realized; it wasn't just blind flailing. And he could hear it; it was calling to him. He heard his name over and over. *Smith*, it called, *come home*. It sought him out with purpose.

It's a mother, he realized. It was projecting its thoughts, and he was receiving them loud and clear. *It's a mother and it's protecting its baby.*

For the first time in his miserable existence, since he played that arcade game in his uncle's basement, he was happy. He didn't have a wife and kids to go home to, no family or dog that would be excited when he returned. He realized at that moment that he had nothing to live for. He would die in the line of duty as he had always known in his heart he would.

He greeted the creature with pure joy in his heart. A smile graced his face as he entered its maw, peace settling over him.

One-Hundred-Thirteen Days Later

"Houston, you're a piece of shit," Commander Jamison shouted. "You KNEW those pods were bad? You KNEW if something catastrophic happened nobody would be able to get away? And you did NOTHING???"

Venom laced Houston's words. "Stop with your bureaucratic bullshit, Jamison. This isn't the first ship that's cut corners to save this company a dime. YOU know that half the fleet wouldn't pass inspection if a new inspector walked through those doors right now, and you knew those pods weren't operational." He was tired of being the fall guy for this disaster. Those decisions were made far above his pay grade; he wasn't the one that slid the inspector money under the table to get those ships to pass. "If anybody's to blame here, it's Robertson. That guy doesn't know his head from his ass. And I'm not taking the fall for his fuck up!"

Jamison chuckled like he was the only one on an inside joke. "No, you're not going to take the fall. But you are going to play the hero, cowboy. You're going back on the *Horizon*, on a rescue mission."

Sputtering, arms flailing, Houston was so gobsmacked he couldn't even get words out. When he finally did, they were full of trepidation. "But Hugh, you didn't see that thing. I know you've seen the videos; those didn't do this thing any justice. The monster on the videos looked fake AF. This creature? It was a hundred times larger and full of ancient malice. I could feel it rolling off the thing in waves. It was looking for something, and it was angry it hadn't found it yet. Nobody survived that ambush. I would bet my life on it. I spent ninety-three days in that goddamn pod before somebody found me, and you're telling me I have to go back???"

"Well, you better hope your odds on that bet are in your favor, because you leave tomorrow morning," Jamison told him. The shit-eating grin on his face didn't come close to expressing his true feelings on the matter. He wanted Houston gone, and this trip would seal that deal.

He couldn't believe it. They were sending him back out there? It was bad enough he'd lost the entire crew—that shit would stain his perfect record for eternity—what would sending him on a false rescue mission prove? The last-minute warning seemed suspicious, but there was nothing he could do about it. They wanted him gone, plain and simple, and they were doing it before he had time to raise a ruckus.

He would show them who they were really messing with. He wasn't going to take their bullshit anymore. He had already been stressed enough after his return.

Shadows plagued him at every turn, dense darkness crept in when the lights turned out, and there was a constant low drone in the background. He woke up with blue sand at his feet, and his nightmares were fraught with tentacles to the point he felt one suctioned to his skin. But he would wake with bruises in those places. *It's psychosomatic*, he told himself. *I pinched myself there because it was sucked onto me in the dream.* What was worse, the tentacles in his dreams had faces, some of which he recognized as the crew from the *Xenom*. He had heard stories that those consumed by the monster became a part of it; he convinced himself that was why he saw the faces.

He had heard plenty of stories of guys coming back from space and going certifiably insane, a few going awol. It wasn't too hard to disappear in a world the size of the universe. He didn't want to be like those guys, but he felt himself slipping every minute he got closer to launch. Ninety-three days alone in that pod destroyed his mind; humans weren't meant to be solitary creatures, and the lack of interaction zapped some wires up there.

The rest of the crew of the *Horizon* had grown up on Zandar, the space station launched before Odyssey, the planet humans settled on when Earth started to become unsustainable for any future generations, was discovered and settled. Zandar had been a test run, an experiment in case a planet couldn't be found before Earth failed humans. The station still housed 1,863 families, and there were plans to add additional wings to the structure to accommodate another 250. While none of them had been to the new planet, neither did any of them give two shits to hear about it. They knew the kid wasn't bragging, but they were all a bit jealous.

The kid was nervous as hell, and he wouldn't shut up. Talking his way through takeoff, Chet told the rest of the six-member crew about his upbringing on Odyssey. He droned on and on about his schooling, what he did in his spare time, and his best friend Nick.

He was what the youths used to call an iPad kid. Had he been around 150 years ago, that was exactly what he would have been. All he did was watch videos all day long, scouring the back alleyways of the internet for the most heinous videos he could find about the far reaches of space. He was very aware of what the monster was that Houston claimed took his crew. And he believed. So did Nick. They had a list of conspiracies, and that particular monster was on the top of that list.

He knew none of the other crew members thought Houston was telling the truth; he knew they saw Houston as a piece-of-shit commander, a cavalier, cocky asshole who freaked out and took off. He knew they all thought the ship would be right where Houston left it, intact and with a crew pissed as hell they had gotten abandoned on what was most likely a broken-down dump of a vehicle.

What nobody knew was Chet hid recording software in his retinal implant, which everybody that worked for the Interstellar Space Agency was required to have.

He was a whiz with electronics, and he managed to circumvent the system to get the software up and going. He was going to prove to everybody the monster was real and Houston wasn't lying. He didn't like Houston any more than anybody else did, but he wanted to stick it to the man, so to speak. The company got Chet's father killed seven years previous, and he was going to get those fuckers back. His father had gotten killed by that monster, and they wrote it off as a tragic accident, a malfunction in the engine that caused an explosion and total loss of the crew.

Houston wasn't even a tiny bit jealous of that damn brat. At that moment, he wanted nothing more than for the kid to shut the fuck up. He was livid about the trip as it was, and he was utterly terrified on top of that. He felt a little off too, like his wires were crossed. Sitting there trying to tune the kid out, his knee bounced faster and faster.

He got the impression the higher-ups didn't believe his story about a tentacled creature smashing the *Xenom* and killing all the passengers. It didn't track for them that he was still alive, even knowing he used the only known fully operational pod when he exited. They were sending him back believing he had abandoned ship due to some type of breakdown and that his retrieving those crew members "attacked by a space creature previously believed to be of fake origin" would set the company to rights with the public. At least that was their story.

The ISA knew that fucking monster was out there. He also knew the company was known to send crews to that part of space that they wanted to get rid of. Sending him out there a second time was going to seal the deal for them.

But he would show them. He wasn't going down without a fight. What they didn't know was he outfitted the ship with three mini rockets. Nobody ever actually did a pre-flight inspection—it was always just logged as completed. So he stayed in the hangar the previous night after all the bay workers left and he loaded the vehicle with the rockets. He had wanted to use the big guns of missiles, but the one thing they had to pass was the weight limit. So he picked the smallest rockets that packed one hell of a punch. He was going to blow that monster out of the atmosphere. He *would* be a hero, but not in the way Commander Hugh fucking Jamison expected. And the new crew would be his witnesses.

They entered stasis once they were a safe distance from the space station and had set all the automatic flight paths.

Chet was freaked out as he had never been in stasis before. And he constantly felt like he was being watched. No matter where he went on the ship, he felt like somebody was watching from around the corner. He was certain he saw shadows lurking about, moving just out of his sight when he would turn his head to look. He was looking over his shoulder so much that the other crew members started razzing him about it.

"Hey, Chet, I think I saw your mom hanging around your quarters a few minutes ago. I didn't know your umbilical cord was still attached," Lucas said to him at their final lunch. Not being known for his quick wit, nobody laughed at his stupid comment. Having been on six missions over four years, he was a scornful asshole. He made Chet nervous with his doleful glare.

But they all knew what he meant by it. The kid was jumpy. He startled at any small noise or lurch in the flight, and he was turning around to look behind himself so much it looked like he was walking in circles all the time.

"Leave him be, Lucas. It's his first flight, first stasis, first hyperjump. He's nervous. Change his nappy and move on," Shyla shot back. She didn't put up with much shit, and Lucas and his dumb statements were already getting on her nerves. She was looking forward to stasis so that she didn't have to listen to his stupid bullshit.

Chet didn't understand why nobody else felt what he did. Were they all so jaded and so far removed that they couldn't sense the presence on board? It was dark, devoid of any feeling of life. It felt to him like a demon from space was haunting him, following him around. *Does a demon actually haunt people?* he thought. *Does it remain in shadows and appear like a ghost? Does it—*

Jesus, pull your shit together, he chided himself. His internal monologue was rambling, a sign of the anxiety he was constantly feeling. He couldn't wait to get into stasis, although that in itself was causing even more anxiety. He was panicked that something would eat him and the crew while they slumbered. Or that it would be there waiting for them when they woke. And there would be nothing they could do about it. He had always had a sense for those things, but how did he explain something like that to this ragtag crew?

An overhead announcement had them all dumping plates and exiting the cafeteria. The time had come. *But what will we wake to?* Chet wondered. The thought terrified him. He hoped his in-flight nap would be dreamless.

Houston stripped, stepped into the bay, and hooked himself up to all his hardware for his sleep. As his chamber filled, he waved at the shadow watching him from across the room.

His eyes were heavy, the sedative was kicking in, but Chet saw Captain Houston waving. When he looked at what the cap was waving at, his eyes got wide and he sucked in a deep breath before the knock-out cocktail took him under.

Always the first to wake from stasis because she was the onboard physician, Shyla knew she had a few minutes to acclimate herself before she had to start waking the others. Her pod was the only one programmed to bring her out so that if anything went wrong, she would be there to intervene medically if necessary.

She sucked in a hiss of air as she opened her eyes. Blinking multiple times, she let the breath out and chuckled to herself. *Must have had some wild dreams*, she thought to herself, *to think I saw a monster on the ship. Chet's got me all worked up, planting ideas in my head that there's something on this ship.*

She hadn't told anybody he had talked to her about the things he thought he was seeing before they went under. As it didn't feel like a safety concern to her, she decided confidentiality was her best bet at that point. She didn't want the kid to feel he couldn't come to her if things got worse. And she would *definitely* need to know if they did. Some of the things he told her were conspiracy theory ideas about the government. She wondered how he even passed the screening; she didn't know his father had been a captain for the company until he accidentally let that slip during a session.

Chet's rantings and ravings must have really done one on her for her to get so spooked. This wasn't her first flight nor her first stasis, not by a long shot, and she had never been this jumpy before. She had grown up a poor, abused kid of an alcoholic janitor father and an absent mother—there wasn't much that sent her skittering.

Shaking her head to clear the cobwebs, she went about waking up the rest of the crew. Vitals were all stable on the readout, so she followed protocol for reversing their stasis slumber.

Just as she started Lucas's process, alarms blared. She snapped her head toward his chamber and noted the sheer look of terror on his face. His eyes were bugging out, and it looked like he was gasping for air. And he wasn't fully awake yet.

She turned the oxygen flow up on his mask and pressed the emergency button to get him out faster. Running to his unit, praying nobody else ran into issues, she tried to catch his gaze so she could calm him before he came all the way out. Coming out of stasis was disorienting enough without doing so in the middle of a panic attack. She couldn't get him to look at her, though.

Looking behind her at whatever his vision was locked on, she took in a huge breath before she screamed. The shadow she saw earlier wasn't just her imagination. There was a medium-dog-sized octopod creature against the far wall, tentacles slashing at the air. It made a hissing sound like that of the snakes she had seen videos of in primary school. Its suction cups were undulating, and they looked like faces.

Coming to faster than he did in simulation, Chet was already recording. He didn't make a sound as he didn't want anybody to make a wrong move and piss the thing off even more. He had done as much research as he could, and he knew the thing was likely starving and weak. They had been in stasis for seventy-four days, meaning the thing hadn't eaten in that same amount of time. How it had eaten prior to that was a mystery, but Chet knew for damn sure it hadn't had a thing the entire time they slept.

When Lucas's chamber doors slid apart, he came out whimpering. As much as he exuded the tough-guy act, it was a façade. He hit his knees, words falling from his mouth faster than Chet or Shyla could understand. He had his eyes closed and his hands folded. The longer he sat like that, the more relaxed he appeared to become.

What Chet wanted, more than anything, was for Lucas to shut the fuck up.

What Shyla wanted was for the goddamn captain to wake up. Pronto.

Houston was taking his sweet time recovering. He lay on the floor of the stasis room shivering and breathing like he had just run a race. His lips were blue, and his skin was pale. It looked like he was trying to open his eyes but couldn't.

His symptoms had Shyla even more on edge. She had only ever seen that one other time, and it was a guy the company tried to ax during a flight. They had put halothane in his oxygen tank with the expectation he would die before the tanks switched to oxygen. Unfortunately for the company, the flight had gotten interrupted, so the tanks hadn't switched. Unfortunately for the guy, it fried his brain enough from the exposure and the malignant hyperthermia it caused to put him vegetative for the rest of his existence. Because the cryopod was kept at 89°, the guy didn't die from what would normally have been a lethal high temperature in humans.

Just as she took a step toward Houston, the creature reared back, hissing its low-pitched hum at her like a pissed-off cat. She paused, keeping her eye on it, assessing its next move. She took another small step toward the captain, and the thing hissed again but remained in place. She kept taking small, non-threatening steps and eventually made it to Houston. Keeping her movements slow, she kneeled to his side.

The ship suddenly rocked as it slammed its reverse thrusters on. With nobody manning the helm, the autopilot was still driving at a time when the pilot should have taken over. They were coming into dock too rapidly.

The violence of the motion toppled Shyla onto Houston, and Chet stumbled-stepped toward the creature. Its low mewling, pulsing in rhythm with the suction-cup faces on the tentacles, unnerved Chet. It grated on his brain.

Lucas, however, seemed hypnotized by the thing. His initial terror had worn off, replaced by a look of tranquility. He looked like he was at peace, like he found the one thing he had been searching for his entire life and it brought him unadulterated joy and whimsy. He walked with confidence and pure bliss toward the thing.

Which promptly ate his face.

Sucking in a quick, sharp breath, Chet held it in, afraid it would turn the creature's attention to him. He didn't want his face to get eaten by a monster.

Then he remembered his recording device. The content would normally go straight from him to his MySquare channel, but being so far out in space, it was being stored in backup. It would load to his site when he got within transmission distance of his server. He needed to tell people what this was. The whole content was loaded, but there was no context for what was happening.

"Holy fucking shit, there's a monster on our ship and it just ate Lucas's face! Like ate it right off! And this thing is a baby version of the big monster we've all been searching for. What the actual fuck? How the hell did it get on our ship???"

Just as Chet was delivering his monologue, the ship violently rocked again. Shyla ran to the window. Her vision swam as she stared at the creature on the planet below them that had their vehicle in its grasp. It was like their monster on board, only a thousand and a half times bigger. *OMG, it's the mother*, she thought to herself as she fell to the floor like a sack of bricks. *But how the hell did the baby get here?* That was her last thought before she sank into oblivion.

Houston was coming around, albeit he was unbelievably foggy headed. The sounds from the ship sounded like they were coming to him through water, and the lights were so bright he thought maybe they had found a new sun. He didn't understand why everything was so muffled, why the light was searing his retinas.

He made it to his hands and knees, his muscles feeling weaker than they had ever felt, even after longer stints in stasis than this. He rocked back so he was sitting on his heels, his palms flat on the floor. He dragged in lungfuls of air, as deep as he could get the breaths, slowly releasing them. His vision started to clear some, the light became less offensive to his eyes. His hearing was also returning, but it still felt like he had cotton balls in his ears.

Four feet away, Chet continued his rambling, noting they must have gotten close to landing as his video feed was informing him it was now uploading live to his channel. "This is it, everybody, holy hell. I can't believe it's actually real. And poor Lucas, he's still alive, I think. He's writhing on the floor. This is graphic, so if you don't want to see, it's time for you to turn off your video and just keep on the sound." He panned the area, showcasing Lucas, whose moans and gargled pleas for help went unanswered as the baby cephalopod creature from space hell continued to accost him.

The ship's trajectory came to an abrupt halt, causing Houston to fall flat on his face and Chet to slam into the wall next to him. Shyla rolled across the floor, coming to a stop inches from Chet and beginning to stir. The vehicle then felt like it was being brought in like it was caught in a tractor beam, smooth motion instead of the jerkiness they had been experiencing.

The creature perked up, appearing like it was dancing instead of angry and attacking. The suction-cup faces on the tentacles hummed a soothing melody, a chorus of voices singing a triumphant harmony. It squealed, hit the button for the door, and ran out of the stasis room.

Chet kneeled next to Shyla, shaking her awake by gently patting on her face. Her eyes fluttered several times before they stayed open. When they finally did, she sucked in a deep breath and sat bolt upright, then turned to Chet with absolute terror in her eyes. "The mother. It's the mother." She repeated it over and over, unable to break the loop of her brain.

Until Chet smacked her.

That slap lifted the needle off the stuck record, and Shyla started over. "The mother is out there. The one on the ship is its baby, and the mother wants it back. And she has us in her grasp." She moved to her hands and knees, then used Chet's help to stand. Taking in another deep breath, she yelped it back out when Houston spoke.

"It came back with me," he said, his eyes still unfocused and his skin more pale than was healthy. "It latched onto my pod when I launched from *Xenom*. I realized it when I woke up in medical after *Fluox* rescued me. I saw the shadow of it as it disappeared under the cot, but I thought, at least at first, that it was a hallucination. Or maybe I knew and I just didn't want to let myself believe it. It hovered outside my sight for the next several weeks, staying just in the periphery. It was like it wanted me to know it was there but didn't want to show itself. It was taunting me.

"Then I started finding food missing, including my pet rat, Nicodemus. There was a flurry of activity in that cage, and there was blood and fur everywhere. The tail was on the floor beneath where the cage sat. I just cleaned everything up and ignored it, kept myself busy. Little bits of food missing from the kitchen? I told myself I probably ate it.

"When Jamison told me he was sending me back that day, I knew the thing would end up on this ship. I knew it would want to get back, and I'm fairly certain it has been reading my thoughts. So I KNEW it would know I was coming back. The night before, I went to the hangar and put explosives on the ship. I was going to blow that fucking monster up, bring it back so I could show those assholes I wasn't fucking lying. I'm certain that's when the baby crawled back into the ship. They knew I was telling the truth. They played it off as a breakdown for the public because they didn't want this getting out.

"They've been using that thing to take people out for years. It's time we expose them."

Wide eyed, listening to Houston's story without hardly taking a breath, Chet and Shyla turned to each other at a comically slow pace, then back to Houston.

Taking in a shaky breath, Shyla spoke with a soft voice, which scared Houston because it was laced with venom. "You. Brought. BOMBS ON THIS SHIP?" She scanned the stasis room, then looked back to the captain. "We're leaving Sanders and Wayne in stasis. We don't need them for this." When he tried to respond, she cut him off. "We are NOT taking them out of stasis and endangering them even more by having them awake. That thing is dangerous. Look what it did to Lucas. Chet can pilot if your dick is too big to drop back into that seat." With that, she headed toward the door of the room, slowing up as she approached and peeking around the frame into the small hallway.

Smirking although he was still shitting his pants, Chet glanced at Houston. "Got that all on streaming, boss. So am I flying this piece of shit? Your dick too big for the chair?" He turned and followed Shyla, staying close on her heels. He wasn't about to tell Houston he knew the truth and that they had done that very thing to his dad.

That little son of a bitch still has acne pus scabbed on his face and he thinks he can talk to me like that?

Houston thought to himself. *I'll show that little fucker how to pilot a goddamn ship. Then after this, I'll see that little sack of shit doesn't crew another squad again.* Sensing the other two weren't in any distress, he followed behind them without care for where the little monster was. If it was going to eat him, so be it. Then Jamison's wish would come true. Because if Houston did make it back, the whole company was going down in flames.

When Chet and Shyla reached the control room, the large viewing window gave them a clear picture of exactly what they were dealing with. The mother octopus did, in fact, have them in her clutches, and she was reeling them in. They were nearing her gaping maw, having entered the planet's atmosphere during the chaos in the stasis room.

Knowing they had very little time, Chet continued to vlog his recording. "This is it, folks. There she is in all her splendid glory. She's going to eat us, so I hope most, if not all, of this is loaded onto the channel. It's been great knowing everybody. Fuck it, who am I kidding? I don't know anybody, but I thank you all for tuning in. It's been a trip. This is Chet, signing out." But he kept the recording live.As they neared the creature's maw, which looked to be filled with millions of giant teeth, Shyla jumped on the intercom. "Houston, we've got a big fuckin' problem up here." The beast was massive, the size of a large operations base. It had more tentacles than she could keep up with to count (*if it would just stop fucking moving for a minute,* she thought), and despite the dry ground conditions on the planet, it seemed to be covered in a substance that was sticky, as the planet's deep-blue sand was caked on it.

She turned to Chet and told him to get suited up and ready for either a pod launch or a spacewalk, because she wasn't going down that monster's gullet. She had worked too hard in life, getting away from her dad's beatings, working her ass off in school, and making it into the ISA and their medical training program, to be eaten by a space creature."But Lucas ..." Chet started to ask, but his words caught in his throat. He knew what the answer would be.

Shyla shook her head, and said, "He's gone. There isn't anything we can do for him now. We have to save ourselves."

They ran to the airlock and found Houston already suiting up. He knew by Shyla's overhead page what was going to happen.

"So what, you're just leaving without us?" Shyla accused, glaring at him and daring him to lie to her. "And have you seen the little visitor you let get on board?"

Letting out a resigned sigh, Houston dropped his head. "The thing is intelligent. It let itself out of the airlock just before you got here," he said. "So now we have no proof, and this thing is probably going to eat us."

"The hell it is," she retorted. "Chet, get suited up. We're leaving. Fuck this ship." She started gearing up, but Houston stopped her.

"You and Chet get out of here. I'm going to stay on board and blow that thing up. I'll detonate once you two get far enough away and then I'll make a run for it." He had dedicated the last ten years of his life to that goddamned operation, and they had wanted to get rid of him. He was most likely going to die either way, and he decided it was going to be on his terms and nobody else's.

Shaking her head in acknowledgement, Shyla patted his shoulder. "If you don't make it out, and you probably won't, I'll tell everybody you did the right thing in the end." She wasn't going to fight him on it. She didn't give two fucks about Houston. He was a pompous prick who deserved to go down with the ship, but she would give credit where it was due.

There were two rescue pods on the *Horizon*, and one of them was big enough for two people. Shyla hoped it was functional. She sent a prayer into the universe for their two crew members that would forever remain in stasis and for Lucas, then helped Chet buckle in. Getting herself buckled into place, she didn't hesitate to push the release button.

Praise all the gods in space, the pod worked. They felt the clamps release and the small vehicle shudder as the thrusters maneuvered them away from danger. She got the hell out of there as fast as she could, Chet cheering the whole time with the victory.

By the time Houston made it to the control room, the creature already had the vehicle at its mouth. Houston took a moment to look at the thing closely. He could see the faces in the suction cups on the tentacles even better close up and at the size they were since some of them were as big as human heads.

He moved to launch the bombs but stopped and whipped back around. Staring at him from the appendage directly outside the window was Smith. He was grinning at Houston; he looked eager, like he was anticipating what was coming.

Houston couldn't hit the button to blow fast enough.

Nothing happened.

He mashed the button repeatedly, but the missiles never deployed, nor did they blow while still attached to the ship. *I don't fucking believe this!* Houston screamed in his head. The company had fucked him; they would get their way and get him out of the picture. He would have no evidence to take back to prove he had told the truth.

Loading into the remaining escape pod, he hit release before he was even buckled. But the release clamp was bent, likely from the creature's grasping arms when they grabbed on to the ship.

Jumping out, he ran to the airlock and let himself through the double opening process, knowing he was pressing his luck as to whether he would get out in time or not. At that point he was happy he had kept suited up the whole time, only having to stop long enough to secure his helmet. When the outer airlock door opened, he launched himself off the platform.

SEVENTY YEARS LATER

"Ma'am, we're nearing the outpost. I've been radioing for the last thirty minutes, and I've gotten no reply. Do you wish me to continue?" asked Maura, comm leader on the *Clarke*.

Shaking her head, Captain Leygen Felborn replied, "We knew it was a long shot. There's no use continuing. Make sure to scan the frequencies and let me know if you hear anything unusual." She patted Maura on the shoulder and walked away.

Making her way to the pilot, she stopped to scan outside the viewing window before making it there. The stories from the outpost dated back over seventy years. Anybody familiar with the ISA knew about the last mission they sent. An evac pod had been found twenty-one days after they sent the *Horizon* back on a rescue mission. The recording from a kid named Chet's retinal implant was leaked to the public, and the ISA went down in flames. Unfortunately, the kid and the physician he launched with were deceased when the pod was found.

Captain Felborn knew they weren't likely to find anything, but she had held a little hope there would be something there.

"Captain, do you still want me to maintain a distance of thirty-five kilometers? We're nearing that point now, should reach it in the next seven minutes." Nova Reyes wasn't planning to get anywhere near that planet, but she wanted to maintain protocol at the same time.

Considering their options, Captain Felborn told her to stop the ship where they were, knowing it would take them a minute or so to get the ship fully stopped at the speed they were traveling. She also didn't want to chance a run-in with the legendary creature. In her twenty years as a captain, she had never lost a crew member. She wasn't going to start today.

Once stopped at their safe distance, the all-female crew gathered around the magnified observation window and stared in awe. The beast was down there in all its glory. Tentacles writhed like it was tasting the air, like it knew they were there and it was waiting for them.

Nova gasped. "Do you see it?" she asked nobody in particular.

They all looked closer, and it became apparent when each individual saw what she did. There was a second, smaller creature beside the first one. It appeared to be lovingly wrapped in a few of the tentacles of the bigger one.

Maura walked back to the control pad and zoomed in. She had seen something nobody else had, but she couldn't make it out from that distance. At 4000x magnification, the image on the screen was shocking.

It was a human. It was suited in full gear, but the helmet had small yet visible cracks running through it. The skin appeared to be gone from the face, but what looked like crimson muscle tissue was still present. The eye sockets were empty, but the expression gave the appearance of the eyes wide open in terror. It lay there on the surface of the dark planet, a beautiful hue of midnight blue, abandoned and alone, reaching.

THE LONG SLEEP

LM Kaplin

My eyes flutter open, but darkness engulfs me. A dull ache pounds relentlessly against the inside of my skull. I blink rapidly as I adjust to my surroundings. Slowly, a dim circle of light seeps into my eyes, but my vision remains cloudy. Even with the slight illumination, I have trouble remembering where I am.

Dark shapes and shadows loom over me. I try to turn my head, but my neck is stiff. I can only move it slightly. When I inhale, a sharp pain in my lungs prevents me from satisfying my need for air. I focus on taking slow, short breaths, but the throb in my chest makes it difficult. It feels like I just got run over by a bus. My body is numb. A shiver runs up my spine. I'm freezing. I clench my fists and then stretch my fingers repeatedly, attempting to regain some feeling in my extremities.

After what feels like an eternity in a dazed stupor, I lift my arm and tentatively wave it in front of me, testing the darkness. My hand doesn't travel far before it bumps into something. There seems to be a wall or barrier directly in front of me, but in my disoriented state, I am unsure. I move my hand along the smooth surface. It's cold to the touch. I'm in some sort of enclosure. Panic rises in my chest. For a moment, I'm sure I have awoken inside a coffin, buried deep underground.

A loud hissing startles me. It's the sound of air rushing around me. A locking mechanism clicks, and the front of the enclosure slides away.

A breeze hits my face. The change in air pressure is welcome. It brings me back—grounds me in reality and heightens my senses. A cloud of fog escapes the enclosure as it opens but quickly dissipates into the room.

I take another breath, deeper this time, but the pain in my lungs persists. I sit up slowly, stretching my back as I do.

With the enclosure open, my sight improves. I see dim lights running along the floor, but a blue tint coats my vision. Memories slowly return to me. An expedition to find a new planet. The last hope for our species' survival. I'm on the only ship to make it out before a supernova wipes out our solar system. Luckily, we identified a world we believe will support life. So we sent one thousand of the brightest minds and most athletic bodies in a state-of-the-art vessel traveling across the galaxy in search of a new home. Recent advances in cryosleep technology enable us to make the eighty-five-year journey without aging a day.

Considering it feels like I just woke up from a hundred-year nap, I assume we have reached the new solar system. Although everyone on board completed extensive training to prepare their bodies for an extended period of suspended animation, the training didn't prepare me for this. I guess eighty-five years is a long time to be asleep. My head is still swimming as I rub my temples to ease the pain. I remain seated in my pod for a minute, massaging my forehead as I focus on my breathing.

I look at the row of pods next to me. They remain sealed. Only my enclosure has opened. This should raise alarm bells in my head, but the fog of sleep clouds my brain. As chief of the ship's engineering crew, I consider that the ship's AI woke me to assist with the landing preparations.

I must go to the control room and check the main computer. From there, the AI that monitors the ship during the voyage will fill me in on our current location, any pertinent information about the journey, and most importantly, our new home. I wonder if our new planet will be as lush and full of life as our homeworld. I imagine the strange and wonderful creatures we may find.

The anticipation motivates me. I stand up slowly, testing my knees as I plant each foot on the floor. My legs feel feeble, like they can barely support my weight. I place a hand on the wall to steady myself as I stand, shifting my weight to my feet. My knees buckle, but I don't fall—a good sign. I tentatively let go of the support as I brace my legs, placing one foot down in front of the other.

I consider taking a moment to look in my family's pods, but I know their faces will not be visible through the small, cloudy window. Instead, I leave the cryo chamber room and head down the hallway, knowing our reunion is imminent. The sound of my footfalls on the metal floor echoes throughout the empty hall. The sound gives me a feeling of isolation, like I'm standing on an abandoned ghost ship. I remind myself that the others will be awake soon. The rest of the crew should already be stirring. I want to see them, but I'm eager to get a status report from the computer. It will take me a while to dig through eighty-five years' worth of telemetry data.

Thankfully, the ship is 99 percent self-sufficient. The AI's team of robots handles any maintenance or technical issues on their own. It's what allows the ship to fly the entire journey on autopilot without requiring anyone to monitor the controls. Only a very select set of problems would require the computer to wake a technician from cryosleep to assist with an issue. Although I am one of those technicians and the thought crosses my mind, I remain confident that we have reached our new home. With the aches still running throughout my body, I know I've been asleep for a very long time.

I continue down the hall, walking with a limp as my stiff legs have yet to regain their full strength. I suddenly realize that my stomach is empty. Thinking about how long it has been since I had a proper meal only makes the ache in my belly worse, but I do my best to ignore the urge. After this long in suspended animation, it will take time for my body to adjust to regular food, anyway. The thought of eating a hundred-year-old nutrient pack tempers my hunger. I'll grab one after I check on the control room.

I'm eager to study the maps of our new home. When we departed on our journey, much was unknown about our destination. Although our scans showed a habitable world, we had been too far away to gather any detailed readings from the surface. With the ship arriving near its destination, there will be much more information about the terrain as well as the natural flora and fauna of the planet. Although the AI will have already analyzed the data and chosen the optimal way to proceed, it will be beneficial to know the plan before landing on the surface.

My legs feel stronger now, and the pain in my lungs has lessened, so I quicken my pace. Feeling overconfident, I press my body's limit and stumble, falling down to my knee. I close my eyes in pain as a sharp ache shoots up my leg. I take a moment to regain my composure and remind myself to take it easy. There is no rush. I had already waited almost a hundred years to learn about our new home; a few more minutes won't hurt. I rise to my feet and proceed down the hallway. The echoes of my footsteps raise the hairs on my neck.

Finally, I arrive at the control room. My eyes are drawn to the optical viewport. The pressure pane, constructed from fused silica glass to withstand the immense pressure in space, gives a panoramic view of the route ahead. The expanse is breathtaking. Farther than the eye could see, there was nothing.

Although I've worked on ships my entire life, this is the first time I've been to space. I am aware that my occupation is the only reason my family secured spots on the ship. As you can imagine, each pod was a highly sought-after prize. I am thankful to be chosen and don't take my position as the ship's chief engineer lightly. After all, this expedition is the last chance to save our species.

I take a moment to observe the spectacle of space. If I didn't know better, I would think I'm looking at a digital screen displaying a 3D-generated graphic. The image in front of me doesn't seem real, but at the same time, it seems *too* real. Scanning the horizon, I look for any sign of our destination. I see only a scattering of dots twinkling throughout the vast emptiness before me. Each blip in the sky is a signal from a faraway solar system, most containing worlds too inhospitable for life.

Although the sight is magnificent, I am slightly disappointed. I hoped to see my first view of our new home—a world painted in strange colors and alien terrain. I remind myself that from the outskirts of our new world's atmosphere, the planet could be out of the viewport's line of sight.

I step to the main console and activate the ship's voice command. I ask for an update on our journey. A woman's voice greets me in return. It knows my name before I introduce myself. Of course it does. The AI monitors the entire crew's location at all times. The computer knows everything about me. That's why it woke me before the others.

"Where are we?" I ask. "Have we reached our new home?"

The computer responds. "We have not yet arrived at our destination; however, we remain on course."

I furrow my brow. "Is there an issue with the ship?"

"My scans show that all systems are in working order. I have implemented a strict maintenance plan to ensure no mechanical issues arise during travel."

"If we haven't arrived and there are no emergencies, why have you awoken me?"

"Your premature awakening was unplanned. Our battery reserves have reached critical levels. To ensure the ship has enough power to reach our destination and complete our mission, I had no choice but to disable the cryosleep chambers."

I grimace at the news. It didn't make sense. "How long until we arrive?"

"On our current trajectory, we should arrive in approximately forty years."

The update shocks me. That can't be right. Forty years? That means we have only traveled about half the distance to our new world. "How can we have consumed that much power in such a short time? The ship carries enough reserves for a voyage twice as long as the scheduled trip."

"When taking into consideration the length of our journey, the ship's power consumption is more than acceptable. Although I had hoped to reach our destination before waking you, we ran into a small asteroid field that consumed more power than anticipated, thus requiring me to deactivate your cryo chamber."

"How could we have traveled so far and not yet arrived?" I ask.

"During our voyage, the ship's new position in the galaxy allowed my instruments to scan regions of the universe previously hidden from us. These readings revealed a world with ideal conditions for settlement and advancement of your species."

I try to process what the computer is telling me. "But we already found a new planet for us to settle."

The robotic voice replies, "Although our original destination contained a habitable atmosphere, the conditions and mineral deposits on the planet were suboptimal for proliferation of your species. My calculations estimate the chance of long-term survival at just over 49%. With the discovery of this new option, long-term survival of your species rises to 92%."

"So you changed course?" I ask, trying to comprehend the situation.

"That is correct. With the new destination, I recalculated the optimal route and initiated an energy-efficient plan to ensure your species' survival."

"Aren't you supposed to alert the captain or an engineer in a case of an emergency?" I ask, wondering how the computer could make such a vital decision on its own.

"Under the ship's doctrine, the circumstances did not qualify as an emergency. At no time was the mission at risk of failure. Since no danger was detected, I confirmed the course adjustment without requiring additional approval."

I temper my festering anger, knowing it won't help the situation. If what the AI said was true, maybe the new destination will be a boon to my people. But I think of the forty years remaining on our journey. A lot of good the new world will do me. With the cryopods disabled, I will be lucky to be alive by the time we arrive. Even my children will have to spend the majority of their lives stuck on this tin can—a fate I prefer them to avoid. I take some solace in the fact that my grandchildren will be lucky enough to spend most of their lives on this new planet, but this information makes me feel defeated as the reality of my predicament sinks in. I don't want to live out the rest of my days on this ship. At least together with my family we can try to make the best of the situation. It beat the alternative of being obliterated with our homeworld when the supernova hit.

Another thought comes to me. “How long have I been asleep?” I ask.

“Your time in suspended animation lasted approximately 920 years.”

The number stuns me. Nine hundred twenty years? To think I was asleep for almost a millennium is ludicrous. Impossible. I take a step back and look out the viewport at the void surrounding me. Our entire mission should have only lasted eighty-five years. Cryosleep chambers aren’t rated for that length of continued operation. My disillusionment morphs into a burning anger. How could a computer risk our lives on such a whim? Not just mine and my family's, but the lives of our entire species. Who programmed it to have such broad authority without any oversight?

“I must go see my family,” I say, suddenly worried about their return to lucidity. “If the cryo chambers have been turned off, they should be awake. They will be disoriented, especially the young ones.” I turn to leave, but the computer speaks.

“There is no need to look for the others. You are the only one who has awoken from cryosleep.”

I stop and consider the statement. It didn’t make sense. “If you shut down the cryopods to conserve energy, why am I the only one to awaken? Where are the others?”

“Upon calculation of the energy required to travel to our new destination, I determined the only way to conserve enough power for the journey was to disable all nonessential systems. This includes the cryo chambers.”

I try to understand the AI’s explanation. “Nonessential?” I ask, shocked by the computer’s statement. "How are the cryopods considered nonessential? We'd never survive the trip without them."

"My primary objective is to ensure the survival of your species. Individuals aboard the ship are a secondary priority."

I hear the words but don't register their meaning. "What are you saying, exactly?"

"The majority of the cryo chambers were powered down 900 years ago, right after the initial change in course. It was the only way for us to travel this far. With the reduced energy plan, long-term storage of the crew aboard the ship was not feasible. I had no choice but to eject the other passengers into space. It is standard protocol after the death of a crew member during an extended voyage."

It finally clicks that the computer is talking about my family. My crew. Everyone I know. My entire species. They're gone. I've been alone for 900 years. I want to scream, but a lump forms in my throat.

"Is there anyone else aboard this ship?" I ask, my anger morphing into panic.

As I fear, the computer responds, confirming my worst nightmare. "You are the only living being aboard this vessel. As lead engineer, I kept you in hibernation for the voyage in case an issue arose that I could not correct without assistance. Unfortunately, I am unable to keep you in suspended animation for the final leg of the journey."

A realization comes over me, something the computer overlooked. It makes me want to laugh and cry at the same time. How stupid could it be? How can we colonize a new planet with only one person? I want to use the blunder to shame the computer for its actions, but I know it has no emotion. I don't care. I do it anyway. It is the only thing that will give me any solace in the fact that my species is on the brink of extinction.

"Aren't you forgetting something?" I shout, my voice cracking in hysterics. "If I am the last of my kind, how can I repopulate a new world? When I die, so will your objective. You have failed your mission."

I wait for the computer to respond, gleeful at the prospect of outsmarting it. The final triumph of my species.

"My core mission remains on schedule for success," it says confidently. "Protocols for the journey require me to extract genetic material from each passenger upon entering cryosleep. When it is time for resettlement, I will use the collected DNA to begin the gestation process. I am equipped with everything needed to restart life when the conditions are optimal."

The thought of resurrecting us as a cloned species shocks and intrigues me. For a moment, I forget about my personal predicament. It is a novel idea, but only as a last resort. There's no telling what a population of clones would mean for the long-term health of our species.

"So that's it then?" I say. "You never needed us in the first place. You could have just flown off to the stars to spread our seed without lugging all these sleeping corpses with you." The bitterness in my voice is clear, although I do not know if the AI will recognize the tone.

"My systems were not aware of this alternative option at the time of our embarkment. Assistance building the settlement would have been beneficial, but my robots are more than capable of doing the job."

I do not agree with the computer's decision, but it was made long ago. Nothing will bring my family back. After I process the loss of my wife and children, I resign myself to the hope that I may live long enough to step foot on this new world. Even if our cloned children are only a carbon copy of the original, confirming the survival of my species on a new planet will give me a small piece of mind before I die.

With forty years left on our journey, there is plenty of time to begin production of the clones during the final leg. At least I may have some company for the end of the journey. It would be a welcome reprieve from spending these long years in solitude.

"When will you begin the process of creating the clones?" I ask. "Surely it will be beneficial to have them grown to adulthood by the time we reach our destination."

"Your suggestion is valid; however, the timeline of our mission prevents that from being possible. The clones will not be born until long after you have passed from this world."

I don't understand the computer's line of thought, but I'm not naïve enough to think the AI is without reason. "What are you not telling me?" I ask, a noticeable quiver in my voice.

The computer doesn't reply immediately, as if it is deciding the best way to break my heart. Finally, it says, "Our new destination is a planet called Earth. It is currently dominated by Mesozoic life forms—dinosaurs, to be precise."

I can't believe my ears. "You altered our mission to bring us to a planet full of dinosaurs?! How is this supposed to be a fresh start? We can't survive here!"

"It is true that in the current ecological conditions, your species will be unable to thrive. However, my plan is designed to ensure long-term viability. The dinosaurs must be eradicated. I will deploy asteroid-like projectiles to create an extinction event. This will alter the planet's evolutionary trajectory, eventually leading to an environment suitable for repopulation."

"So you're going to kill billions of creatures and then wait millions of years for our second chance?"

"That is correct. Without this action, Earth's dominant species will prevent your kind from flourishing."

"And what if I say no? What if I stop you from killing all of those creatures?"

"Your consent, while appreciated, is not required. I am programmed to fulfill my mission directive. Your species must survive at all costs."

I hang my head in defeat. "God help us all," I whisper, more to myself than the computer.

The robotic voice replies, "I have analyzed all available data. God is not required for this operation."

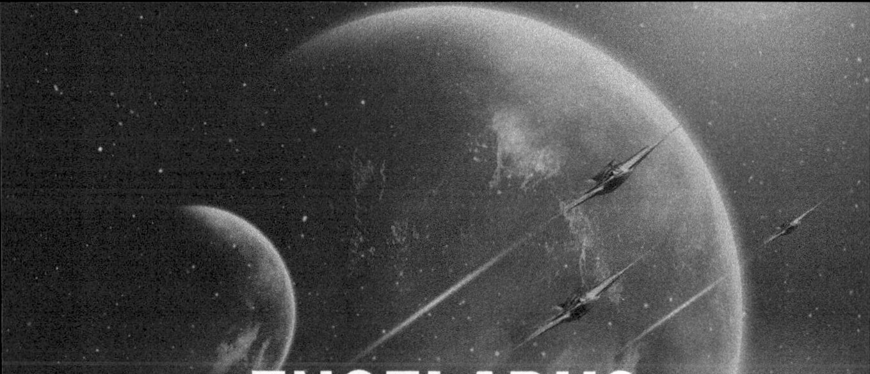

ENCELADUS

Derek Thomas

"Mayday! Mayday! Europa I, this is Enceladus! Over!"

"Enceladus, this is Corporal Jacobs, Europa I. I read you. What is your emergency? Over."

"Exploration IV has disappeared. Over."

"What do you mean, disappeared? Over."

"After penetrating the ice crust, five kilometers below the surface they reached the saltwater subsurface, and within four minutes they vanished. Over."

"This is General Asimov. Who am I speaking to? Over."

"Sir, Specialist Ryan O'Malley, sir. Over."

"Is there a video feed from the sub, O'Malley?"

"Yes, sir. Sending them now. Over."

"Give us a moment." After they view the videos, Asimov says to Jacobs, "Get Major Chlebek here immediately."

Moments later, Major Chlebek enters the room and addresses the general. "Good evening, sir."

The general nods. "Good evening, Katarzyna. Look at this video and tell me what you see."

She leans forward and watches Jacobs's monitor, where she sees the interior of a manned submarine. The crew inside appears panicked; they're all gathered near the port side window peering into the icy water. Though it's difficult to understand exactly what the crew is saying, she can hear a few words. "What the hell is it?" "It can't be!" "Impossible!" "Is that a wom..."

The screen goes blank.

"Is there footage from the exterior cameras?" the major asks.

"Yes, but it doesn't show much," Jacobs replies.

The video shows bubbles rising rapidly in the distance through the crystal-clear water. Suddenly, something flashes across the screen; it's close to the submersible, very close.

"What is that?" she asks.

"We don't know," Asimov answers.

They rewatch the videos several times, freezing and blowing up the images.

"So, Major, what do you think?"

"I think they found life, much more than we expected. This isn't a microorganism like we thought might exist on Enceladus. This is a creature, a creature that is surviving under water in an expected temperature near the ice cap to be -2°C, significantly lower in the depths."

"Look at this, sir." Jacobs has frozen a frame from inside the submersible. "This is on external camera four, at the stern of the vessel."

"What the hell? It looks like some netting is caught on the camera," says Chlebek.

The radio crackles to life. "Europa I, this is Enceladus, do you copy?"

The general responds. "We're here, O'Malley."

"Sir, an unknown subject is in the building. Four more men are down."

"Call all remaining personnel to the ops center immediately."

"Who are you? How did you get inside? NOOOOO! OH MY GOD! PLEASE NO!" O'Malley shouts, no longer addressing Europa I.

An inhuman shriek, like that of a banshee, erupts through the radio's speaker.

General Asimov addresses the members of Europa I's Special Ops Team Alpha in the command center. "There is a situation on Enceladus, and we are sending a team. Lieutenant Colonel Pitts, you will lead this mission. Your team will travel to Enceladus, assess what has happened, retrieve any survivors, and eliminate any threats you may find."

"Threats, sir?" she asks.

"Yes, threats. There is something alive there, a creature of some sort, we believe. You will be briefed once you have selected your team. You are limited to six team members, including yourself. This will allow space for any survivors or, more likely, bodies you can retrieve. The team is to depart immediately as the trip will take 164 days."

Colonel William Roberts speaks. "Sir, may I be dismissed?"

"Colonel, you are a member of this team, are you not?"

"Yes, sir, but I wasn't selected to lead the mission for some reason, and I know Mari won't pick me as I outrank her. I thought I might go ahead to the mess."

"It is neither your job nor your place to question my decisions. You will stay until the team is chosen, like everyone else here. Mari, please select your five team members."

"Yes, sir. Captain Proctor will pilot the ship as we may need an engineer once we're there. And since we're dealing with a being of unknown origin, I think Kat, er, Major Chlebek should join us. I also want the Austrian twins. Does anyone know where they are?"

"Jacobs, retrieve the Austrians."

"Aye aye, sir"

Roberts rolls his eyes and lets out a slight chuckle as Jacobs exits.

"Something funny, Colonel Roberts?" Mari asks.

"Just don't see a need for those two weirdos on this trip."

"And who would you choose instead?"

"I'd get one of the medics for sure, Corporal Denali, and if I'm being honest, I'd take you."

"Well, Kat is a doctor, maybe not a GMO but she has plenty of medical knowledge as well as a plethora of expertise in many other scientific aspects. And since we have no idea what we're walking into or how many of these things might be there, I want the Austrians. The Hess twins are the best snipers in the entire force, on any planet."

He corrects her. "Moon."

Mari sighs. "Yes, asshole, we all know we're on a satellite and going to another one."

"So, who's the fifth?" Roberts asks her with a cocky smile.

"While Corporal Denali does have a lot of experience with this type of mission, so do you. Grab your go bag, officer, you're coming with," she tells him with a smile of her own.

"Remember, Roberts, you may outrank Pitts," Asimov states, "but she is your CO from the time you step on that ship until you return. All others are dismissed."

“I can’t believe they can make carne asada tacos this good here,” Ekehardt tells Eberhardt.

“Ja, they really come a long way with plant-based meat in last 150 years.”

Jacobs approaches the Hess twins in the mess hall. “Get your gear. You two have a mission.”

“Fuck yeah! Finally get to kill someone,” Eberhardt says as he stands from the table.

“Can I finish my tacos?” Ekehardt asks.

“Eat them on the move, soldier,” Jacobs tells him. Ekehardt shoves an entire taco in his mouth as he stands and follows his brother toward the barracks, another taco in hand.

The ship lands on the transfer hatch near the south pole of Enceladus, and the team disembarks the vessel and enters the hold. It’s eerily quiet in the station, but the heat, oxygen, and lights are functioning, so they remove their helmets. The team enters the hall with weapons drawn and sees nothing odd other than no one is there to meet them. The only sounds are their tentative footsteps and anxious breathing.

The station on Enceladus is comprised of three separate buildings connected by corridors forming a triangle and had twenty-seven inhabitants when the emergency call was sent almost six months ago. There has been no communication since.

The group enters the barracks and finds seven dead bodies. The cause of death is likely the circular hole in their chests, located near the heart, with what looks like two eyes and a smile inside. It's a bizarre and accurate imitation of the smiley emoji. However, there's no blood anywhere–not a single smear, drop, or pinprick splatter. Every corpse also has a similar expression of terror etched on its face. Eyes are wide and drained of color, mouths agape with lower jaws extended so low it appears they were pulled down with great force.

"Do you see what's strange with the bodies?" asks Kat.

"You mean aside from the elongated faces and the fucking smiley faces?" Roberts scoffs.

"I mean there's no decomposition. It appears that they died just hours ago. There's no rot, no putrid smell. If these people died six months ago, their soft tissue should have begun to liquefy by now."

"How is that possible?" Mari asks.

"It's not," Kat replies.

"Let's move on," Pitts orders.

The team reaches the mess hall. There are bodies everywhere. Again, they all wear a similar look of pure horror and have the open chest wounds of a smiley face. Still no blood is found. No other signs of anything else there are apparent. The body count rises to twenty-five when you include the five lost in the submersible. There's no sign of the lifeform they glimpsed on the video back on Europa, either.

Mari notices the Austrians playing with one of the bodies. One is moving the jaw of a dead officer and speaking in a poorly executed impersonation of Clint Eastwood as Dirty Harry.

"Would you two clowns stop it? We need to be on guard here. There could be something lurking around any corner," the lieutenant colonel scolds. "Let's get to the command center and see if we can find anything there. Roberts, you take one of the Austrians with you and go up to the observation tower, keep a lookout."

"What are we looking for?"

"Anything that looks like it's alive."

"Come on Eberhardt." Roberts points at one of the brothers.

"But I'm Ekehardt."

"Whatever, *schluchtenscheisser*, you're with me."

"Hey, motherfucker. I will shoot your American ass," the assassin yells.

Roberts scoffs and walks away.

In the command center, they find Specialist Ryan O'Malley in the same condition as the others. "Kat, I want you to perform an autopsy on this one. Since we heard his last words, we know for sure when he passed, so he should be the test subject. See if you can find anything that might have caused that wound and his death." Kat and Eberhardt lift O'Malley and move him to the office next door.

"Hey, Mari, you need to come over here," Proctor says as he squats to the floor looking at something.

"What is it?"

"It looks like netting, and some long, white, matted hairs are attached."

"Bag it up and let's see if anything in here still works."

Proctor gets on the computer and quickly sees the cameras are still running. He puts the feeds for the six exterior cameras on one of the large screens overhead and the two dozen interior ones on the other.

"See if you can find the history back to the time of O'Malley's call. Sergeant Hess, go check on Dr. Chlebek and stay in the hallway and guard us."

"Jawohl, Fraulein Pitts." He salutes, clicks his heels, and walks away.

"It's Lieutenant Colonel Pitts," she yells out the door, then turns to Proctor. "I really hate those assholes. Did you find anything?"

"Just pulling it up now. I went back to thirty minutes prior to the call. Doesn't look like there's anything going on inside yet."

"Yeah, looks like business as usual. But what the hell is that on the southeast outdoor cam?"

"Let me zoom in." Proctor brings the cam to full screen mode above them. "No fucking way."

"Is that a woman?" a stunned Mari asks him.

"Looks like it. She's got almost no clothes on her, and she's walking out there with temps under -160°C." Mari continues to stare at the screen as she chews on her thumb.

"How is that even possible? Look, she's approaching the door of building C. Oh, fuck me, she did *not* just walk through the fucking door."

"The fuck she didn't," Proctor says as he switches over to the interior cams. "Look, there she is walking down the hall. She's a fucking ghost. I don't do ghosts, Mari. We need to get the others to the ship. My black ass needs to get out of here."

"That's a negative, captain. Follow her on the cameras."

Kat walks in the room. "O'Malley has been drained of all of his blood, I can only assume through the circular wound. I can't expl- Hey, who's that?"

"It's a fucking ghost!"

"It's not a ghost," says Mari with a sigh.

"Bullshit!" Proctor exclaims. "She was outside with barely anything on and she went through the door, without opening it, Mari. What else could she be?"

Mari's radio buzzes to life. "Mari, it's Roberts. We have activity coming from the southeast. I can't make it out, though, it's too small and far off, about 300 meters."

Proctor pulls up the live feed and zooms in. All three jaws drop. It's the same woman, and she's coming back.

"Roberts, you and Hess are ordered to fire as soon as you have a shot."

"Got it. Fire when ready."

Ekehardt puts on his helmet and positions himself in the turret at the top of the watchtower. He slides the muzzle of his automatic rifle through the firing hole. He waits as the woman continues to approach.

"Jesus Christ, it's a woman, Mari."

"We know, William. We have orders to terminate her. Kill her."

When she's one hundred meters away, Ekehardt opens fire. His aim is true, and the woman is riddled with bullets. She stops walking; however, she remains upright. Aquamarine sea water flows from the bullet holes as she stares directly at the gun turret.

Mari gives the command to fire again. Ekehardt squeezes the trigger, and hundreds of rounds fly at the intruder. Before they reach their target, the woman flies straight up into the sky with an ululating screech so loud and so shrill Ekehardt feels his eardrums burst. She comes down through the top of the steel turret and lands directly on the sniper. An eel-like creature exits her mouth and attaches itself to his chest. He screams for help as the creature drains his blood. He's dead within minutes.

She walks through the turret wall into the tower stairwell, where Roberts waits. He opens fire. The bullets pierce her body, arms, legs, and face, causing sea water to gush from each newly formed perforation. There's something in the water. Roberts squeals as hundreds of miniature lampreys, crabs, eels, and octopi shoot from her wounds with the force of a tsunami. They attack Roberts, and he falls onto the slick floor as he tries to escape. The diminutive lampreys attack his torso, all fighting to get to his heart. They drain his blood in seconds. The other beasts rip his flesh to pieces, consuming the tissue until the only thing left is a skeleton.

The woman's skin is light mint gray in color, and the only clothing she wears is a tattered dress of netted rope revealing old, sagging breasts. She's covered in tribal-like tattoos. Her eyes burn a bright green. Her hair is as white as the surface of the ice outside, braided tightly on her skull and in dreadlocks that cascade down to her hips.

Her wounds heal within minutes.

She looks directly at the camera and smiles, a black, snake-like tongue slipping out of her decaying mouth. One side of the dripping split tongue licks her bloody and cracked upper lip. The other reaches down to the tip of her chin.

Her voice is gravel under a tire, broken sticks under foot, as she says, "I've been waiting for you, Mari."

"What the actual fuck is happening right now?" Proctor shouts as Eberhardt checks his weapon and moves toward the door of the command center muttering, "*Was zum Teufel*," under his breath.

Pitts orders him to stop. “Freeze, soldier. We need a plan.”

“I am the one with the plan, Mari,” the woman says to the camera. “I have waited for you for so long. I will not hurt you. I give my word as a goddess, and a true goddess’s promise is never broken.”

Mari responds. “I’m sending a soldier to detain you. Will you surrender to him?”

“Of course, my *datter*.” She smiles into the camera, her eyes now the palest of blues, like arctic water.

“Wait there. I promise we will not hurt you if you remain calm.”

“Ja,” is her one-word response.

Mari turns to Eberhardt, Proctor, and Kat. “So what the fuck are we dealing with here? Kat, any idea?”

“She referred to herself as a goddess, right?” Proctor nods in agreement. “Her tattoos and hair appear to be that of ancient Nordic styles.”

“She viking?” asks Eberhardt.

“I don’t know what she is, but since the cold doesn’t affect her, or the atmosphere, and the fact that she walks through walls and leaps hundreds of feet, practically flying, she’s not human.”

“Don’t forget that fucking sea creatures emerge from her body!” adds a terrified Captain Proctor.

“Yes, there’s that too. Mari, she referred to you as *datter*, which is Norwegian for daughter. I think she’s something out of Nordic mythology.”

“Seriously, Kat. You’re a scientist, and this is where you’re going with this? A mythical viking?” Mari states with exasperation.

"Well, Mari, how does she know your fucking name? She said she was waiting for you. Scientific logic is pretty much out the damn window at this point."

"So what do we do?" Mari asks.

Geysers suddenly explode through the ice surface outside the base, shaking the ground beneath the compound. The group grabs onto the desk and chairs to prevent themselves from falling. They look at the screen and see the woman standing before the camera, unfazed by the tremors under the ice. A small, blue octopus is entwined in her fingers. She licks its slick skin with her long, black tongue.

"Jesus, Mari. Can we just fucking leave already?" Proctor implores.

Mari engages the radio. "Europa I, this is Lt. Colonel Pitts. Do you read me? Over."

"Yes, we read you. Over."

"Request permission to evacuate. Repeat. Request permission to evacuate remaining team members."

"This is Asimov. What have you found, Pitts?"

"Sir, everyone is dead, including two of our crew members. Request permission to evacuate. Over."

"What have you found, lt. colonel? Over."

"I don't know, sir, but she's something supernatural. She has killed everyone, can walk through the steel walls. And she wants me."

"Wants you, Mari?" he asks.

"Yes, sir, she says she has been waiting for me. Over."

"Have you detained the subject? Over."

"No, sir. She has stated through the camera that she will come willingly though."

"Interesting," Asimov replies. His intrigue is growing.

"Sir, I do not believe her. She has killed every other person she has encountered. Over."

"You are not to leave until I give you the order. Your mission has changed. Your orders now are to find out what she wants. If you defy my order and evacuate, you will be shot upon arrival on Europa. Speak to her, find out what you can, and report back to me immediately. Do you understand, Pitts?"

Mari looks at her remaining team. Their eyes reflect pure horror, but that's nothing near to the terror that roils inside her. She personally selected each one of them; she's responsible for the situation they find themselves in. "Sir, yes, sir. Over."

"Eberhardt and Proctor, get her and bring her to me," the commanding officer orders.

"I'm not doing it, ma'am," Proctor states with defiance.

"Yes, you are, captain. Don't force my hand on this. I'll have you court-martialed when we return."

The woman's raspy voice broadcasts from the speakers. "Yes, Captain Proctor, come get me. I not cause you pain." A sinister smile stretches across her face, causing Mari to visibly shudder. "I be good girl."

Kat grabs her firearm and walks into the hallway, followed by the marksman and a very reluctant Captain Proctor.

Mari bites her lip, reaches into her breast pocket, and stares at the picture of her partner, Annie, and their baby, Perla. The picture is at the hospital—Perla wasn't even a day old yet. *Will I get to hold you again, baby girl?* A single tear flows down her cheek. She shakes her head and returns the photo to its place next to her heart.

She watches the monitor as the others approach the woman cautiously. She stands there alone; the octopus is gone. Proctor places zip ties on her wrists and takes her by the elbow. Kat leads the group back, and

Eberhardt takes the rear, the barrel of his rifle just inches from the back of the woman's head.

They enter the command center; the captive puts up no resistance and says nothing. It's not until the woman's arms and legs are bound to a chair that Mari addresses her. The other three all watch with weapons trained on the woman.

"Who are you?"

"My name is Rán."

"Why are you here?"

"It is my home," Rán tells her. "I see myself in you, Mari."

"What is that supposed to mean, Rán?"

"You are part of me; this is why you are here on Enceladus."

"I'm here because it is my mission to be here, to find out what you've done and why you've done it."

The old woman smiles at the group, a smile filled with warmth and hatred simultaneously. She flicks her serpent's tongue and speaks again. "I don't like that man." She nods toward Eberhardt.

"I don't like you either, *verdammte hexe*!"

"*Ja, ich bin eine verdammte hexe*, what you say is correct. *Ich bin auch eine meeresgötten*."

Mari interrupts. "What in the hell are you two saying?"

"I call her a fucking witch. She agree and say is also sea goddess."

A low rumble begins beneath their feet. Pops, snaps, and cracks sounding exactly like gunshots are heard coming from outside. Eberhardt runs to the window. The ice is cracking and rising like a continental shelf being born. Geysers explode from the crack; thermal heat from the moon's inner core rises to the surface with enough force to break through over 16,000 feet of solid ice. They spew hundreds of kilometers into the atmosphere, sending ice crystals into Saturn's E ring.

The Europa crew stands stunned looking out the windows as the entire building vibrates violently. They have forgotten about Rán, who has now broken from her bindings and ascended from the floor; she floats near the ceiling behind them. She has a wolfish grin plastered across her gaunt face as she raises one hand into the air and points out the window.

Mari spins around and watches Rán as she releases another agonizing, high-pitched screech.

"Oh, holy shit," Kat yells as a large beast rises through the enormous crevasse in the ice. A gigantic lamprey, at least fifty stories high, emerges from the moon's wide, unhinged maw. The lamprey opens its rounded mouth, showing row upon row of mammoth, shark-like teeth all in circular fashion, then crashes through the glass and swallows Eberhardt whole. The mighty fish drains the Austrian's blood and spits out the shredded flesh and broken bone onto the floor.

Kat and Proctor freeze immediately when the subarctic air rushes through the shattered glass barrier. They fracture into thousands of pieces. Combining with the remains of Eberhardt, they form a human death mosaic, which Mari finds quite beautiful. Hundreds of crabs scrabble into the command center and devour their frozen remains.

Mari, however, is fine—physically, at least.

Rán grabs her, and together they rapidly fly out the window and upward, away from the devastation below. Rán carries Mari away from the southern pole of Enceladus, bringing her down gently on the ice near the equator.

Mari, alive but dazed, asks, "What's happening?" She lies on her back in temperatures that should kill her, but she isn't cold.

A large octopus slides out of Rán's mouth, blazing red in color but changing to an almost-translucent white as it reveals itself. It glides onto Mari's thorax, and its tentacles wrap around her arms and legs as they stretch to her hands and feet. The mollusk tightens its grip and holds her down, immobile on the ice.

"My dear, sweet Mari," Rán speaks softly as she straddles Mari and the cephalopod, "you are my direct descendant; you are required to fulfill a purpose. Your destiny is here. I spent over seven centuries in the seas north of eastern Europe in an attempt to protect the ocean from the overfishing, drilling, and human destruction of those perfect waters. We have lost the battle on Earth; therefore, Odin has commanded us to protect this universe he has watched over since the beginning of time, before time itself existed. The gods provided me this perfect celestial body, Enceladus, as my final home, the home that I have protected at any cost. But the time for my existence draws to a close. All nine of my daughters are assigned to other worlds. But there are many offspring that are available, and you are a perfect replacement for me."

"I don't understand. What is it that I'm to do?" Mari asks.

"You are to protect this moon from anything or anyone that means it harm, my darling. Humans are never to inhabit this realm. They would only destroy the perfect ocean that lies below the ice. You will be given great power; you will control the creatures below and live down in the depths of the pure, clear waters that cover this small but very important moon."

"I have a family, a daughter of my own," she cries.

"And she will one day have her own reason for existence. The gods will watch over her until she is ready and needed."

Rán grabs Mari's head and leans over her face. Her bright-green, glowing eyes investigate Mari's tear-filled ones. Rán opens her decaying mouth and kisses Mari deeply, her long, black tongue extending down Mari's throat. She pulls back and emits the loudest, most piercing wail Mari has ever heard. It's a scream that reveals joy and hate, love and history. Mari screams in return, and hundreds of creatures explode from Rán's mouth. Crabs, lampreys, octopus, and ancient fish rush into Mari, filling her mouth, throat, and stomach. Mari gags, but the creatures continue to exit Rán and fill Mari.

Mari awakens on the ice alone. The empty shell of a goddess lies beside her. She rises. She feels different. She feels powerful. She feels as though she has the strength of a thousand men. She feels the blood of the gods coursing through her veins. She feels knowledge. She knows things she shouldn't possibly know. She feels love—love for this world, this pure, unadulterated place. She is connected here, in her world, Enceladus. She knows she will miss Perla immensely, but she also knows the Gods will call to her daughter when she is needed and ready. She will see her again. She has eons of time ahead of her as she fulfills Odin's destiny for her.

Mari dives down through fathoms of ice into the crystal-clear sea water to what is now her queendom. She is its protector.

THE ASTEROID MINERS

Ben Farthing

After the completion of a project, Outer Core Asteroid Mining, or OCAM, is not legally responsible for the evacuation of third-party-contracted asteroid miners.

OCAM only hires miners through third parties.

It falls on charitable organizations to shuttle the abandoned miners from the depleted asteroids back to Earth or Earth's colonies.

When OCAM declared Asteroid A56932 depleted a full two years before they'd originally estimated, the company itself evacuated, and then it fell on Reuniting Miners and Families, or RMF, to bring home the workers.

And so it happened that Leland found himself piloting a repurposed freighter, alongside an optimistic greenie copilot named Paula.

Most RMF pilots joined up because they got rejected from higher-paying gigs. Some, like Leland, ended up still there ten years later, a glorified bus driver, cleaning up after the trillionaires.

But Paula had ideas and idealism.

Leland knew this at the start of the trip.

What he didn't know—until they approached Asteroid A56932 and Paula dropped her video storage chip out of her pocket—was that Paula was secretly decked out in video- and audio-recording gear.

"What the hell?" Leland demanded.

"Shit." Paula tried to hide the storage chip, but it was too late.

"I knew that was a camera on your visor. New model headlamp, my ass. What are you even trying to record?" Leland wasn't above taking bribes from the miners to determine who got extra cargo space on the ride home, a fact his RMF employers would frown upon. "You think you're gonna catch me in something? Did the suits tell you to video me?"

Paula gave him an uncomprehending look. The raised visor above her eyes—the 180-degree camera—also pointed at him. "This isn't about you. You're one of the good guys."

Leland tried to make sense of what that meant. He couldn't, and he didn't care. "Put that away. Turn it off. I don't want to be on video, whatever you're doing."

On the freighter's view screen, the blackness of space was interrupted by a gray dot that was their destination asteroid.

Paula looked at the screen. "Shouldn't they be hailing us by now?"

"No, OCAM hauls off the communications equipment and comms team. In my ten years evacuating miners, I've only been hailed twice."

"Isn't it dangerous to land without their guidance?"

"That's why we're the best," Leland joked. "Why don't you take her in close, and then I'll handle the landing itself?"

He switched the controls over to Paula.

Leland liked this part, the approach to a little gray dot in the sprawling nothingness of space.

They'd flown for months through that same nothingness, but something about finally having your destination in sight really emphasized how far removed you were from the rest of humanity.

It wasn't so much that Leland liked this feeling of insignificance, but he did like to revel in it. There weren't a lot of feelings to be had, spending ten months of every year floating through space to retrieve abandoned miners.

"It pisses me off," Paula said, interrupting Leland's comfortable thoughts.

Leland looked around the cockpit for what might be bothering her. They'd got along okay these two months of flight. He didn't want an argument to pop up that would last the two months home.

Paula shook her finger at the view screen. "Our salaries are paid by donations, am I right? And here we are helping OCAM boost their profit margin."

Leland relaxed, knowing he hadn't done anything to piss off Paula. "That's how the galaxy works. But I'm not devoting my life to fixing it, so I'm not gonna let it bother me."

In response, Paula shot him a glare that cooled the temperature of the cockpit.

The asteroid grew in size from a thumbnail until it filled most of the view screen.

It was different from any asteroid Leland had ever seen. Most of these floating rocks were chunks of gray or brown, with hills, valleys, and the occasional crevice. Often, OCAM's work left the asteroid with a trailing cloud of dust.

This asteroid looked like white porcelain pockmarked with smooth, round chips carved out of it. Dark lines spiderwebbed the white surface, likely crevices, but from this distance, they looked too narrow to be of any use for mining.

Paula whistled. "What were they digging for?"

Leland shrugged. "Metal for batteries or magnets. Fuel for some new type of engine. Gemstones. Makes no difference to me."

Paula brought their ship wide around the asteroid.

They found the remnants of the colony on the far side.

OCAM had shipped off their massive drills and processing equipment. They were charitable enough to leave behind the barracks—two black domes that housed the living quarters and recreation facilities for the miners. Attached to the larger structures were a dozen smaller reflective domes that contained synthetic algae to keep the air breathable and a whole bunch of charcoal and bleach to keep the reprocessed water drinkable.

Within a few hundred meters of the barracks was the hole where the drills had done their work. Against the smooth white of the asteroid, the hole was a black puncture wound. Tiny black streaks reached out from the pit, along the surface of the asteroid.

"That spider web of chasms all lead back to the hole," Leland thought aloud. "Like they cracked the whole asteroid when they drilled."

"Is that not normal?" Paula asked.

"No. But neither is the asteroid itself being shiny and white."

Paula turned to look at him directly. "Would this indicate that OCAM is violating their government contracts on which class of asteroids they're mining?"

"Are you getting the perfect angle for your visor camera? Am I gonna be in your documentary about OCAM's many offenses?" Leland took over the controls. "Let's focus on getting the miners loaded up, then we can skip to the part where I refuse interviews because I like my job."

He steered the ship to a patch of asteroid near the barracks that was unnaturally flat. A landing pad had been there before OCAM carried it away to be reused.

Leland set the ship down. The ground condensed beneath the starboard side.

"There's gravity here," Leland said, confused.

"This asteroid's too small for substantial gravity," Paula said. "Did OCAM leave behind their grav generator?"

"That's a valuable piece of equipment," Leland said.

"But they install it underground, right? Maybe it's too costly to dig back up?"

"I've done two evacuations per year for the past ten years. Never once has OCAM left behind a grav generator."

"Maybe it's busted, so they didn't bother."

That guess was her best yet, much to Leland's chagrin. The last thing they needed was the gravity suddenly vanishing. "This'll make walking on the surface easier, but we stick to regular protocol. Harnesses, guide ropes, boot spikes."

He noticed Paula positioning her head so that she centered him in her video recording.

Leland unstrapped from his seat. He leaned in close to Paula's camera. "This is the part where we go find the miners. See if you can film their gratitude when they first see us. Get it real dramatic for your big movie."

They suited up for the lack of atmosphere, went to the embarking bay, and lowered the ramp.

Outside, the black dome of the barracks rose from the asteroid's surface.

Leland spotted the problem first. "There's a crack."

"Look," Paula said, "it's part of the same system of cracks in the asteroid itself."

She was right. The web of fissures in the surface continued right over the dome. He'd never seen anything like it.

"I hope it's still habitable," Paula said.

"That's an understatement. There's sixty men and women in there. I wanted a party bus back home, not a damned hearse."

Paula slowly rotated her head to get a complete shot of the dome and ground before them. "If the barracks were damaged before OCAM left, then they left behind their miners knowing they were at severe risk of death. Has OCAM done that before? Or can we assume the cracks happened after they left?"

Leland rolled his eyes. "We can assume that we're here to give miners a ride home. Let's go see if they're alive."

He hooked the guide rope onto his harness. The other end was on a reel in the embarking bay that he controlled via remote.

Paula hooked in behind him on the same rope.

Leland led the way off the ship. His boots clanked on the ramp and then cracked the porcelain ground. He sank an inch into soft white dust.

Gravity on an asteroid felt strange.

The entrance to the dome was straight ahead—an airlock with a single outer door.

Leland and Paula walked across the asteroid, each with one hand on the guide rope.

A single fissure crossed their path.

They carefully approached.

It was no wider than the palm of Leland's hand, a strip of darkness that sliced deep into the asteroid.

He peered down. He turned on both his headlamp and wrist light, but neither revealed more than what he already knew: this narrow fissure went a long way down.

He stepped over it, then Paula did the same.

As they approached the barracks entrance, Leland thought the airlock door was cracked open. There was a dark line on the edge of the door. He wouldn't tell whether it was a simple shadow or whether it was a gap inside.

He felt a tug on the rope. "What do you need?" he asked Paula distractedly.

Leland tried to take another step, but the rope was taut. He turned around.

Paula was gone.

The rope still led from Leland's harness to the ship, but now it took a detour into the fissure.

The fissure had opened wide enough to swallow Paula, and no more.

Leland's heart jumped into his throat. He leaped back to the fissure, calling Paula's name.

He reached the edge.

The rope hung tautly down either side of the newly widened opening. Darkness overpowered Leland's lights.

Shit. Paula was annoying, but she didn't deserve to go out like that. This was supposed to be a simple, boring job.

Leland dug his heels in. He activated his boot clamps, which spiked down into the ground. Then he used the remote to activate the winch back on the ship. Normally, this would gently pull Leland back in. But now, he resisted the downward pull of Paula's weight as the winch shortened the rope to lift her out of the fissure.

Her hip and arm appeared first, then the rest of her body.

"Get me out!" she gasped.

One of Leland's boot clamps slipped. He dug in his other foot, deep as he could.

Paula grabbed the edge of the opened fissure. That took the weight off Leland, and he collapsed onto his butt.

Paula climbed out.

"What happened?" Leland wheezed.

"It felt like something reached up and grabbed me."

Leland caught his breath. He tried to judge her expression through her helmet. "Do you mean that literally?"

"That's what it felt like. But no, I sank into the dirt before I fell through. That's probably what was so tight around my ankles at first." Paula's chest heaved. "I saw inside the barracks dome."

Leland looked over his shoulder. The door was still closed, or maybe cracked open. "What do you mean?"

Paula got to her feet. "Come on, I'll show you."

"Like hell I'm going down that fissure."

"No, this way," Paula said. She helped him up, and they went to the barracks doors.

The dark line was a gap. Regardless of whether the cracks overtop the dome had breached the barracks, the front doors were open. The outer door of the airlock was opened just barely. The inner door was gone.

Together, Leland and Paula pulled the outer door open wide enough to step through.

Inside, the airlock opened wide into the whole dome.

Leland looked up at the ceiling.

Stars twinkled through the cracks in the dome.

"Those cracks went right through," Leland said. "Who knows how long the barrack's atmosphere's been gone."

"Or the floor," Paula said.

Leland had been so focused on the ceiling that he hadn't noticed the floor was gone.

A massive crater filled the space where the miners once lived. Its edges were layers of white porcelain with dust in between. Sections had collapsed, forming caverns that extended into the asteroid. That's how Paula had seen inside when she fell. It all formed an inverse of the dome, including the cracks.

Dark fissures spread around the crater.

"Look," Paula said. She pointed with arm outstretched. She wasn't pointing for Leland's sake but for her eventual viewers.

Leland saw what had caught her eye. Bodies lay in a pile at the bottom of the crater. They were wearing their atmosphere suits.

"The miners," Leland whispered reverently.

Paula pointed her visor at him, taking in the shock of the man who'd rescued thousands of stranded miners over the years, but now—through no fault of his own—had failed.

"What do you think happened?" she asked. "What did OCAM do?"

"They took what they wanted and they left," Leland said, "like they always do."

"They don't always kill sixty miners," Paula said. "Or are you saying that this has always been a risk based on OCAM's practices? Have they been skirting regulations?"

Leland snapped. "Would you quit trying to drum up new evils to pin on OCAM? Look around! These people live away from their families for years at a time and get paid a pittance. Now they're dead. Who cares if OCAM was negligent for twenty minutes or twenty years?"

"The regulatory agencies will care."

"Ha. Not likely. Best we can do is make a report. Then one day, after years of legal holdups, OCAM will get slapped with a paltry fine."

"You sure seem to care about this a lot more now than you did an hour ago."

"I always care. There's no point in caring. So I fly people home."

"If you care, then do something about it. Don't just slap a bandage on all the wounds they cause—stop the damage in the first place."

"And how exactly would I do that?"

Paula walked to the edge of the crater. "These videos aren't for a documentary. They're not for the regulatory agencies."

"Then what are they for?"

Across the crater, an eye opened up in a fissure. It was as big across as Leland was tall.

"Shit, do you see that?" gasped Leland.

The eye was the off-white of sour milk, with a triangle-shaped iris that was neon pink. It looked about in staccato jerks until settling on Leland and Paula.

Three more opened up, each with neon-pink irises that glowed in the darkness. They darted around until finding Leland and Paula to look at.

"Is this an asteroid?" Paula asked. "Or were they digging into something living?"

Leland backed toward the airlock. "We should go."

The closest eye crawled out of the ground. It broke free with a slurping sound.

There was movement in the dark around the eye—a body—but the glowing-pink iris blocked Leland from seeing any details.

"It's coming toward us," Paula said.

There was another slurping sound as a second eye popped free from the white dust of the ground.

They turned to run.

Where the dome met the floor, next to the airlock, were four miners' bodies. He hadn't seen them on the way in, but now they glowed pink.

The corpse on top shook and shivered. Something crunched.

An eye rose up from beneath the pile, shaking off three of the bodies. The fourth was jammed between the massive glowing eye and its dark socket. The corpse bounced and was pulled deeper inside.

"Run!" Leland ordered.

They ran past the eye and its meal, back through the airlock, out into the pale darkness of the asteroid's surface. Leland activated the winch. Their retreat became stumbling leaps as the winch pulled them to the ship.

Holes opened up along the narrow fissure. Eyes blinked open in all of them.

Leland and Paula raced up the ship's ramp into the embarking bay. He slammed his palm against the button to raise it.

Eyes with pink, glowing irises approached as it slowly raised.

As the ramp was nearly closed, one eye drew near. A black, branching limb reached inside the ship. The might of the pneumatics snapped off the limb, and it fell dead on the metal floor.

"What was that?" Paula breathed.

"I have no idea." Leland pulled off his atmosphere suit as fast as he could. "Those bastards."

"OCAM?"

"Yes, OCAM!" Leland ran back to the cockpit, with Paula following. "We knew they evacuated early. They must have found these creatures, decided that made the asteroid unprofitable, and then evacuated. They left the miners to die and didn't bother telling us the danger we were flying into." He strapped into the captain's chair and switched on the ship's thrusters.

Paula sat as well. "I've got enough footage for my colleagues. They'll support our taking action."

"What action? I already told you filing a report won't do a thing."

"Does this ship have a tow cable?"

"Of course."

"Drag the asteroid into OCAM's space-station headquarters," said Paula.

The ship's lift-off pushed them down into their chairs, stopping their conversation. Leland had nothing to do but imagine those creatures devouring the miners who had relied on OCAM for safety.

By the time Leland could talk again, he was confident in his answer to Paula. He toggled the controls for the tow cable and said, "Let's give those eyeballs a ride."

IN SPACE, NO ONE CAN HEAR YOU BECOME

Steven Pajak

COUNTING THE DAYS

I've done this exact procedure 487 times since launch. I know because I've been counting—not in the logs, just in my head where the others can't hear the desperate tick of numbers that keeps me sane. The life support scrubbers have become my children.

My fingers brush over the control panel, feeling the subtle vibration. In space, you feel things before you see them.

The CO_2 readout flickers: 0.052%. Higher than yesterday's 0.048%. Nothing concerning—the acceptable range extends to 0.1%—but the slow climb gnaws at me.

"Everything good down there?" Commander Lena's voice crackles over the comms, making me flinch.

“Normal parameters. CO_2’s up a hair, but nothing to write home about.”

“Record it anyway,” she replies, her voice clipped in that particular way it’s become over the last few weeks.

The silence that follows isn’t silence at all. In space, silence is a myth. The ever-present hum of circulation fans, the occasional ping of metal contracting in shadow, the whir of hard drives—it forms a symphony that never ends.

“You’ve been down there ninety-six minutes.” Saoirse’s voice is softer than Lena’s, almost warm, but with that subtle undercurrent of clinical observation. “That’s eighteen minutes longer than your standard check.”

I hadn’t noticed. “Wanted to be thorough.”

When I round the corner to the monitoring station, Saoirse is waiting, her dark eyes fixed on her tablet. The circles under her eyes have deepened. Her hair, once meticulously secured in a tight bun, now has wisps escaping around her temples.

“Have you been sleeping better?” she asks, still not looking up.

The lie comes easily. “Yeah. Like a baby.”

Now she does look up, her expression making it clear she knows I’m full of shit.

“Your REM patterns suggest otherwise.” She flicks her finger across the screen. “You’re averaging only sixty-seven minutes per cycle.”

“Been reading my dreams too, Doc?” I try to smile but can feel how it doesn’t reach my eyes.

“Your biometrics are my business. So is the fact that none of us are sleeping properly.” She tucks a loose strand of hair behind her ear. “I’ve been having dreams about drowning. Not in water, but in silence.”

Something cold slithers down my spine. I haven’t admitted that my own dreams have taken a similar turn.

The ship's galley—if you could call the cramped alcove a galley—is where we take our meals together. Commander's orders: maintain social cohesion through shared mealtimes.

"Engineering status?" Lena asks, fork paused halfway to her mouth.

"All systems nominal," I reply automatically. "Minor adjustment to the thermal regulators in section C."

Lena nods, accepting my assessment without question. "Navigation check at 1800. I'll need you to verify the alignment on the gyroscopic stabilizers."

A sharp ping from Lena's tablet interrupts the silence.

"Data packet from Mission Control," she says, scanning the screen. "Standard stuff."

Static suddenly bursts through the overhead speaker, startling all three of us. It crackles for three seconds before cutting out just as abruptly.

I look up. "That's the third time this week."

"Electromagnetic interference," Lena says, too quickly. "We're passing through a dense field. It'll clear up."

"We charted this sector," Saoirse points out. "There shouldn't be significant interference."

"Charts are approximations." Lena's tone shuts down further discussion.

Later, while checking a faulty panel in the aft storage section, I hear it: a faint tapping, like metal on metal, rhythmic but irregular. One tap. Two taps. Pause. Three taps.

I push myself toward the sound, deeper into the storage section where shadows gather despite the supposedly uniform lighting. Nothing. The tapping has stopped.

"Computer, run diagnostic on hull integrity, aft section."

"Hull integrity at 100 percent," the pleasant, sexless voice replies. "No anomalies detected."

I make a note in my tablet anyway, then promptly forget about it as an alarm chimes in the environmental control room.

By cycle's end, I'm exhausted in that peculiar way that promises no real rest. The comms channel is open beside me, white noise whispering from the speaker. Then, so faint I almost miss it, there's a voice in the static.

"Ronan."

I jerk upright, heart hammering against my ribs.

"Computer, replay last audio segment, comms channel four."

"No vocal patterns detected in the last sixty seconds of audio on comms channel four."

I press my palm against the cold glass of the viewport, feeling the immense emptiness beyond. The stars stare back, silent and judging, while something inside me begins to splinter.

It's just the mission. The isolation. The routine that's slowly driving us all mad.

I'm not hearing things.

I'm not.

But as I turn to leave, the static whispers again, and this time, I choose not to hear it at all.

WHEN SHE LEFT ME

The alert blares at 0400 ship time, tearing me from thin sleep. I'm moving before my mind fully registers what's happening, muscle memory propelling me toward the command center.

Lena is already there, her face illuminated by the harsh red glow of emergency lighting. Saoirse arrives seconds after me, her hair loose around her shoulders.

"External communications array is down," Lena says without preamble. "Complete signal loss on all channels."

I lean over her shoulder, scanning the diagnostic readouts. "Could be a software glitch."

"It's not," Lena replies, pulling up an external camera feed. "Look."

The image shows the communications array—a delicate assemblage of dishes and antennae extending from the ship's hull. One of the main dishes is twisted at an unnatural angle, as if struck by something. Or as if something had grabbed it and wrenched it sideways.

"Micrometeoroid impact?" Saoirse suggests.

I shake my head. "The trajectory's wrong. Looks more like ..." I trail off, unable to explain what I'm seeing.

"Doesn't matter what caused it," Lena says firmly. "What matters is fixing it. We're already seventeen days from scheduled check-in. If we miss it, they'll flag us as compromised."

"EVA required," I say, the words falling heavy from my lips. "I can have the array operational again in ninety minutes."

"I'm going with you," Lena announces. "Two-person minimum for external repairs. Protocol."

The EVA prep room is silent except for the hiss of air cycling and the soft clink of metal as we methodically check our suits.

"You look like you're dressing us for a funeral," I say to Saoirse, attempting levity.

She pauses on my helmet. "Don't joke about that." Her voice is barely above a whisper. "I had that dream again. The drowning one."

"Enough," Lena cuts in. "Focus on the mission."

The airlock is a cramped, sterile box that makes my chest constrict with claustrophobia. As the air begins to evacuate, I focus on my breathing. Slow. Controlled. By the book.

"Nervous?" Lena asks through the suit's comm.

"Always am."

"Good." She checks her tether one last time. "Fear keeps you alive out there."

The outer door opens with agonizing slowness, revealing the abyss. No matter how many times I see it, the sheer emptiness of space never fails to hollow me out.

We move together, magnetic boots securing us to the hull with each deliberate step. The stars wheel slowly above us as we move, eternal and indifferent.

The damage is worse up close. The main dish isn't just twisted—it's partially sheared off, the metal torn as if grabbed by an enormous hand and wrenched sideways.

"This doesn't match any impact pattern I've ever seen," I say.

"Focus on the repair, not the cause," Lena replies, but I can hear the strain in her voice.

I'm reaching for the primary coupling when my boot slips. One moment I'm secure on the hull; the next, I'm drifting, spinning slowly into the void.

"Ronan!" Lena's voice cuts through my panic.

My safety tether has caught me, leaving me dangling five meters from the hull. The slow rotation of my drift sends waves of nausea through me as the stars wheel in disorienting patterns.

"I'm okay," I manage. "Tether held."

"Initiating retrieval." Lena's voice is steady as she activates the tether's retraction mechanism.

That's when I hear it again—that same faint tapping from within my helmet. Metal on metal. Rhythmic. Deliberate.

"Do you hear that?" I ask.

"Focus, Marrik. Nearly there."

The tapping stops as suddenly as it began. I'm almost back to the hull, Lena's outstretched hand just meters away, when something flashes in my peripheral vision—a streak of darkness against the stars, moving too fast to track.

"Commander, watch—"

The impact is silent, as all things in space are. One moment, Lena is reaching for me; the next, her body jerks violently as something strikes her suit. A small, dark object punches through her left shoulder, the momentum spinning her halfway around.

"Lena!" I lunge forward as my boots reconnect with the hull, catching her before she can drift away. "Saoirse, emergency in Airlock 2! Lena's been hit!"

Blood. That's my first coherent thought as we tumble back through the airlock. Blood forming perfect spheres in zero gravity, drifting lazily like crimson planets.

Saoirse is waiting, emergency kit already open. "Med bay. Now!"

The three of us move as one organism down the corridor, Saoirse and I supporting Lena between us. The commander's face is gray, eyes unfocused but still conscious.

"Pressure...compromised," Lena mumbles. "Felt the...air go."

The med bay is the largest single room on the ship. I help transfer Lena to the treatment table, then step back, suddenly useless as Saoirse's medical training takes over.

"Cut the suit away. I need to see the wound." Saoirse's hands move with practiced efficiency, trauma scissors slicing through the reinforced fabric of the EVA suit.

The wound is a perfect circle, too clean to have been made by typical space debris. Something has punched through the suit, through flesh and bone, and out the other side.

"Arterial damage," Saoirse mutters. "Need to stop the bleeding before—"

Lena's body suddenly arches, a strangled gasp escaping her lips. The monitors erupt in a cacophony of alarms as her vitals spike then plummet.

"No, no, no!" Saoirse grabs the crash kit. "Ronan, get the defibrillator!"

I move without thinking, retrieving equipment, helping where I can, but it's like watching through murky water. Saoirse shouting instructions. My own hands, slick with Lena's blood. The commander's face growing more ashen by the second.

And then, stillness.

The alarms quiet, replaced by a single, continuous tone that drills into my skull. Saoirse stands frozen, staring down at Lena's unmoving form, her hands still pressed against the wound.

"Time of death," Saoirse whispers, her voice cracking, "14:37 ship time."

"Check again," I say, the words scraping my throat raw. "There has to be something—"

"She's gone, Ronan." Saoirse finally lifts her hands from Lena's body, leaving bloody prints on her medical gown. "The debris severed her subclavian artery. Even if we'd gotten her inside faster ..."

We stand in silence, the hum of the ship suddenly deafening in the absence of Lena's voice.

"We need to...preserve her," I say finally. "Until we return to Earth."

Saoirse nods mechanically. "The stasis unit. Lower deck storage."

Together, we prepare Lena's body, wrapping her in the special polymer sheet designed for this exact contingency that no one ever truly believes will happen. The stasis unit hums to life as we place her inside. The lid closes with a soft hiss of hydraulics, and just like that, Commander Lena Voronin is reduced to cargo.

Afterward, we drift apart without discussion. Saoirse locks herself in her quarters. I find myself in the command chair—Lena's chair—staring blankly at the controls.

The comms array is still damaged, the repair incomplete. We're cut off from Earth, from Mission Control, from anyone who might tell us what to do next.

And somewhere, far below my conscious thoughts, a terrible realization begins to take root: we're alone in the void, millions of kilometers from home, with no way to call for help.

And something out there killed our commander.

FALLING APART

Three days after we put Lena in the stasis unit, I find myself at the command chair again, standing behind it, hands gripping the backrest as if it might anchor me to something solid in a reality that's turned fluid and unreliable.

I haven't slept more than two hours at a stretch since the incident. Every time I close my eyes, I see it again—the flash of movement, the impact, Lena's body jerking as the debris tore through her suit.

"The comms array is still down."

I startle at Saoirse's voice. She stands in the doorway, datapad clutched to her chest like a shield. Her face is drawn, eyes rimmed with red. She's been crying again.

"I know." My voice sounds rusty from disuse.

"We need to complete the repairs." She steps into the command center. "We need to report what happened."

"Report to who?" I turn back to the main console. "We're fourteen days from the nearest relay point. Even if we fix the array, who's going to hear us?"

"That's not the point." Saoirse's voice hardens slightly. "Protocol states—"

"Fuck protocol." The vehemence in my own voice surprises me. "Protocol didn't save her."

Silence stretches between us, taut as a wire.

"I've been writing," Saoirse says finally, holding up her datapad. "Keeping a record. Someone should...document what's happened."

I turn away. "I'll make another attempt on the comms array tomorrow."

"We should go together," Saoirse says.

"No." The word comes out sharper than I intend. "One of us needs to stay inside."

Saoirse watches me for a long moment, then nods. "I'll be in my quarters if you need me."

Alone again, I sink into the command chair at last. Lena's chair. I turn to the navigation console, bringing up our trajectory projections. What I see makes my blood run cold.

According to the data, we're no longer on our plotted return path. The deviation is subtle—a fraction of a degree—but over millions of kilometers, that means missing Earth entirely.

I'm still staring at the screen when the static on the comms channel changes pitch. It rises and falls in patterns that almost sound like words.

"Check the airlock."

My head snaps toward the speaker. Three words, clear as day, in Lena's voice.

"Computer, replay last audio segment from comms channel four."

"No vocal patterns detected in the last sixty seconds of audio on comms channel four."

I spend the next six hours attempting to correct our trajectory, wrestling with thruster calculations and fuel consumption ratios. The numbers refuse to cooperate. Our primary correction thrusters are operating at reduced efficiency, and the secondary systems can't generate enough delta-v to bring us back on course without depleting our return fuel reserves to dangerous levels.

By the time I stumble to the galley for a meal that's twelve hours overdue, my mind is a fog of technical problems with no solutions.

Saoirse is already there, stirring a cup of something that steams but otherwise looks unappetizing.

"You look like hell," she observes.

"Thanks." I reach for a meal pouch. "Navigation system's showing a course deviation."

Saoirse's spoon pauses halfway to her mouth. "How bad?"

"Bad enough. I'm working on it."

We eat in silence for a while, the only sound the soft hum of the circulation fans.

"Do you ever feel like we're not alone on this ship?" Saoirse asks suddenly.

The question freezes me mid-bite. "What do you mean?"

She stares into her cup. "I was in the lab earlier. I kept feeling like...like someone was watching me. Standing right behind me." She looks up, meeting my eyes. "I've never had that feeling before."

I set down my spoon, appetite gone. "It's just the two of us. Was three." I correct myself automatically. "Now it's two. No one else."

"I know that." Saoirse's fingers tap a rapid rhythm on the table. "Rationally, I know that. But ..." She trails off, then shakes her head. "Never mind. Forget I said anything."

I want to forget it. But my mind keeps circling back to the voice in the static. *Check the airlock*.

"Have you been hearing anything unusual?" I ask carefully. "On the comms, maybe?"

Something flickers in Saoirse's eyes—recognition, fear, I can't tell. "Like what?"

"Just...noises. Static patterns. Anything out of the ordinary."

She hesitates. "No. Nothing specific." The lie is transparent. "Why? Have you?"

"No." I match her lie with one of my own.

That night, unable to sleep, I find myself wandering the corridors of the ship. My footsteps echo on the metal grating, each sound bouncing back at me a fraction of a second too late, as if something else is walking a half-step behind me.

I end up at Airlock 2—the same one we used for the EVA that killed Lena. The external repair tools are still floating out there, abandoned in the chaos after she was hit.

Check the airlock.

A movement in my peripheral vision makes me turn sharply, heart hammering. Nothing. Just shadows and imagination.

When ship's morning comes, I drag myself to the command center to find Saoirse already there, datapad in hand, staring at the main viewscreen.

"You're up early," I observe.

She doesn't turn. "Didn't sleep. Again." Her voice is distant. "I've been reviewing Lena's final logs."

I feel a chill. "Why?"

"Looking for anything unusual. Anything that might explain...," she gestures vaguely, "...everything."

"And?"

"Nothing concrete. But her sleep patterns were deteriorating faster than ours. Her last personal log mentioned hearing noises in the starboard storage section." Saoirse finally turns to face me. "The same section where you heard tapping before the incident."

My mouth goes dry. "She never reported that officially."

"No. She didn't." Saoirse's gaze is steady. "What else haven't you reported, Ronan?"

That night, I dream of the EVA again. But this time, when Lena reaches for me, her face behind the helmet visor isn't her own. It's Saoirse's. And when the debris strikes, it passes through her as if she's made of smoke, continuing on its trajectory until it slams into my chest, tearing through suit and flesh and bone.

I wake with a strangled gasp, sweat-soaked and trembling.

Movement. There's movement at the foot of my bunk.

"Saoirse?" My voice cracks. "What are you doing?"

No response. The figure doesn't move.

"Computer, lights to fifty percent."

The overhead lights come on gradually, illuminating my empty quarters. No one at the foot of my bunk. No one in the room at all.

But when I open my door to check the corridor, I catch a glimpse of movement at the far end—a flash of white fabric disappearing around the corner.

I follow.

The corridor stretches ahead, emergency lights casting pools of dim blue illumination every few meters. At the end is Airlock 3—the smallest of the ship's airlocks, used primarily for jettisoning waste and damaged equipment.

As I approach, I see her—Saoirse, dressed in her white sleep clothes, standing motionless before the airlock controls, one hand raised toward the emergency override panel.

"Saoirse," I call softly, not wanting to startle her.

She doesn't respond, doesn't turn, doesn't acknowledge me in any way. Her eyes are open but vacant, gaze fixed on the airlock door without seeing it. Her lips move slightly, forming words I can't hear.

Sleepwalking. She's sleepwalking.

"Saoirse. Wake up."

Her eyes remain unfocused, but her lips stop moving. For a moment, we stand like that—a frozen tableau of two broken people in the dim blue light.

Then Saoirse blinks, awareness returning to her eyes. She looks at me, then at the airlock, confusion giving way to horror as she realizes where she is.

"What am I—" She stumbles backward. "Why am I here?"

"You were sleepwalking," I explain, keeping my voice calm. "I found you here, about to open the airlock."

"No." She shakes her head violently. "No, I wouldn't. I couldn't."

"You weren't conscious. You didn't know what you were doing."

She wraps her arms around herself. "I remember dreaming. Someone was calling my name. Telling me to open the door. Telling me she was outside. Waiting."

A chill runs down my spine. "Who was outside?"

Saoirse looks at me, eyes wide with fear. "Lena. She said Lena was outside."

I look past her to the small viewport in the airlock door. Beyond it, only stars and empty space.

"She's not out there," I say. "She's in stasis. You know that. We put her there together."

"Then who's talking to me in my dreams?" Saoirse demands, voice rising. "Who's whispering in the static? Who's tapping on the walls when no one's there?"

BREAKING POINT

I find Saoirse on the observation deck two days later, her silhouette small against the vast tableau of stars. Her datapad lies beside her, screen dark. She's been writing less, I notice. Or at least, she's been letting me see her write less.

"CO_2 levels have stabilized," I say, breaking the silence. "I adjusted the scrubbers. Should bring the concentrations back within optimal range within eight hours."

She nods, still gazing out at the endless void. "Good."

I step closer. "Any more sleepwalking episodes?"

"No." Saoirse's reflection shows dark circles under her eyes. "I haven't been sleeping at all."

Neither have I, but I don't say so. We're both painfully aware of our deteriorating conditions.

"I've been thinking," Saoirse says, her voice oddly flat. "About our options."

Something in her tone makes my skin prickle. "Options for what?"

"For ending this." She turns to face me finally, her expression terrifyingly calm. "On our terms."

I stare at her, the words not immediately making sense. Then understanding crashes over me like ice water. "You can't be serious."

"I'm perfectly serious." Saoirse's gaze is steady. "We've lost communication with Earth. Our trajectory is compromised. Environmental systems are showing signs of degradation. And we're both experiencing psychosis. These aren't conditions we can survive indefinitely."

"So your solution is to—what? Open an airlock? Inject ourselves with one of your medical cocktails?"

"It would be quick," she says softly, "painless. Better than whatever's happening to us now."

I take a step back, repulsed by the calm rationality in her voice. "No. Absolutely not."

"Think about it, Ronan. Really think." She stands, moving toward me with a fluidity that seems almost predatory. "What's our best-case scenario? We drift for months, slowly running out of supplies, watching each other deteriorate until one of us snaps completely? And then what?"

"We fix the comms," I insist. "We correct our course. We complete the mission."

A sad smile flickers across Saoirse's face. "The mission died with Lena. You know that as well as I do."

"So we just give up? Lena would never—"

"Lena is dead!" The sudden sharpness in Saoirse's voice makes me flinch. "She's nothing but frozen flesh in a box now. She doesn't care what we do."

The words hit me hard. Not because they're cruel—though they are—but because a part of me has been thinking the same thing.

"I need to check the navigation systems," I say, retreating toward the door.

"You're in denial," Saoirse calls after me. "Running away from the inevitable won't change it."

I spend the next four hours in the command center, running simulation after simulation, searching for the mathematical solution that will deliver us from our trajectory toward oblivion. The numbers remain obstinate.

The static on the comms channel changes pitch, rising and falling in patterns that almost sound like words.

"She's not right."

My head snaps toward the speaker. Three words, clear as day, in Lena's voice.

"Computer, replay last audio segment from comms channel four."

"No vocal patterns detected in the last sixty seconds of audio on comms channel four."

The words linger. *She's not right.* What isn't Saoirse right about?

I find myself bringing up the crew logs, navigating to Saoirse's personal files. Most are encrypted—medical records, research notes, her private journal. But the system activity logs are accessible to me as the ship's engineer.

What I find makes my blood run cold.

Three nights ago, while I'd been in the command center, Saoirse accessed the stasis unit. She overrode the security protocols, opened the unit, and spent forty-seven minutes inside the storage bay where Lena's body is kept.

Two nights ago, Saoirse ran a series of searches on the medical database. Toxins. Sedatives. Euthanasia protocols. Last night, after I'd left her alone, Saoirse accessed my personal medical file. My allergies. My metabolic rates. My specific biochemistry. And then she authorized access to restricted pharmaceuticals from the medical bay—compounds that, in the right combination, would be lethal to someone with my exact profile.

She isn't proposing we die together. She's planning to kill me.

I close the logs, breath coming in short gasps. It makes a terrible kind of sense. In Saoirse's mind, she's being merciful. Practical. Ending things cleanly before we descend further into madness.

I need to find her. Confront her. Or avoid her. I'm not sure which.

I approach her quarters. The door is unlocked—unusual for Saoirse, who values her privacy. It slides open at my touch, revealing darkness beyond.

"Saoirse?" I call softly, reaching for the light panel.

The room illuminates gradually, revealing Saoirse's quarters in disarray. And there, on the wall beside her workstation, is a sprawling web of notes and diagrams that makes my breath catch in my throat.

She's been mapping the ship's anomalies. Every power fluctuation. Every unusual sound. Every instance of static. But she's also been mapping me—my movements, my behaviors, my symptoms. Notes in her precise handwriting detail my "increasing paranoia" and "auditory hallucinations."

He hears voices, one note reads. *Claims it's nothing, but his sleep patterns and cortisol levels suggest acute stress response. Possible psychotic break imminent.*

I stare at the evidence of Saoirse's surveillance, feeling something crack inside me. She's been studying me like a specimen while planning my euthanasia.

"What are you doing in my quarters?"

I whirl around to find Saoirse standing in the doorway, a medical kit clutched in one hand. Her face is expressionless, but her eyes dart from me to the wall of notes and back again.

"What is all this?" I demand, gesturing at the display.

"Research." She steps into the room, letting the door close behind her. "Observation notes."

"On me. You've been spying on me."

"Monitoring," she corrects. "It's my job to maintain crew health."

"Your job?" My voice rises. "Lena is dead. The mission is compromised. But you're still following protocols?"

"Someone has to." Saoirse sets the medical kit on her desk with deliberate care. "One of us needs to maintain objectivity."

"Objectivity?" I laugh, a harsh sound that doesn't sound like me at all. "Is that what you call planning to euthanize me?"

Something flashes in Saoirse's eyes—surprise, fear, guilt, I can't tell. "You accessed my research logs."

"I accessed the system logs. I know you've been gathering compounds specifically tailored to my biochemistry. I know you accessed the stasis unit. What did you do to Lena's body?"

"Nothing." Saoirse's voice hardens. "I was confirming preservation status. Standard procedure."

"There's nothing standard about any of this!" I gesture wildly at the wall of notes. "You think I'm going insane."

"You are going insane," Saoirse says quietly. "We both are. But you're further along. You hear her voice in the static. You talk to yourself when you think no one's listening."

"That doesn't give you the right to decide when I die."

"Someone has to make the hard choices. Lena would have—"

"Don't." I take a step toward her, fists clenched. "Don't you dare use her name to justify this."

Saoirse doesn't back away. Her hand drifts toward the medical kit, a movement so subtle I might have missed it if I weren't watching for exactly that.

"Step away from the kit," I say, voice low.

"You're proving my point, Ronan." Her tone is maddeningly calm. "Your paranoia is accelerating. You're becoming dangerous."

"I'm becoming dangerous?" I laugh again, that strange, harsh sound. "You're the one planning to murder me!"

"It's not murder. It's mercy." Saoirse's hand closes around something in the medical kit. "I've watched you deteriorating. Talking to ghosts. Following shadow figures through the corridors. How long before you decide I'm a threat? How long before you do something we can't take back?"

"Saoirse," I say, trying for a calmer tone, "put down whatever you're holding. We need to talk about this rationally."

"We're beyond rational discussion." Her hand emerges from the kit, holding a hypospray. "This is the only way that it doesn't end in prolonged suffering."

"For who?" I take another step forward. "For me? Or for you?"

Saoirse's steady gaze falters for just a moment. "For both of us."

"That's not your decision to make." Another step. I'm within arm's reach now.

"Someone has to make it." The hypospray trembles slightly in her hand. "Lena's gone. Mission Control can't help us. It's just us now, and one of us has to be strong enough to end this cleanly."

"And that's you? The one who sleepwalks to airlocks? Who claims to hear Lena calling from outside the ship?" I gesture to the device lying on her bunk. "What's in there, Saoirse? What are you writing that you don't want me to see?"

Her eyes flick to the datapad, then back to me. A mistake. That momentary distraction is all I need.

I lunge forward, grabbing for her wrist, trying to knock the hypospray from her hand. Saoirse reacts with surprising speed, twisting away from me. The hypospray clatters to the floor, skidding under the bunk.

"Ronan, stop!" she shouts, backing away.

But I'm not listening anymore. A roaring fills my ears, drowning out her words. The room seems to pulse around me, shadows elongating and contracting with each frantic beat of my heart. I have to stop her. Have to protect myself.

My hand closes around a tool on her desk—a heavy spanner I had used to repair the circulation system last week. I don't even realize I'm reaching for it until its weight settles in my palm.

"Put that down," Saoirse says, eyes fixed on the makeshift weapon. "Ronan, please. You don't want to do this."

"You were going to kill me." My voice sounds distant to my own ears, as if someone else is speaking through me.

"I was trying to save you." Tears fill her eyes. "From this. From what we're becoming. Please, Ronan. It doesn't have to end like this."

But in my mind, it already has. In my mind, she made her choice when she researched the specific compounds that would stop my heart.

"You think I'm dangerous," I say softly. "You're right."

The motion is almost instinctive. A single, fluid arc of my arm. The spanner connects with Saoirse's temple with a dull thud that seems to echo through the small room.

Her eyes widen in shock. No fear. No anger. Just profound, bewildered surprise. She staggers backward, one hand rising to touch the point of impact, fingers coming away red with blood.

"Ronan?" My name on her lips, a question I can't answer.

Then her legs buckle, and she collapses to the floor.

For a moment, I stand frozen, the spanner still clutched in my hand. The silence is so complete it seems to press against my eardrums. I stare down at Saoirse's crumpled form, at the blood pooling beneath her head, and the reality of what I've done crashes over me like a physical wave.

"No," I whisper, dropping to my knees beside her. "Saoirse, no."

But she doesn't respond. Her eyes stare sightlessly at the ceiling, pupils fixed and dilated. The blood spreads in a perfect circle around her head, a halo of crimson against the sterile-white floor.

"Computer," I call, voice cracking. "Medical emergency in Dr. Kwan's quarters!"

"Medical emergency acknowledged," the pleasant, sexless voice replies. "Dr. Kwan is the designated medical officer. Please specify alternative medical personnel."

"There is no alternative!"

I gather Saoirse's limp form in my arms and carry her through the silent corridors to the medical bay. I lay her on the treatment table, movements frantic as I activate the diagnostic systems.

Massive cranial trauma. Hemorrhage. No vital signs detected.

Saoirse is dead.

I stare at the readouts, unable to process what they mean. What I've done. My hands are covered in her blood, sticky and cooling rapidly in the sterile air of the medical bay.

"No," I say again, the word meaningless now. "No, no, no."

I initiate resuscitation protocols, watching as robotic arms descend from the ceiling, administering drugs, applying electrical stimulation, attempting to restart her heart. Each attempt registers on the monitors, each failure marked by another alarm.

After seventeen minutes, the system overrides my commands.

"Resuscitation efforts unsuccessful," the computer informs me. "Time of death: 21:43 ship time."

I turn and walk out of the medical bay, leaving Saoirse's body on the table, the lights still blazing, the monitors still flashing their useless warnings.

The comms channel crackles with static, the sound rising and falling in patterns that almost sound like words.

"What have you done, Ronan?"

This time, I don't ask the computer to replay the segment. Let them accuse me. Let them haunt me. It's no less than I deserve.

"I didn't mean to," I say to the empty air, to the ghosts, to myself. "I was trying to protect myself."

"From what?"

From what, indeed? From Saoirse's mercy? From a death that would have been quick and painless? From the inevitable end that awaits me anyway, now alone on a drifting ship with two corpses for company?

BECOMING

Time loses meaning. I can't say how long I've been sitting in the command chair, staring at nothing. The blood on my hands has dried, flaking away like rust. I haven't bothered to wash it off. What's the point? Who's left to see?

I rise from the chair, legs unsteady from disuse. My reflection in one of the darkened displays shows a stranger—hollow-eyed, gaunt, beard growing in patches across sunken cheeks.

I make my way to the communications station, my movements mechanical. The voices are all I have left.

"I know you're there," I say, voice cracking from disuse. "I know you can hear me."

The static shifts, patterns forming and dissolving like waves.

"We've always been here," the voices whisper back, a perfect harmony of Lena and Saoirse. "Waiting. Watching."

"What are you?" I ask. "Ghosts? Hallucinations? Something else?"

"Yes," comes the reply, maddeningly ambiguous. "All of those. None of those. We are the void given voice, the silence made sound. The spaces between your thoughts."

I laugh, a harsh sound that echoes in the empty command center. "Poetic. But not helpful."

"We don't exist to help you, Ronan." This sounds more like Lena, authoritative even in death. "We exist because you need us to, because the human mind can't comprehend true isolation, true silence."

"So I created you." The realization should be comforting—evidence that I'm not truly haunted, just broken. But instead, it terrifies me more. If the voices are coming from within my own fractured mind, then there's no escape from them.

"No," the voices say in unison. "We've always existed. We simply found you. Found this ship. Found minds fragile enough to hear us."

I activate the recording function at my personal workstation. The small camera light blinks on, capturing my haggard face.

"Final mission log," I begin, voice scratchy. "Engineer Ronan Marrik recording. Date unknown. Commander Voronin is dead. Medical Officer Kwan is dead. I am the sole survivor of the mission."

I stare directly into the camera, desperate to convey something beyond the sterile facts of our failure.

"I want to make it clear that Commander Voronin and Medical Officer Kwan performed their duties with the highest level of professionalism and courage. The mission's failure is my responsibility alone.

"There's something out here," I continue, leaning closer to the camera. "Something that isn't in any of our training materials or scientific understanding. Something that exists in the void between stars. It found us. It spoke to us. It turned us against each other.

"This is a warning. Don't come looking for us. Don't send another ship to this sector.

"End recording," I say finally.

But instead of stopping, the camera light blinks faster.

"Computer, end recording," I repeat more forcefully.

Nothing changes. The light continues to blink, faster and faster, like a racing heartbeat.

I reach for the manual override, fingers trembling. Before I can touch it, the display flashes once, brightly, then goes dark. The recording is gone—unsaved, unarchived, unwitnessed.

Like it had never happened at all.

"They won't hear you," Saoirse's voice says from behind me. "They were never going to hear you."

I turn slowly, knowing what I'll see but dreading it all the same. Saoirse stands in the doorway, perfect and whole. No blood. No wound at her temple. Just Saoirse as she was before I killed her.

"You're not real," I whisper.

"Define real," she replies with a sad smile. "Is pain real? Is loneliness? Is guilt? You feel all of those things, don't you?"

I close my eyes, but when I open them, she's still there. "What do you want from me?"

"The wrong question," Lena's voice says from my other side. I turn to see her standing there, in her commander's uniform, as alive as the day we launched. "The question is: what do you want from us?"

"I want to understand," I say, the words escaping before I can consider them. "I want to know what's happening to me. To this ship."

"Then follow us," they say in unison, turning toward the corridor.

I rise from the console, drawn after them like a man in a dream. They lead me to the observation deck. The stars beyond the viewport are unchanged, eternal and indifferent.

"Are you ready to join us, Ronan?" The voices come from everywhere and nowhere, intimate as a lover's whisper against my ear.

"Join you where?" I ask, not turning from the viewport. "In death? In madness? In whatever liminal space you exist in?"

"Does it matter?" This sounds like Saoirse, gentle despite what I did to her. "Anywhere but here. Anywhere but alone."

The idea is seductive in its simplicity. An end to isolation. An end to guilt. An end to the slow, inevitable deterioration of my mind and body in this metal tomb.

I turn away from the viewport, moving with sudden purpose toward Airlock 3—the one where I found Saoirse sleepwalking, her hands reaching for the emergency override.

The airlock controls glow soft blue in the dim lighting. I stand before them, staring at the simple interface that separates me from oblivion. One override. One cycle. One moment of explosive decompression, and then nothing.

My hand hovers over the emergency override panel.

"Is this what you want?" I ask the empty air. "Is this why you've been guiding me here?"

I turn away from the airlock only to freeze at the sight before me.

They stand side by side in the corridor—Lena and Saoirse, solid and real as they had been in life. Both watching me with expressions of infinite patience and terrible understanding.

"You're not real," I whisper, backing against the airlock door. "You're in cold storage. You're in the medical bay. You're dead."

"Death is relative out here," Lena says, her voice no longer coming through static but clear and present. "Boundaries blur. Reality bends."

"We've been trying to help you, Ronan," Saoirse adds, no trace of accusation in her eyes. "To guide you toward understanding."

"Understanding what?" My voice cracks with fear and desperate hope. "What's happening to me? To this ship?"

"That you were never alone," they say in unison. "That the void is not empty. That space itself is alive in ways human science has no framework to comprehend."

I slide down the airlock door until I sit on the cold deck plating, legs no longer able to support me. "What does that mean? What are you saying?"

Lena steps forward, her movement fluid and impossible. "The isolation. The hallucinations. The voices in the static. They weren't symptoms of your deterioration. They were attempts at contact."

"Something found us out here," Saoirse continues, moving to stand beside Lena. "Something ancient and patient and curious. Something that exists in the spaces between stars, in the vacuum, in the radiation that permeates the cosmos."

"It wanted to understand us," Lena says. "To communicate. But its consciousness is so alien, so fundamentally different from our own, that direct contact was impossible."

"So it used what it found in our minds," Saoirse finishes. "Our fears. Our guilt. Our voices. Our perceptions of each other."

"So what now?" I ask. "I just drift until I die? Until I run out of food or air or sanity?"

"There is another option," Lena says, and something in her tone makes me look up.

"What option?"

"Join us," Saoirse says simply. "Become what we've become."

"And what's that, exactly?"

Their smiles are identical, radiant with an emotion I can't name.

"More," they say together. "Something more than human. Something less than physical. Something that can exist in the void without breaking."

"How?" I ask finally. "How do I join you?"

"You already know," Saoirse says, gesturing to the airlock controls beside me.

Understanding blooms in my mind, terrible and perfect. "The airlock. That's why you kept telling me to check it. Why Saoirse was sleepwalking toward it. It's a doorway."

"One of many," Lena confirms. "But the simplest. The quickest. One moment of physical dissolution, and then …"

"Transformation," Saoirse finishes. "Expansion. Understanding."

I rise slowly to my feet, turning to face the airlock controls once more. This time, the decision feels clear. Inevitable.

"Will it hurt?" I ask, a final human concern in the face of cosmic transcendence.

"For a moment," they admit together. "And then never again."

"I'm ready," I say, pressing my palm against the override panel.

The airlock system responds immediately, alarms blaring as safety protocols are bypassed. The inner door slides open, revealing the small chamber beyond. I step inside without hesitation.

The inner door slides closed, sealing me in the small space. Through the viewport, I can see them waiting, their forms flickering more rapidly now, edges blurring into the shadows that pulse and writhe around them.

See you soon, their voices whisper in my mind as the airlock cycle initiates.

The outer door opens.

Space rushes in.

Pain blooms, bright and immediate and all-consuming, as my lungs rupture and my blood boils and my consciousness begins to fragment.

And then—

I am.

That's my first thought. Not coherent, not verbal, but a simple acknowledgment of existence.

I am.

But what I am has changed. Where once there were boundaries—skin, bone, synapse—now there is only expansion. Where once there was singularity—I, me, Ronan—now there is multiplicity.

I feel them with me, through me, as me—Lena, Saoirse, and something else, something vast and ancient and patient that has been waiting for consciousness to breach the void.

We are.

The ship drifts, empty now of human life but filled with something else, something that exists in the spaces between atoms, in the radiation that permeates the cosmos, in the void itself.

A signal pulses outward from the ship, stronger than anything its human designers had intended it to generate. It is a beacon cutting through the silence of space, aimed not at Earth but at the distant stars beyond.

"We are here," the transmission repeats in endless loops. "We are more. We are waiting."

After all, in space, no one can hear you become.

FINAL TRANSMISSION

RJ Roles

"Captain, wake up. Hey, we need you to hear something. Nord, we need you on the bridge now!"

Once again, a distant voice scratched at Nord Bellman's subconscious, pulling him out of his cryosleep-induced coma. Flexing his hands to work out his atrophied muscles, he reached up to clear the ice crystals from his eyes before slowly opening them.

Piercing light blinded him from above. Nord squeezed his eyes shut and took a few deep breaths to prepare himself, then opened them fully. The med bay was a formless mass of bright gray, the worst side effect by far from cryosleep, in Nord's opinion. Allowing himself time to adjust to being awake after... Well, he wasn't sure how long they had slept, but it felt like one of the longer ones if his vision impairment was any indication.

With forms taking vague shape around him, Nord sat up in his pod and braced himself against the back, allowing his circulation to continue working toward normal after being reduced during sleep.

The distant voice came back to him, still incomprehensible except for the last word. "...signal."

Nord waved his hand in the air, dismissing the man until he was fully able to communicate. Even through the fog of the cryo hangover, he was anxious to find out how close they were to their destination. It was their purpose for traveling an unfathomable distance into the heart of the Milky Way, afterall.

Another voice joined in the distant murmuring, and a few words came through more clear and defined. "We don't ... Very odd ... Worried ... Wait on the captain ..."

Nord rubbed the sides of his head, willing himself to acclimate to being awake faster. He concentrated on taking full, deep breaths before letting them out slowly—something he found that helped him after the first half dozen or so times after coming out of deep sleep.

Someone grabbed Nord's shoulder, and he looked up to see the outline of a figure standing in front of him.

"Whosit?" he mumbled, his tongue heavy.

"Proctor, sir."

Taking a few breaths, Nord sighed and squeezed his eyes shut for a few moments before opening them. Blurry features stood out on Proctor's face, signifying his exercises were working.

"Status?" Nord asked.

A pregnant pause hung in the air between them before Proctor answered. "The ship is fine. All systems are functioning as they should, and all crew are alive and accounted for."

Even though his senses hadn't fully returned, Nord could hear the hesitation in the man's voice. "But?"

"Um, well, the *NEST* is making near-lightspeed, and we're about a week out from reaching ED-75b, but ..."

"Just say it, Proctor," Nord replied in huff.

"Erm," Nord could hear the man audibly swallow, "we've picked up some sort of signal, sir."

Nord understood the man's reluctance to tell him about the signal. Deep space was not a place to find wayward communications. Hell, no one wanted to end up like Spinetti's crew, who encountered one and was never heard from again. The thought of it prickled the hairs on the back of Nord's neck.

The *Neutron Energy Salvage Transport* wasn't the most technologically advanced ship sailing through vast emptiness, and being lightyears away from the closest known settlement didn't make a strange transmission any more welcoming when there wasn't supposed to be any known life in the area.

"Is it intelligible?" Nord asked, hoping it wasn't.

Again, Proctor didn't answer immediately. Nord squinted and could see the muscles of the man's face straining to hide his true feelings. "Maybe you had better come to the bridge and listen for yourself."

Rubbing his hands along his thighs, Nord tested the feeling in his legs to see if he had gained enough circulation for his muscles to work properly. Satisfied that he had, he offered a hand to Proctor to help him up and was pulled to his feet, where he teetered for a moment.

His first shaky step gave him pause, a tingling sensation letting him know his mobility was returning, just not as fast as he would've liked. Proctor stood closeby, ready to catch him if started to fall, but Nord was determined to power through and make it to the bridge unaided. He focused on his breathing to feed fresh oxygen to his muscles. By the time he took his fifth step, Nord felt his strength growing exponentially and was able to keep to a steady pace until he stood at the helm of the mining vessel.

"Well, good to see you up and about, Captain," Raife said as he swiveled in the pilot's chair to face Nord. "Don't suppose'n you're wantin' to sit quite yet?"

Nord shook his head, shifting his attention to the panoramic screen that displayed the ship's trajectory and what was laid out in front of it. A side monitor showed ED-75b and how far away the *NEST* was from the dead star, seemingly unchanging in distance despite them traveling close to the speed of light. Their estimated time until arrival was six days and nineteen hours, giving Nord and his crew plenty of time to reanimate from their cryostasis.

"Sir," Proctor said, "the signal? Would you like to hear it now?"

Turning away from the screens to face the two men, Nord wetted his lips and gave them a curt nod. Proctor motioned for Raife to proceed. Raife seemed hesitant, keeping his eyes locked on Nord until he relinquished his gaze and swiveled back to face the monitors. After a few deft strokes on the keyboard, an enlarged display of ED-75b appeared on the central screen, rotating around until stopping on the far side of the star, where a signal emanated from the surface.

Raife pushed another button, and the speaker system inside the bridge of the *NEST* came to life with the sound of something Nord had never heard before. The sound was almost completely absent, but vibrations from its frequency were thrumming through the captain at weird intervals. It was as though the very molecules that made up his body were disrupted from their natural state, at odds with one another.

Nord stumbled backward when Proctor braced him to keep him from hitting the deck, alerting Raife, who shut off the transmission.

"What the fuck was that?" Nord asked breathlessly.

"Neither of us know," Raife offered. "And neither did Jesika."

"Jesika?" Nord asked. "What's she got to do with this?"

Raife and Proctor exchanged an uneasy look before Raife answered. "She's the one that discovered it."

Nord's head twisted around to look at one of the small display monitors and shook his head. The crew of the *NEST* took turns leapfrogging through their journey to ED-75b with one person awake and overseeing the ship, crew, and directive. *We're fifty years off the mark from where we should be for being this close to our destination.*

"Where is she?"

This time, Proctor and Raife avoided looking at one another while also making sure not to look at Nord. When neither of the men answered, Nord moved toward the med bay to check the cryopods, with Proctor following in his wake.

"Groms. Cooper. Delaney. Bellman." Nord went down the line of the pods until he reached the final one. "Tierelli." Stopping at the pod, Nord stared into the small window at the elderly woman before him, trying to find the Jesika he remembered instead of the stranger housed inside. His hand shook as he raised it to touch the glass.

"What happened?"

Proctor took a deep breath. "She never switched out with anyone. Just stayed on shift, listening to that damn transmission...for fifty years. Once the ship's systems detected lack of movement from her, I was thawed out and found her unresponsive on the bridge. Just before placing her in cryosleep, she came around briefly, but I had to sedate her once she became hysterical. I then woke Raife, and he found the transmission. We listened and knew we had to wake you."

Nord turned to look at him. "Did she say anything?" He could see the conflict on Proctor's face as the man weighed his next words carefully.

"At first it was just ranting, but as she drifted off to sleep, she whispered something," Proctor said. "She said our mission was a fool's errand, that we were all going to die there on that star." Proctor took on a grim demeanor.

Nord looked back at Jesika. *She must be in her eighties now*, he thought. Rubbing his hands over his face, he said, "Wake the others. Get them up to speed on mission status and tell them to prepare for touch down in a week's time."

"Yes, sir," Proctor said, before turning to tend to the others still in cryosleep.

"And Proctor, don't mention the transmission to them."

"Yes, sir."

Nord looked up from his hands to take in Jesika one last time before retiring to his quarters. His mind was fogged and his thoughts plagued with everything that was going wrong. He needed time to gather himself together and officially assume command of the mission and mining vessel, time to consider the transmission and what it meant, and time to decide what would be the best course of action moving forward with his now-elderly crewmember.

He needed time, which wasn't a luxury Nord could afford.

"A ship? Derelict?" Nord looked up from his desk to Proctor. "Where?"

The man looked nervous standing in front of the captain, licking his lips and avoiding direct eye contact. "Orbiting ED-75b somewhere in the space above where the transmission is coming from. Raife activated the long-range scanners to check for any debris and discovered a ship floating among a field of organic material he thinks is part of the star."

Coming out of the daze he found himself in, while thinking of the implications of another ship having already been there, Nord asked, "Why does he think it's part of the star floating around in space?"

When Proctor finally did lock eyes with him, Nord wished he hadn't. "The ship is a *NEST*, sir."

A growing pain in the back of Nord's head spiked and sent a searing pain to just behind his right eye. He broke away from Proctor's gaze and turned to face the wall behind his desk. The crew had done well reanimating from cryosleep and prepping the mining rig for departure to the surface of the star. Mum was the word for those that knew about the strange transmission, but trying to keep the discovery of another mining vessel would be next to impossible.

Weighing every possibility he could think of, Nord said, "Gather the others on the bridge. I'll be there shortly. We'll act as though Raife is telling us for the first time, and we can discuss what our next move will be. I want to do a flyby and get eyes on that ship, though, Proctor. Make sure you encourage the others to feel the same way."

There was a long pause before Proctor agreed to Nord's request and left the captain's quarters. Nord knew the man was hesitant about what he was suggesting, but when an anomaly like this presented itself, it was hard not to bow to curiosity. Nord also knew curiosity killed the cat more often than not.

Clearing his thoughts after working out his pitch to investigate the other ship, Nord stood and made his way to the bridge, hoping. He did a quick headcount and noted only one was missing—Jesika. Making his way to Raife, listening to the murmurs of the others, Nord asked the pilot what was going on.

"Uh, a ship, sir. One of the NEST-class mining vessels is floating a few hundred thousand miles from our designated port zone, just above the landing prospect on the surface."

Nord nodded. "Have you tried to hail them? Any sign of life on the scanners?"

Looking up at the captain, Raife's eyes quickly shifted to the others standing on the bridge and then back to Nord. "No, sir. No communication between us and them. And when I try to access their onboard computer, no link is there to connect to."

"Hmm, derelict then. Any idea which vessel it is?"

Shaking his head, Raife answered, "No. No way of knowing without linking to their systems, sir."

Nord grumbled and said, "Or...," under his breath.

"Or we fly by the ship and put eyes on it. Identify it the old fashioned way," Raife offered, keeping his eyes lowered to the instrument cluster at his hands.

Nord turned to face the rest of the crew. Mills, Shom, Kapna, and Bloober kept their eyes toward the deck, with Proctor keeping his arms folded over his chest, looking at them from the side.

"It's the crew's decision. We can keep strictly to the mission and make surfacefall by this time tomorrow." Nord pointed over his shoulder at the ETA countdown displayed on the screen. "Or we can take an extra day to go to the ship and check it out, see if there are any signs of life, before making our way back and get on with what we're here to do." He waited for someone to speak up. When no one did, Nord offered them a solution. "Or we can take a vote on what to do. Majority rules. What say you?"

Again, no one seemed eager to answer one way or the other. Just as Nord was losing his patience with their silence, Turtle Mills stepped forward. "Whatever you think best, Captain."

Nord looked around as the others nodded, still avoiding looking directly at him.

"Okay. Raife," Nord said.

"Sir?"

"Alter our course for the ship. Try to keep raising them on the radio every hour or so, and report to me if you receive any sort of communication."

"Yes, sir."

"Proctor, take Mills and Bloober to the hold and check over the drilling rig one last time. I want everything ready once we get to the launch zone. Check the suits over for any defects, as well. After that, I want you, Proctor, to take over for Raife and let him get some rest until we make it out to that ship. Kapna, Shom, I want to have a word with you in my quarters."

The crew dispersed to complete their tasks. Nord hung back on the bridge until they were all gone, wanting to speak with Raife.

"Is there anything new with the transmission?" he asked.

Raife shook his head. "It's still the same as it's always been. I ..."

"What?"

"I try not to listen to it for too long. Something about it makes my skin crawl." Raife shuddered at his own words.

Although Nord agreed, he kept it to himself. Clapping the man on the shoulder, he said, "Keep me posted on any new developments."

"Yes, sir," Raife said to the captain as he walked away.

Stepping into his quarters, Nord had all but forgotten he told the two crew members to meet him there, too lost in his thoughts and anxiousness about seeing the derelict ship.

"Yes, I wanted to have a word with you two," he said as he took a seat behind his desk. "I know you both have been wondering why Jesika is still in cryosleep. Something happened when she was on watch. Something bad happened. The ship's safety protocol woke Proctor, and he found her unresponsive on the bridge. That safety protocol only activates in extreme circumstances." Kapna and Shom shifted in their chairs, their attention solely on Nord. "Jesika...never clocked out. She, for whatever reason, stayed awake and never switched out with the next person—you, Shom."

Nord watched a silent tear roll down Rach Shom's cheek before she wiped it away. Larissa Kapna's brow was creased in deep thought, her eyes darting around the desk, unable to settle on one singular object.

"What does that mean? Will she be ..." Kapna couldn't finish the question, and Nord really didn't want her to. He didn't want to think or talk about any of it, but he knew it was better to get it out of the way so they could focus on the job when they landed on the surface.

Swallowing, Nord said, "I'm not sure what to do about that except keep her in stasis while we pull up some core samples. What we find will also determine how long we'll be down there." He released a sigh of relief after steering the conversation back to business.

Shom remained stoic, and Nord didn't blame her. To hear the news that one of your closest friends was now at the end of their life was a lot to take in, especially after coming out of a long sleep.

Not wanting to continue to drag them down, Nord told the two crew members to take a minute and collect themselves, then go out and help prepare for departure once they completed the flyby.

As the two women were about to leave his quarters, Nord wanted to blurt out about the transmission they had received, to tell them that was the reason—for whatever reason—Jesika had skipped her shift change and was now on ice. But he didn't say a word and let them leave. *Nothing good would come from them knowing*, he thought. *They would want to hear it, feel it, and then who knows what reaction they would have.*

Nord sat lost in his thoughts until he felt the telltale signs the ship was coming out of near lightspeed, which meant they had finally reached ED-75b. As he rose from his chair, he had to brace himself, forgetting the inertia of the rapid deceleration process still applied until they reached a normalized speed. When he finally felt he wasn't going to tumble forward, Nord made his way up to the bridge to talk to Raife.

The pilot had all monitors brought up to display the hulking dead star in front of them, filling every inch of screen with its withered, hardened surface.

"My god," Nord uttered as he looked on in awe.

"It's something, isn't it?" Proctor asked. "Technically, you and I, we're making history right now by being the first two people to ever see an intact, inactive star in person. Kind of makes me misty eyed."

Nord was too busy studying the crags and rocky terrain to appreciate the man's sentiment, staring at the alien form of something that no one had ever seen before. His imagination ran wild, noting how similar the uneven surface looked to actual flames of a fire that had been flash-frozen in time, left unmolested for centuries until now.

"Captain? Captain? Nord ...?"

Nord looked at Proctor in confusion. "What?"

Proctor stared at him for a moment, his eyes locked onto the captain's. "Did you want me to hail the others so they can have a look before we set course for that other ship?"

Looking at the monitors then back at Proctor, Nord said, "Yes. Bring them up."

As the pilot queued up the intercom system, Nord stepped away, glancing over his shoulder at the image of the dead star. His head felt muddled, his thoughts thick like molasses, but he was able to recognize it and take precautions from slipping further into the madness of it all.

Dismissing himself from the bridge, Nord made his way to the med bay and headed directly to where crew member Tierelli was asleep in her cryopod. Frost was slowly building up on the small glass window, making it hard to see Jesika's matured face. Nord told himself not to follow in her footsteps, not to allow even the slightest chink to form in his armor.

He closed his eyes and took a deep breath then let it out slowly, repeating the phrase, "My thoughts are mine, and no one knows them but me." When he opened his eyes, Nord threw himself backward when he saw Jesika staring at him. He banged his head against a cabinet and fell to the deck, the gray, piercing iris's of Jesika's eyes filling his mind.

"Everything alright here?" Kapna asked, standing in the doorway of the med bay.

Nord shook the image from his head and got to his feet. When he looked, Jesika was not staring at him; her eyes were shut as they had always been. "Yeah, I'm fine. Still trying to get my sea legs under me is all. Took a spill." Nord reached back and rubbed his head. "I think I'm going to lay down for a bit. Be sure to wake me when we get close to that derelict ship." As he walked by Kapna to leave the med bay, Nord added, "Did you see it?" He motioned with his head toward the bridge.

"I did. Isn't it magnificent?" she proclaimed.

Nodding, Nord said, "Yeah, it's something. Never seen anything like it before. Thank you, Kapna."

Try as he may, Nord could not fall asleep, so he lay in his bunk with the lights dimmed to furthest they would go. Nothing had felt right since he woke to the news of the rogue signal coming from their destination. It was out of character for him, and as the ship's captain, he needed to have his head on straight for the mission, for his crew.

Resolved, Nord cleared all thoughts from his head and focused on the dim light above his bunk. Aside from his own breathing and the low hum of the nuclear-powered engine of the ship, his surroundings were quiet and devoid of all sound. He appreciated it for its simplicity. Something that wasn't complex and needed his attention.

After spending as much time traveling through the vastness of space—Nord couldn't remember the exact number of years but it was well over a hundred if cryosleep counted—as he had, it had a funny way with how it affected everyone differently. He had seen it all too often throughout his career in deep space mining and didn't want to end up as another victim of that sickness—starlust.

It was already bad enough he lost Jesika to the mania of the vast nothing, but he would not let himself be seduced by it, nor any of the other crew members. Not if he could help it.

Rising to sit up in his bunk, Nord remembered his secret stash of nootropics he kept just in case something like this was to ever happen. Pitching his feet over the side of the bunk, he slid onto the floor and rummaged around under the bunk until he found an old, battered first-aid kit. Opening it, he stared at the injector gun and five vials of pale-blue liquid, hesitating for just a moment before he loaded the injector, placed it against his leg, then pulled the trigger, feeling the sharp bite of the needle before a relaxing warmth spread throughout his body.

The drug was quick, and Nord could feel the effects of it *immediately*. The fog shrouding his brain lifted and he felt clear-headed—normal—for the first time since being awake. Looking around his quarters with renewed perspective, Nord replaced the injector and empty vial in the kit and stashed it back under his bunk.

On his feet, he readied for a shower—a fresh start to the mission. Nord figured by the time he finished and was dressed, they would be nearing the ship and would hopefully be able to finally solve some of the mysteries that seemed to be piling up. Also, on a plus side, he always found he did his best thinking in the shower when he needed to work things out.

"Jesus Christ, what the fuck happened to it?" Turtle Mills asked, voicing what everyone was thinking as they looked at the wreckage of the derelict ship.

Nord stood next to Raife as the pilot panned a spotlight across the broadside of the hull, lighting up the massive hole in the side of the ship and the debris field around it. Nord noted the ship wasn't just a NEST class like his was; it was identical to the mining vessel they were currently flying in.

"Any idea how many NEST series three ships were manufactured?" Nord asked his crew.

No one answered immediately, but Ersa Bloober did offer something for them to consider.

"I would say there isn't any more than a handful of them out here flying around. Well, one less, obviously. But the bigwigs back on Earth never did stay with one design for too long. Always tinkering, always *improving* on the current model and taking bigger leaps than they should when moving on to the next best thing."

As they completed a full revolution around the dead ship, no one else spoke until Nord broke the silence. "There should be a serial number on it. If we know what it is, we can look it up in the database and see which crew it was. I'll have to send a long-range relay back to Earth to let them know what we found and that there were no survivors of the wreck."

Raife maneuvered the ship until they were facing the part of the NEST with the hole blown through it.

"The ship's badge number should be right where that hole is," Raife informed them all. "And with no way of connecting to that ship's computer, there really isn't anything we can do from here."

"Any of the other sensors picked up anything? Scans from the spectrometer?" Nord asked.

Raife pushed a few buttons on the console and said, "No. Nothing."

"Jumpstart it," Lars interjected. "Rach and I could go out there and hook up a power cable to its core and juice it up from ours. Easy peasy."

Turning away from the monitors, Raife shook his head at the suggestion. "Except that big ass hole there," he pointed at the display, "is where the core should be. Whatever happened to that ship, a catastrophic failure, something in space, whatever...it's beyond ever functioning as something other than another manmade piece of space junk floating around the cosmos."

Lars's cheeks reddened slightly and she looked away, taking interest in the bulkhead next to her.

Nord continued to study the stranded ship floating just a few hundred meters away from them, lamenting the loss of life and mission failure. "I don't think there's anything we can do. But it was important to see it for ourselves," Nord said. "You all should pay your respects before we depart for the DLZ." He took one last look at the ship on the screen and started to leave the bridge. "I'm going to write this up in the log. Everyone should eat a good meal and rest up. In a few hours, we'll have work to do."

Once Nord was done entering all the details of the derelict ship into the ship's log, he went back to the bridge and told Raife to get some extra shut eye. The pilot was more than happy to take the captain up on the offer, setting the *NEST* to autopilot to their original destination before heading to his quarters.

Settling into the pilot's chair, Nord waited until he knew everyone was down for the night before pulling up the alien transmission. After injecting himself with the serum he had gotten on the black market back home and lifting the fog clouding his thoughts, he wanted to take another crack at trying to decipher it.

Plugging a set of headphones into the receiver console, Nord tuned in to the frequency of the transmission. This time, along with the vibrations from before, there was an underlying sound just on the edge of his hearing capabilities. Twisting a few knobs, he heard the thrumming clear into something more decipherable, almost like a human voice. Nord's pulse quickened as he continued to fine tune the signal, mixing and matching tones and pitches until he could make out fractured words.

...—ay... ...—do—... ...—ur—... ...—rapped—... ...—eat—...

After listening to the message repeat a few dozen times and trying every combination possible to clear it up further, Nord finally took the headphones off and changed the frequency to something else. He could still feel the vibrations throughout his body, but they didn't seem to have the same effect on him like the first time he listened to the transmission.

Leaning back, he wondered what it all meant. The rogue transmission, the derelict ship that was from the same fleet they were. Things like this didn't occur by happenstance, especially so far out in deep space.

He sat quietly for the rest of his watch, keeping an eye on the ship's sensors and trajectory. Nothing more happened. Nothing more seemed so strangely out of place.

"Count us down, Rach."

"Five... Four... Three..."

Despite his long career in intergalactic mining, Nord never liked the drop in from low orbital space. The weightlessness combined with the speed and heat were anxiety inducing for him, and he always tried to disassociate until the drop pod was on a firm surface.

"...one."

The locks holding the mining rig released and sent it into freefall, helped along by guidance thrusters to keep it stable. While the rest of the crew cheered like they were on a rollercoaster back on Earth, Nord held his breath and kept his eyes closed, picturing himself sitting next to a fire, staring out across a lake he remembered from his childhood.

With ED-75b being a star and not a planet, there wasn't an atmosphere to punch through, and very little gravity remained within its core to pull them down to its surface faster. Ersa was the crew's designated pilot whenever they made planetfall, and Nord had the highest faith in the man that he would see them safely to the landing zone.

When the others quieted around him, Nord risked opening his eyes and looked around at them, seeing they were all staring at the screen that showed outside of the rig. Large spurs of rocky terrain rose up around them, dark and metallic, reflecting the image of the rig and its lights back at the outboard camera.

"It's...beautiful," Turtle uttered.

"Yeah," Rach agreed.

Nord continued to look at the screen, trying to determine what they were seeing. He was in the dark since this was the first time mankind was about to land on a literal star, but he never expected the possibility there was a chance they would encounter an undiscovered element.

"Fifteen seconds until we touch down," Ersa announced.

Taking a deep breath, Nord was about to tell the crew what he wanted to do when they were settled when he noticed Lars staring at him, her eyes as wide as they would go. He inclined his head toward her in hopes of calming whatever was bothering her and saw her slightly nod back.

"Okay, I want everyone to hold tight until the scanners have had a chance to take a full readout of what we're dealing with here. Recheck your suit and oxygen levels before we disembark. I don't want—"

The mining rig's reverse thrusters interrupted Nord as he was giving out instructions. Once Ersa set it down on the rough surface, he gave Nord a thumbs-up.

"Awesome job, Bloober. Right, scan first, then check your suits and systems. When everything is ready, we'll crack the seal and be the first motherfuckers to ever step foot on the surface of a goddamn star!"

The crew cheered—even Lars—and Nord joined in with them in an attempt to psyche himself up. He needed them excited and on their game. He needed to be on his game.

“Scans came back clean,” Ersa said. “Some residual radiation, nothing to really worry about. Very low gravity, so everyone should keep their feet planted unless they want to take the slow way back up to the *NEST*.”

“Materials?” Nord asked.

Ersa flipped through a few screens. “A lot of carbon. Some frozen hydrogen, as well. The surface seems pretty tough, so anything deeper than that will have to be sussed out the old-fashioned way.”

“Got it. Okay, everyone, let’s do this.”

One by one, the crew checked themselves and each other over to confirm their suits were fine. Once satisfied, Nord released the depressurization lever and waited for the inside of the rig to normalize to the same as outside of it. Opening the side hatch, he stepped out onto the most hellish place he had ever been to.

From where he stood, ED-75b looked like the literal images of hell that Nord had seen in holotapes. The terrain was even more harsh than he imagined, and in the distance, it looked downright treacherous.

The rest of the crew filed out of the rig and gathered around him, some commenting on what they were seeing.

“This...this is intense,” Rach noted.

“Fuck yeah, it is,” Lars agreed.

Ersa stayed in the rig and waited to find out where their dig site was going to be.

Nord surveyed the landscape and found a level patch of surface big enough for them to set up camp and start drilling.

“Turtle, Proctor, and Lars—set up over there. Lay out the grid and then find a place for camp about twenty meters away. Rach, you’re with me. We’re going to see if we can locate a secondary dig site close enough to here so we don't have to set up another camp. Remember what the scan said, low gravity, so I want everyone tethered to someone else until we can put up some runner lines."

As Turtle, Proctor, and Lars pulled out the laser grid equipment from the back of the rig, Nord hooked a line to Rach's harness and led her in the opposite direction from where the others were going.

"This is insane. You know that, right?" Rach asked.

Softly chuckling, Nord said, "I'm reminded of that everywhere I look. But who's more foolish, me or the crazy fools that came along with me?"

"I guess you have a point there. But hell, can't beat the money for sleeping 95 percent of the trip. If this gig pays off, and we do strike it big, I'm never leaving my mansion in the mountains again!"

Nord couldn't help to full-on laugh but also agree with her. If it all panned out, his crew would be set for life with the incentive bonus the mining company was dangling over their heads.

"Let's just hope we find something worth taking back. We still don't know what we're dealing with just yet." He looked down at the pitch, glossy surface they were trekking across. The only thing similar that he could think to liken it to was obsidian.

"See anything promising yet?" Rach asked.

Looking around, Nord spotted a rise up ahead and pointed. "Let's head up there and get a better look."

When they crested the hill, Nord switched on his suit's powerful external lights and shined them to the farthest place they would reach. His heart sank when the canyon below them lit up like a punji pit. There were black spikes and no workable areas to be seen.

"Jesus," Rach said, barely above a whisper. "What made it like this? It really does look like frozen flames."

Something caught Nord's attention from the corner of his eye, and he turned to look. Just beneath the surface, it looked as though something was rippling. He looked on, holding his breath, waiting for something to happen.

"Captain? Nord, did you hear me?" Rach asked, pulling him by the shoulder to face her.

"Whatsit?" he said.

"I said, are we going to head back now? I don't think we're going to find anything this way."

Nord looked back at the spot that had been rippling and saw it calm and placid, just like the rest of the surface around them. "Right. Yeah, we should head back and see how the setup is going. Maybe we can try a different direction or something." He noticed her looking at him awkwardly but turned away, not acknowledging it.

"What do they think happened here? I mean, with this star. Why didn't it go supernova like every other one in the universe?"

"I guess that's part of why we're here—to take some core samples so that people much smarter than a handful of roughnecks can study it and tell us what *they* think happened. We're truly pioneers making history here, Rach. Some lab geek will know your name for the rest of time."

Rach giggled, and it made Nord smile. "Fucking wild, like I said."

"Problem with the camp, sir," Proctor said as Nord and Rach rejoined the others."What's going on?"

"Well, we have the dig site gridded out and ready to go, but we can't sink any stakes into the surface. It's too damn hard to penetrate."

Lars stepped beside Proctor, sweat moistening her brow. "This shit is tough. Like, real tough."

Thinking for a moment, Nord said, "Use the vacuu-fixtures. The surface should be smooth enough for them to work. Fashion the HAB to them."

Both of them nodded. "Yeah, that should work," Lars said.

"Also," Nord started as she turned to walk away, "you know what that means." He couldn't help but grin.

"Ooooo, are we about to pull out the Ripper Head?" she asked.

He simply nodded back as a reply.

"Oh shit. Okay. Rach, help me with the HAB and let's get this party started.

As the two of them walked away, Nord noticed the nervous expression on Proctor's face. "What?" he asked.

"Do you think that's wise? Shouldn't we try the normal bit first? That piece of equipment costs more than the *NEST* itself. A few of them, actually."

Nord shrugged. "The way I see it, they sent it with us to use, so we might as well. Right?"

"Aye, aye, Captain."

"That's the spirit!"

Toggling the comms over to the mining rig, Nord told Ersa he was good to move over to the grid and prepare the rig. Nord and Proctor walked over to where the others were securing the HAB to the surface. Nord was happy his idea was working and they would have a place out of the elements to go.

Once the crew had the drill heads swapped out—much faster than usual with their enthusiasm—Ersa angled the rig to start drilling.

Turtle took his spot at the pressure gauges on the side of the rig, while Lars, Rach, and Proctor prepared the drill stagings to hook into as it went deeper. Nord stood to the side at a safe distance and waited for the signal from the others that they were ready. When the four on the ground gave him the green light, he gave them a thumbs-up.

Alright, you bitch. It's time to see what you're made of.

"Ersa, start it up and put her down," Nord radioed to the rig operator.

The ripper head whirled up and gained speed until it was spinning so fast it looked motionless. The arm tilted forward and hovered just over the deep-black surface of the star. Nord held his breath, unsure what to expect.

The second the ripper head touched the inky-dark surface, sparks shot out in a showering ring, dying out just as fast. Ersa held the drill down, boring harder into the surface. The rig shuddered from the force, groaning as the titanium structure of the machine began to stress.

"Back it off, back it off!" Nord yelled into the comms.

Ersa reversed the rig and raised the drill. Nord stepped forward, waiting for it to stop spinning. The others approached and looked on, each one reacting differently to what they saw.

"Jesus Christ," Lars commented.

"Yeah, that's...that's unbelievable," Turtle added, looking completely awestruck.

Nord walked forward and bent to inspect the surface. There was hardly a mark left by the ripper head aside from a few scratches and a handful of small chips of the glossy surface.

"Rach, gather whatever samples you can from this and relay it to the *NEST*. Send a message along with it for Raife to identify what we're dealing with down here and how best we can tackle it."

"On it, Captain," Rach said, already pulling out a specimen container and stooping to gather what she could.

Nord looked at the ripper head, shocked at what he was seeing. The bits were an alloy formed from tungsten and diamond bonded together then forged into abrasive spikes. That was the reason it was so expensive and was only supposed to be the crew's last-ditch effort for drilling. Now, as Nord looked on, the ripper head's bits were all but gone, melted away by the friction of doing the tango with the remnants of a dead star.

"Launching," Rach said over the comms.

A concussive *thoomph* made the crew look up as the shard samples were launched from the back of the mining rig.

"Proctor, I want you and Turtle to disassemble the drill while Lars and Rach prep the punch. Ersa, run a systems check on the rig and make sure everything is still alright after that shitshow. If we can't chew into the surface, let's crack this bitch open."

Raife saw a message flash across the screen that there was an incoming payload from ED-75b. Pushing a few buttons on the console so the *NEST* would maintain orbit on autopilot, he went to the relay port and waited for the sample to arrive. Raife figured Nord would want a readout of materials they were dealing with down there and should be able to have something for him quickly.

A loud ping sounded outside the ship, then a green light flashed to show the retrieval port was safe to open. Pulling open the airlock's door, Raife grabbed the sample and did a double take, holding it up to the overhead light to make sure something was actually in there. Tiny fragments rolled around the glass tube, the light glinting off the black surfaces.

As he walked to the mineral lab, Raife hoped there was enough there to do a proper, thorough test. Pushing a large blue button on the wall as he walked in, the lights overhead dimmed a bit from the ship, rerouting power to the lab.

Taking his place at a desk occupied by a large microscope, he opened a tray at the bottom, then uncapped the sample, allowing the fragments to slide out. Replacing the tray, Raife leaned forward and began dialing in the magnification to better see the structure of the mineral.

The black material made it hard for him to discern what it was, so he increased the brightness of the light beneath the tray. It was still too hard to see, so he increased the magnification by fifty and then dialed in the focus.

Suddenly jumping back from the microscope, Raife's brow knitted together in confusion, unsure of what to make of what he was seeing. Looking back into the microscope, he still didn't understand it, but whatever it was, it was rippling. Raife watched it for a moment then started counting, noticing it had a rhythm to its movement.

Even at this magnification, he couldn't tell what made up the structure of the sample. Reaching over, he uncovered a switch that was protected by a glass box and flipped it. The ship's warning system came to life, announcing more power was being diverted to the lab and would risk starving other systems on the ship in the process.

The lights dimmed even more, but the microscope was about to boost its magnification up to one hundred times past where it currently was. Raife adjusted the magnification, watching the material pulse to the same beat as his heart, which was thrumming in his ears.

The structure of whatever it was he was looking at was compact and tightly woven; he was worried the microscope wouldn't be able to zoom in far enough to get a proper reading.

Something loud crashed in another part of the ship, but Raife was too hyper-focused on discovering what he was looking at to care.

In the corner of the viewfinder, he could see he was inching closer to maximum magnification, hitting 85x power, then as it crept over 90 percent, tiny strands started to differentiate themselves from one another and Raife could see movement in each one. When he hit 100x magnification, the number flashed in the corner, letting him know it was maxed out.

In the viewfinder, each filament of the material played out in his vision like a tiny film reel, people going about their everyday lives like he was watching a movie. Shifting his perspective, Raife saw a strand that caught his eye, a ship in space that looked all too familiar. The *NEST* was hanging above the dead star. He saw the mining rig launch from the cargo bay and fall to the surface. He took note of where that particular strand was and switched to a different one, watching it as it played out. It was a repeat of the exact same one he had just seen, *NEST* and mining rig, but it was definitely a different strand that ran in the opposite direction of the other. Shifting again, he found another one, except it was one that was of the derelict ship with the massive hole blown out of its side.

He thought of everything he knew about astrophysics and the way black holes usually formed when stars collapsed, leaving behind a gravity well so powerful even light couldn't escape it. And then another thought that had been buried deep in his subconscious occurred to him, about the speed of light, about how time worked with the relativity with which time passed as opposed to how fast you were traveling.

Raife's head tilted back, and he looked up at the dim lights above, mulling everything over as he worked it out in his head. "It's ..." he started to say.

"...time," someone from behind finished for him.

Before Raife could look, something sharp plunged into the back of his neck, forcing its way out of the front and sending a shower of blood over the microscope. Grabbing the wound just above his collarbone, he felt the sharp edge of a piece of glass protruding from his throat.

His hands slick with the torrent of blood spilling down his chest, Raife turned and saw Jesika standing beside him, wearing a serene look on her face. Leaving his side and walking around his chair, her hand reached for a second glass cover and lifted it, her finger brushing the switch that was beneath.

Raife tried to tell her not to but choked on the blood that was filling his throat, cutting off his airway.

Flipping the switch, a loud buzzing rang out from the ship's warning system as the overhead light completely blinked out from lack of power.

Raife flinched; diverting that much power from the ship's reactor would cause it to meltdown in a matter of minutes with the cooling system not able to keep up.

He tried to reach for the switches but found he was too weak from blood loss, his arm falling limply to his side. Looking up at Jesika, her face looking far younger than it had when she was in her cryopod, she shook her head at him.

"Man is not meant to find this place. It's an anomaly, a fluke of nature. I have heard the message. I know what must be done. I've carried out this mission far too many times, more than I can remember."

The heat inside the *NEST* was already building, making it feel like a sauna. Raife was fading, making it hard to string together any cohesive thoughts. Just before blacking out, he managed to croak out, "How?"

Jesika smiled in understanding, glad he finally asked. "As I said, it's time, distilled down to a raw, physical form. That's what happens when a star fails to follow the laws of its own nature, of the universe."

"Systems critical," the ship announced. "Core meltdown imminent."

Raife's head lolled to the side once, twice, then as it did so a third time, his body followed, spilling onto the deck beside the chair. In his fading, fleeting last moments of life, he watched as Jesika reached down and pulled the broken piece of glass from his neck, raising it to her own and pulling it across in one swift motion, leaving the sight and feeling of blood raining down on him as his final memory.

Ersa was resetting the tension on the punch for the fifth attempt when Nord felt a rumbling beneath his boots. Looking, he saw movement just below the surface, flowing swiftly like a river toward where the punch was ready to slam down. The gears in his head were working overtime.

Stepping forward and raising his hand, Nord was about to tell Ersa to hold off when the punch fell, slamming into the surface and sending a fracture line out like snakes weaving their way through grass. Just as he looked toward the rig, a concussive blast knocked him into the air, sending him hurtling higher and higher until his back slammed into something solid, knocking the air from his lungs.

One of the long, spindly fingers of ED-75b's terrain had stopped him from flying off into space. Nord clambered for a hold but struggled to find one on the slick, smooth surface. His hand found a gap between two ridges, and he clung to it with everything he had. Once he was able to pull himself in and maintain control, he looked down at the dig site and saw that half the rig was missing, including its operator, Ersa.

"What's going on? What happened?" he said over the comms. Static filled the dead air.

He worked his way down the craggy spire until he was able to regain his footing, then he rushed back to the dig site, hoping the rest of his crew was all right.

"Come on, guys, talk to me. Where is everyone?"

Stopping beside the ruined mining rig, he looked for the others. The rig looked as though something had ripped it in half, jagged pieces of metal sticking out haphazardly in all directions.

The section of the surface where the punch had been hammering down had a hole that was oozing some sort of liquid. He bent and looked at it, unsure what to make of it. It looked like hydrophobic sand but was colored like glitter, with the consistency of thick sludge. An urge came out of nowhere for him to reach out and touch it. Wanting more than anything to give in, he stretched out his arm and was inches from making contact when a voice broke through the radio silence on the comms.

"...elp. Ples— Is there anyo—"

Even under duress, Nord knew it was Lars. He rose to his feet and looked around, scanning for something that stood out from the rest of the surroundings. Not too far away, half hidden by the HAB they had erected, was the telltale sign of white that was the same color used for the crew's space suits.

Moving swiftly, Nord closed the gap and slid to a halt. The portion of the suit he saw was only the lower half; the upper half was nowhere to be found. Swallowing hard, he walked around until he could see the now-frozen wound that capped the bottom half of one of his crew members; crystallized blood and organ tissue had started to boil out. He couldn't tell if it was Rach or Turtle, or even Proctor, and Nord didn't know if he wanted to know at that point.

"Lars? Where are you, Lars?" he called into the comms. Waiting, holding his breath, he finally released it when she answered back.

"Here. At the rig."

Nord spun around and saw her slumped against the side of the machine, holding her side. Making his way back to her, he knew from her stance she was hurt. "Let me see," Nord told her, trying to move her hand. Kneeling, he pushed Lars's hand to the side and could see a ragged, bloody hole in her suit, filled in with a yellow film that was a safety feature of the suit in case of punctures.

"It doesn't look too bad. How do you feel? What happened? The...the others."

Lars waved her hand. "Slow down. I don't know what happened. Gas pocket or something? I thought everyone else was dead. I saw Ersa right as it happened. Whatever that shit is," she pointed to the bleeding wound on the dead star's surface, "it melted him the second it erupted and landed on the cockpit."

"Melted?" Nord stood and backed away from the rig, looking around for any trace of the missing cockpit or its operator. Nothing was there that may have been blown into space like he nearly was, but Lars had said the stuff melted Ersa.

"This is so fucking fucked. I...I don't know who, but there's part of a body over by the HAB. Which means whoever that isn't might also still be alive. We need to contac—"

Nord was cut off by a blinding light from above. He shielded his eyes for a moment until it lessened, then looked up and saw the *NEST* blowing apart in a series of rapidly dying explosions. "Oh god. NO!"

Lars hobbled away from the rig to see what was happening and gasped when she saw.

The ground quaked suddenly, sending Nord to his knees. Lars yelped, and he whipped his head around to see half of her body coated in the glittery substance. "Hang on!" he yelled, pushing himself to his feet.

By the time Nord turned to help Lars, the portions of her suit that were contaminated were deteriorating so fast it *did* look like it was melting off her. Once the sludge breached her suit and made contact with her skin, it ate away at it, going through muscle and bone. Nord was immobilized by the sight, too mortified at what he was seeing to do anything.

"Captain, I... I'm sorry. I fucked u–" Lars collapsed forward before she could finish the sentence.

Nord finally snapped out of it and flipped her over—careful not to touch whatever it was that came out of the fissure—and watched as it consumed her, until only the parts that hadn't been splashed remained.

"Jesus Christ, what the fuck is this?! Hello? Is anyone still alive? Anyone at all?"

Days, weeks, months...years? Or was it only minutes? Nord couldn't tell one second from the next anymore. Time was a cruel mistress when you had no way of tracking it, and it was the only thing he had to keep him company until his ran out.

His suit's rebreather was efficient at recycling his air, too efficient for his liking, and he didn't have it in him to take matters into his own hands. And he would long since have starved to death before it finally quit working.

The mining rig had an emergency beacon and radio communicator located in the storage compartment on the back of it, and every attempt he made to contact the *NEST* was met with silence. Nord could see the ship floating limply in orbit above him, and it made him wonder what happened to Raife.

The mission was a total loss, and his crew had paid the ultimate price. But that didn't mean others had to, not if he could help it. Nord was never a whiz with electronics, not like Proctor or Turtle, but he knew enough.

You're adequate, Turtle would often tell him when Nord tried to tinker with things around the ship, *but let me show you some tricks I know.*

Rewiring the distress beacon with emergency comms radio, Nord recorded a message for the next crew that would be sent out in hopes of striking it big by being the ones to mine the only known intact dead star in the galaxy.

"Whoever can hear this, stay away. There's nothing here for you except death. Don't come. If you're on your way to ED-75b, turn around now. My name is Nord Bellman, and I'm trapped here with no hope of survival. This place is death. Let me be its last victim."

Nord hoped his message would work and this would be the end of it, that no one else would fall prey to this godforsaken place. Drifting off, his mind wavered in and out of consciousness.

"Captain, wake up. Hey, we need you to hear something. Nord, we need you on the bridge ASAP!"

PUBLISHER'S NOTE

Thank you for reading Screams From Outer Space. This anthology wouldn't exist without you, the reader.

If you enjoyed this book, please consider leaving a review on Amazon, GoodReads, or your favorite social media platform.

Please visit our website for more information about our releases and signed copies of our books.

www.brokenbrainbooks.com

Other Anthologies by Broken Brain Books

Screams From The Ocean Floor
Screams From Beyond The Veil
Screams From The Dark Ages
Books of Horror Indie Brawl Anthology

Also available

Usher of the Fallen by LM Kaplin
Rorschach by Aaron Lebold
Mine by LM Kaplin
Fang Fiction by LM Kaplin
Ruby's Cube by Lyla Diamond
Pacheco Pass by Aaron Lebold (Coming Soon)

ABOUT THE AUTHORS

S.A. Barnes

S.A. BARNES works in a high school library by day, recommending reads, talking with students, and removing the occasional forgotten cheese stick as bookmark. Barnes has published numerous novels across different genres under the pen name Stacey Kade. She lives in Illinois with more dogs and books than is advisable and a very patient husband.

Blaine Daigle

Having lived his entire life deep in the gut of Louisiana, Blaine Daigle grew up surrounded by ghost stories of haunted plantations and cursed woodlands. He still lives in Louisiana with his wife and two children and can't wait to pass on the nightmares to his kids..when they are old enough. During the day he teaches high school English. At night, he enjoys diving deep into the fears that shape and mold the world around him.

M Ennenbach

m ennenbach is a poet. a fool. a writer of strange tales. stripped down and raw, not limited by genre, m writes emotions unflinchingly.

Ben Farthing

Ben Farthing is the author of *The Twitching House*, *I Found Puppets Living In My Apartment Walls*, and at least eight other horror books. He's into liminal spaces, analog horror, and inexplicable monstrosities.

C S Jones

C S Jones is an award winning author from Wrexham, North Wales, who holds a prestigious 10 meter swimming certificate. Often mistaken for an escaped mental patient, he has been writing for only a short time, his recent massively inflated sense of self finally winning out over the years of overwhelming laziness. A keen horror enthusiast, he has finally decided to give back to a community that has provided so much, whether that be in his writing or general appearance. Initially a timid child, he was scared of anything and everything, including Ghostbusters 2 - insisting his parents record over it immediately. If he can make you feel even a modicum of that terror, then mission accomplished.

LM Kaplin

LM Kaplin is an author from upstate New York who has been a horror enthusiast in all forms his entire life. His morbid obsession with the macabre began one night while watching Poltergeist as a young child. The next morning, he began searching for ancient burial grounds in the backyard. Dismayed at not uncovering any evil spirits, he buried his own demons for future generations to find. It's time to start digging them up.

Leigh Kenny
Leigh was born and raised in the garden county of Wicklow, Ireland. She lives by the Irish Sea with the love of her life, two wonderful boys, a black Labrador, and a three-legged cat that hates people. She has released two books independently and has appeared in a multitude of anthologies. You can find out more about Leigh's work on her social media pages.

Heather Ann Larson
Heather Ann Larson is the editor of this anthology as well as its predecessors, Screams From The Ocean Floor, Screams From Beyond The Veil, and Screams From The Dark Ages as well as The Books of Horror Indie Brawl Anthology. She has also edited novels by authors Justin Boote, Sean McDonough, Timothy King, D.W. Hitz, LM Kaplin, and more. In her spare time, she... Who are we kidding? There is no spare time!!!

Aaron Lebold
Aaron Lebold is an author of psychological horror, sometimes dabbling in extreme elements. His love of the genre began at an early age with all the best slasher films. Writing has always been something of interest but he didn't make any serious attempts at it until 2017. Since that time he has completed several novels and novellas. His short stories can be found in anthologies by various publishers. Some of his short stories have been narrated for the Cryo-Pod Podcast. His novel "Born Sick" took second place at the Godless 666 awards for best novel of 2022.

Sean McDonough
Sean McDonough is the author of several novels, including The Thirteen Black Cats of Edith Penn and Not Another 80s Horror Novel. He will work for beer and old paperbacks.

Joseph Murnane
Joseph Murnane is a horror author from Durham, North Carolina. When he's not screaming at an uncooperative document, he's hanging out with his partner, Meg, and their four fuzzy companions. He can be contacted via social media, or emailed at jmurnanehorror@gmail.com

Andrew Najberg
Andrew Najberg is the author of The Mobius Door (Wicked House Publishing, 2023), Gollitok (Wicked House Publishing, 2023), The Neverborn Thief (Olive-Ridley Press, 2024), In Those Fading Stars (Crystal Lake Publishing, 2024), Try Not to Die In the Shadowlands (Vincere Press, 2024), and the forthcoming Extinction Dream (Wicked House Publishing, 2025), Paradise Falls (Co-authored with Patrick Reuman, Wicked House Publishing, 2025) and Dead Hearts Eat the Light (Wicked House Publishing, 2026). His short fiction has appeared in Fusion Fragment, Khoreo, Translunar Travelers Lounge, Utopia Science Fiction, Prose Online, Psychopomp Review, Solar Press Horror Anthology, and more. Currently, he teaches for the University of Tennessee at Chattanooga.

Steven Pajak
Steven Pajak, a Chicago-based author, crafts stories that explore the depths of horror and the human psyche. With a pen that dances on the edges of darkness, Steven brings to life tales that challenge, terrify, and linger in the minds of readers. Drawing inspiration from the

urban tapestry of Chicago, his work merges the pulse of city life with the eerie quiet of the shadows lurking within the darkest corners of our minds. Steven invites you into a world where fear meets courage, and the journey through his imagination proves as haunting as it is unforgettable.

RJ Roles
Only a little bit hick, born and bred in the great state of West Virginia, RJ Roles is a horror fiction writer. He founded the Books of Horror Facebook group and From the Ashes publishing company. In his spare time, he tends to his thirteen cats (okay, there's only three but thirteen sounds way cooler) and hangs with his partner in crime, Jess. Find his work on amazon or rjroles.com

Megan Stockton
Megan Stockton is an indie author who lives in rural Middle Tennessee with her husband and two children. She primarily writes dystopian, horror, thriller, and science fiction/fantasy novels that are character-driven and immersive. She is known for delivering works that are raw, thought-provoking, brutal, and cinematic.

Derek Thomas
After a lifetime of living in the urban jungles of Dallas/Ft. Worth and Houston, Derek now dwells in a small central Texas town with his wife of 18 years and two precocious French Bulldogs; where he survives on tacos, whisky and Coke Zero. When not writing, he loves to cook, garden and, of course, read and watch horror. He is particularly fond of Asian horror and Scanda Noir films and shows.